CEREBRAL LATERALITY: THEORY AND RESEARCH

THE TOLEDO SYMPOSIUM

CEREBRAL LATERALITY: THEORY AND RESEARCH

THE TOLEDO SYMPOSIUM

Edited by

Frederick L. Kitterle
University of Toledo

LEA LAWRENCE ERLBAUM ASSOCIATES, PUBLISHERS
1991 Hillsdale, New Jersey   Hove and London

Lawrence Erlbaum Associates, Inc., Publishers
365 Broadway
Hillsdale, New Jersey 07642

Library of Congress Cataloging-in-Publication Data
Cerebral laterality : theory and research : The Toledo Symposium /
    edited by Frederick L. Kitterle.
            p. cm.
    Papers expanding upon topics discussed at a conference hosted by the Dept. of Psychology
at the University of Toledo.
    Contents: Prosimians as animal models in the study of neural
lateralization / Jeannette P. Ward -- Functional lateralization in
monkeys / Charles R. Hamilton and Betty A. Vermire -- Issues in the
assessment of handedness / M. Phillip Bryden and Runa E. Steehuis --
Handedness, language laterality, and spatial ability / Walter F.
McKeever -- Dynamic temporal-spatial allocation of resources in the
human brain / Dennis L. Molfese and Lisa M. Burger-Judisch --
Cerebral laterality in functional neuroimaging / Frank B. Wood, D.
Lynn Flowers, and Cecile E. Naylor -- Cerebral laterality and
metacontrol / Joseph B. Hellige -- Shadow and substance :
attentional irrelevancies and perceptual constraints in hemispheric
processing of language stimuli / Curtis Hardyck -- The use of
computer models in the study of cerebral lateralization / Michael H.
Van Kleeck and Stephen M. Kosslyn -- Ups and downs in cerebral
lateralization / Justine Sergent and Michael C. Corballis --
Symmetries and asymmetries in the processing of sinusoidal gratings
/ Frederick L. Kitterle and Stephen Christman.
    ISBN 0-8058-0471-4
    1. Cerebral dominance--Congress. I. Kitterle, Frederick L.
II.   University of Toledo. Dept. of Psychology.
QP385.5.c475   1990
152--dc20   89-27540
                CIP

Printed in the United States of America
10 9   8   7   6   5   4   3   2   1

Contents

LIST OF CONTRIBUTORS

M. Phillip Bryden
Department of Psychology
University of Waterloo
Waterloo, Ontario N2L 3G1 Canada

Lisa M. Burger-Judisch
Department of Psychology
Southern Illinois University
Carbondale, IL 62901

Stephen Christman
Department of Psychology
University of Toledo
Toledo, Ohio 43606

Michael C. Corballis
Department of Psychology
Private Bag
University of Auckand
Auckland, New Zealand

D. Lynn Flowers
Section of Neuropsychology
Bowman Gray School of Medicine
Wake Forest Univeristy
Winston-Salem, NC 27103

Charles R. Hamilton
Division of Biology
California Institute of Technology
Pasadena, CA 91125

Curtis Hardyck
Institute of Human Learning
University of California
Berkeley, California 94720

Joseph B. Hellige
Department of Psychology
University of Southern California
Los Angeles, CA 90089

Frederick L. Kitterle
Department of Psychology
University of Toledo
Toledo, Ohio 43606

Stephen M. Kosslyn
Department of Psychology
William James Hall
Harvard University
Cambridge, MA 02138

Walter F. McKeever
Department of Psychology
Northern Arizona University,
Flagstaff, Arizona 86011

Dennis L. Molfese
Department of Psychology
Southern Illinois University
Carbondale, IL 62901

Cecile E. Naylor
Section of Neuropsychology
Bowman Gray School of Medicine
Wake Forest Univeristy
Winston-Salem, NC 27103

Justine Sergent
Montreal Neurological Institute
3801 University Street
Montreal, PQ H3A 2B4 Canada

Runa E. Steenhuis
Department of Psychology
University Hospital
P.O.Box 5339
Postal Station A
London, Ontario N6A 5A5
Canada

Michael H. Van Kleeck
Department of Psychology
William James Hall
Harvard University
Cambridge, MA 02138

Jeannette P. Ward
Department of Psychology
Memphis State University
Memphis, TN 38152

Frank B. Wood
Section of Neuropsychology
Bowman Gray School of Medicine
Wake Forest Univeristy
Winston-Salem, NC 27103

Betty A. Vermeire
Division of Biology
California Institute of Technology
Pasadena, CA 91125

Preface

Research with clinical populations and studies of normal individuals support the conclusion that there are functional differences between the cerebral hemispheres. As a result of these findings there has been considerable, sustained interest in understanding the conditions which give rise to hemispheric asymmetries and in developing models of cerebral functioning that account for these differences in processing.

The chapters presented in this volume expand on topics discussed at a recent conference on advances in cerebral laterality research hosted by the Department of Psychology at the University of Toledo. The chapters are organized into three main categories: recent work using animal models to study cerebral lateralization, further development and utilization of techniques to study hemispheric asymmetries, and finally recent research on selected topics: handedness, metacontrol, the use of computer models in the study of cerebral lateralization, computational modeling in hemispheric studies of mental imagery and mental rotation, the role of attention and interhemispheric transfer in language tasks, and the role of spatial frequency analysis in hemispheric asymmetries.

Ward (Chapter1) presents evidence for behavioral lateralization in prosimian species and discusses the potential usefulness of prosimians in understanding the neural mechanisms and origins of human cerebral lateralization. She describes laboratory tests and investigations of free-ranging behaviors such as hand use, locomotor responses, and postural biases. Beyond simply demonstrating that prosimians exhibit lateralized behavior, this research has identified a relationship for the subject variables of sex and age with the direction and strength of hand-preference lateralization and has furnished considerable evidence that conditions associated with the expression of the behavioral response can exert systematic effects on the strength of lateralized behavior.

Hamilton and Vermeire (Chapter 2) describe research with primates on laterality effects in the processing of faces, line orientation, and the ease of discriminating conspecific individuals and expressions. This work reveals striking parallels in lateralized mechanisms of monkeys and of human beings. It appears that monkeys possess hemispheric specialization with human-like characteristics.

In addition to demonstrating similarities in hemispheric processing by monkeys and man, both Ward and Hamilton and Vermeire discuss the evolutionary implications of their work.

Handedness is regarded as a critical variable in studies of cerebral laterality. However, the relationship between handedness and cerebral specialization is not well understood. Bryden and Steenhuis (Chapter 3) examine some of the common practices for controlling for handedness in studies of cerebral lateralization. They argue that the common practice of restricting one's studies to right handers, or even to right-handed males without a familial history of left handedness, prejudges the procedures as being related to cerebral lateralization and avoids the problem of coming to a fuller understanding of the relationship between cerebral lateralization and such variables as handedness, familial sinistrality, and sex.

In Chapter 4, McKeever reports on an ongoing series of experiments examining individual differences in spatial ability as a function of gender, handedness, and familial sinistrality. Although this approach does not allow direct comparison of RH versus LH functioning, it does allow for investigation of how different patterns of cerebral laterality (as exhibited by males versus females and by left vs. right handers) can affect general styles of information processing. His findings cannot be neatly accounted for by any of the existing theories of gender or handedness differences; however, he reports some intriguing data and speculation concerning the influence of hormonal characteristics on spatial performance that suggest promising avenues for further research.

Molfese and Burger-Judisch (Chapter 5) present the argument that resources of the brain are allocated and reorganized constantly in efforts to deal more effectively with information processing, decision making, and responding. The database upon which the a dynamic temporal-spatial model is based is derived from electrophysiological (event-related potentials) and behavioral research on speech perception. Their work indicates that the brain's response to even simple low-level types of processing is relatively complex. Rather than a simple lateralized model of speech perception, there are complex patterns of unilateral and bilateral processing of speech cues that change over time. Their developmental work also indicates that there are changes in laterality for speech discrimination patterns across developmental periods. Furthermore, from early infancy onward, there are distinct patterns of both unilateral and bilateral cerebral involvement.

Wood, Flowers, and Naylor (Chapter 6) describe experiments that have measured localized functioning of the brain by measuring the amplitude or intensity of metabolic activity (cerebral blood flow) in a given region of the brain and correlating this activity with the demands of cognitive tasks. The two tasks involved processing identical word lists and differed only in what subjects were required to do with the words. One task was to identify words previously heard and repeated aloud (a recognition memory task). The other task involved identifying words of a given length (an orthographic analysis or spelling task). In contrast to typical laterality studies, their experiments have used a large number of subjects so that variance in patterns of activation due to age, sex, intelligence, and anxiety can be considered as well as differences in patterns of intercorrelation due to hemispheric differences in activation. They find differences in localized patterns of activation between and within hemispheres as well as sex differences in activation patterns.   Wood et al. relate these findings to functional and structural models of cortical processing.

Metacontrol refers to the neural mechanisms that determine which hemisphere will attempt to control cognitive operations and derives from studies of commissurotomized patients where it has been found that the hemisphere with the greater ability to perform a task is not necessarily the one that assumes control.   Chapter 7 by Hellige outlines a set of procedures for determining whether metacontrol is a feature of the neurologically intact human brain. Hellige points out that it is important to determine how the hemispheres work together in situations where each has assess to the same stimulus material.   He describes experiments that utilize tasks that are performed in qualitatively different ways by the two cerebral hemispheres and compares performance between unilateral and bilateral stimulus presentations.   By means of this strategy it is possible to determine whether the qualitative pattern of results when both hemispheres are stimulated matches the qualitative pattern of results obtained from one visual field (hemisphere) but not the other.   When this is the case, it suggests that one hemisphere's mode of processing dominates when a choice can be made and, in this sense, one hemisphere exerts metacontrol.

In Chapter 8, Hardyck is concerned with the role of attention in effecting performance differences between the human cerebral hemispheres. He reviews previous experiments that systematically manipulate attentional effects on lexical decisions carried out within visual half fields and new experiments on interhemispheric transfer, stimulus repetition, extremely long exposure times, and variations on stimulus parameters. In all cases, right-hemisphere performance is poorer than left hemisphere performance even when conditions that are maximally facilitative of interhemispheric transfer are utilized.   The fact that hemisphere differences in language performance remain stable despite these manipulations while performance on nonlanguage stimuli is affected by such manipulations is discussed by Hardyck in terms of two possible hypothesis (a) interhemispheric transfer of language information is sloppy and inefficient; and (b) the human brain contains two separate lexicons, one per hemisphere, which do not communicate with each other, with the right hemisphere lexicon being much less capable than the left hemisphere lexicon.

Van Kleeck and Kosslyn (Chapter 9) describe the ways in which computer models can make contributions to investigations of hemispheric functional asymmetry. They discuss how computer modeling can provide insights into the development of lateralization, functional asymmetry in the normal adult brain, individual differences in cerebral asymmetry, the relationship of functional asymmetries to the consequences of brain damage, the structural substrata of lateral differences, and the computational consequences of hemispheric specialization. They show how computer models are well suited for examining how lateral differences can arise from complex interactions among processing subsystems. Van Kleeck and Kosslyn use a computer model of the development of visual cerebral lateralization called BRIAN (Bilateral Recognition and Imagery Adaptive Networks) to explain lateralization in terms of three key ideas: adaptive subsystems that are "tuned" by feedback; interhemispheric processing degradation; and central bilateral control. From high-level explorations of the interactions of multiple processing subsystems, to fine-grained analyses of the structure and function of individual subsystems, computer models allow a level of precision, explicitness, and predictive power that is otherwise virtually impossible to achieve.

Sergent and Corballis (Chapter 10) present a series of experiments that explore the use of computational models to study hemispheric differences in visual imagery and mental rotation. They note a lack of clear-cut findings with respect to cerebral asymmetry in mental rotation and suggest that this could reflect different hemisphere efficiency at performing the various component operations that compose the mental-rotation task. They argue that the computational approach may become indispensable to examine the lateralization of a given operation, as only through an examination of the respective competence of each hemisphere at carrying out each component operation is it possible to identify the stages at which the two hemispheres may be functionally unequal. This issue is explored with a commissurotomized patient in an attempt to isolate some of the components of the task. Sergent and Corballis note that the particular properties of the split-brain allow for the emergence of striking dissociations in hemisphere processing competences. For instance, if the mental-rotation component is predominantly represented in one hemisphere, the absence of direct interhemispheric connections should give rise to a clear visual field asymmetry because the less competent hemisphere would not benefit from the processing resources of the more competent hemisphere as it does in the intact brain. It may thus be through a conjoint examination of the actual operations underlying a given function and of the specific conditions under which those operations are carried out in the brain that significant advances in the understanding of cerebral lateralization will be made.

The experiments described in the final chapter by Kitterle and Christman (Chapter 11) are designed to provide further elaboration of the hypothesis that hemispheric asymmetries in the processing of spatial frequency emerge when processing beyond the sensory level is required. Their experiments show that hemispheric asymmetries arise at both threshold and suprathreshold levels for grating identification. Right-hemisphere advantages are obtained for identifying low spatial frequencies, whereas while the left hemisphere is more efficient in processing high spatial frequencies. However, when the task is detection, hemispheric symmetry is found at both threshold and suprathreshold levels. Kitterle and Christman relate their findings to earlier research with gratings that failed to support the spatial frequency hypothesis. The implications of their results for recent models of threshold detection and identification are also discussed.

ACKNOWLEDGEMENTS

I express my appreciation to the many individuals who helped in the preparation of this book. I am grateful to my colleagues for their prompt response to editorial requests. I am also indebted to Lynn Robertson, Justine Sergent, Stephen Christman, and Joseph Hellige for their comments on selected chapters. I wish to thank Lynne Walker and Dorothy May for assisting in editorial chores. This book would not be possible without the generous support and encouragement of Alfred A. Cave, Dean of the College of Arts and Sciences; Jerry Updegraf of The University of Toledo Alumni Foundation, Vice President for Academic Affairs William N. Free and especially to James D. McComas, University President. All have recognized the importance of our efforts to annually hold topical seminars on advances in biobehavioral research

The continued support and encouragement of my wife, Janet, and daughter, Kristine, on the success of our conference and the resulting book cannot be underestimated.

1 Prosimians as Animal Models in the Study of Neural Lateralizaton

Jeannette P. Ward
Memphis State University

In the search for the origins and mechanisms of human functional capacities, the study of nonhuman species has often furnished invaluable insights. Animal research has the advantage of access to physiological mechanisms and organic subsystems to which experimental questions may be addressed with a thoroughness that the study of humans alone would not permit. More broadly, comparison of structure/function relationships between species, and especially in consideration of phyletic relationships among those species, offers a tool by which function may be understood in an evolutionary perspective.

Human neural and behavioral lateralization is a heavily documented, if poorly understood, phenomenon. The massive literature arising from the study of this phenomenon is testimonial to the interest the topic has inspired for most of this century. The current vigor of this area of inquiry is seen both in the several volumes devoted to some aspect of the topic each year and in the frequent laterality symposia at meetings of psychologists, neuropsychologists, psycholinguists, neurologists, neuroscientists, cognitive scientists, and philosophers. Despite the continuing proliferation of theories and research reports based principally on studies of intact and brain-damaged humans, this literature has a curiously fragmented character. Norman Geschwind noted this state of affairs repeatedly in his final works and made an impassioned plea for efforts to develop a broadly biological theory of neural lateralization (Galaburda, Sherman, & Geschwind, 1985; Geschwind, 1985; Geschwind & Galaburda, 1984, 1985).

One has only to consider the great advances in the understanding of sensory processes made possible by the study of animal models to see immediately how much is sacrificed by neglect of nonhuman animal studies in the exploration of any brain-behavior phenomenon. In the study of sensory processes, for example, it is difficult to imagine how lateral inhibition, opponent cell process, transduction, adaptation, habituation, topographic representation, or parallel process might have been explored fully without nonhuman animal subjects. The study of sensory processes and neural lateralization have been pursued over approximately the same historical period. The extensive use of animal models by the former has been a major factor in advancing sensory research and thus

1

permitting the construction of an integrated body of knowledge.

There has, in fact, been some excellent research with nonhuman primates (see Hamilton, this volume) bearing on questions that are central to laterality research and theory, but this type of work has occupied an undeservedly peripheral position in the area. Basically, the focus of cerebral laterality research on "higher order" functions, functions presumably most characteristic of, if not exclusive to, humans, has given the topic a "top-down" bias that has tended to disengaged it from the potential contributions of the full range of biological constructs.

This state of affairs was enabled by early research that sought evidence of nonhuman primate laterality in laboratory study of the hand preferences of one species of nonhuman primate (Warren, 1953, 1958). Hand preference is a characteristic of humans that is strongly lateralized in most individuals and, in addition, there is a lateral bias for right handedness in the human population. Although in humans the relationship between handedness and other lateralized functions such as language, spatial abilities, etc, is as yet uncertain, the hand preference measure has been attractive as an objective measure suitable for assessing laterality in nonhuman primates. The results of these early studies with one species led to the conclusion that there was no evidence for an evolutionary basis of behavioral or neural lateralization in nonhuman primates (Warren, 1977, 1980). Until very recently that conclusion has been taken as convention. One might wonder at the acceptance of the null hypothesis on such limited evidence and in the face of considerable evidence of lateralization in nonprimate mammals (Collins, 1985; Denenberg, 1981; Glick & Shapiro, 1985) and even nonmammmals (Nottebohm, 1979; Rogers, 1980, 1986).

The study of lateralized behavior in a variety of nonhuman primates was activated in several laboratories in response to the theoretical review of MacNeilage, Studdert-Kennedy, and Lindblom (1987a, 1987b). Their survey and analysis of the existing literature revealed how tenuous were the bases for the conclusion that nonhuman primates had no lateralization relevant to human lateralization. They also proposed the evolutionary development of lateralization within the primate line as an adaptive sequence of hemispheric specialization originating with the most primitive of primates, the prosimians.

As appropriate to an evolutionary scenario for lateralization, the new evidence is based on a broader sample of species than the earlier literature (MacNeilage, Studdert-Kennedy, & Lindblom, 1988; Ward, 1988). The current evidence of lateralization in a variety of primate species is presented by Ward (in press). This chapter presents some of the evidence for behavioral lateralization in prosimian species and discusses the potential usefulness of prosimians in efforts to understand both the neural mechanisms and origins of human lateralization. At the time of this writing, my graduate students and I have evaluated over 300 individuals of 13 prosimian species for laterality using laboratory tests with some and observing free-ranging behaviors with others. We have studied hand use as simple food reaching, duration of food holding, food manipulation, and the patterning between these feeding measures. We have also measured locomotor responses such as leading limb and whole body turning and postural biases such as tail positioning and tonic neck bias. In all these measures, most individuals have been found to be strongly lateralized and, in addition, population level biases have been found with measures for which sample size permitted evaluation. Beyond simply demonstrating that prosimians have lateralized behaviors, this research has identified a relationship for the subject variables of sex and age with the direction and strength of hand preference lateralization and has furnished considerable evidence that conditions associated with the expression of the behavioral response can exert systematic effects on the strength of lateralized behavior. From these studies, I have begun to develop some ideas about the neural mechanisms of prosimian lateralization in relation to the lateralization of vertebrates other than primates on the one hand and of human and other anthropoids primates on the other. It is my hope that prosimians may be useful not only as animal models of human laterality but also as a taxonomic bridge to connect the special lateralities characteristic of the primate order with the more general phenomenon of vertebrate laterality.

In the planning and, especially, interpretation of the prosimian research, I have become aware that there are a number of questions related to this research that require working assumptions if an orderly conceptual framework is to be constructed. My current working assumptions are as follows:

1.   laterality expressed in behavior has a determinable biological basis in structural and/or functional differences in lateral subdivisions of the nervous system;

2.   laterality has its origins in genetic programs but the lateralization of particular behaviors may be modified by the experiences of the organism during ontogeny by environmental pressures and also as a consequence of specific learning or practice;

3.   lateralization is not necessarily a unitary phenomenon in each animal, but there may be two or more response systems with different lateral biases;

4.   when such discretely lateralized response systems are identified, they will be found to serve different adaptive functions in motor control and may be found to occupy different levels of the neuraxis;

5.   each lateralized response system has in a given circumstance a quantifiable strength of lateralization that may be altered by specifiable variables both organismic and environmental;

6.   some type of behavioral lateralization is characteristic of most, if not all, vertebrates and serves a general principle of adaptive significance; and

7.   lateralization is the property of an organism, whereas population level lateralization is an abstraction derived from individuals as samples of a species, and thus whatever proportions of individuals in a population are empirically determined to be lateralized serves as a valid estimate of population laterality for that species (i.e., only if no individual has any lateralized behavior may it be concluded that the population is without laterality).

In the pages that follow, prosimian studies are grouped in terms of what appear to be different types of laterality phenomena. First, research is reviewed that demonstrates the effect of posture on the behavioral expression of lateralized hand preference and a neural model of systemic arousal is suggested as appropriate to this phenomenon. Second, the subject variables of sex and age are shown to be related to prosimian lateralized hand use and these results are interpreted in terms of a model of fetal development of human cerebral hemispheric asymmetries. Finally, the study of whole-body turning in prosimians is reviewed and related to the literature of rotational movement in nonprimate mammals and humans.

Lateralized Hand Use in Prosimians

Laterality in hand use has been assessed as simple food reaching in all individuals of all species studied and preferred hand determined for each individual by z-score analysis. Approximately 80% of all prosimians evaluated have used a preferred hand in food retrieval; of these, most favor use of the left hand. Each hand preference study completed has been conducted with a different species and/or under somewhat different test conditions. Each study has both confirmed the behavioral lateralization of prosimians and furnished fresh insights into the variables that influence lateralized hand use. The research results are thus most effectively presented on a study by study basis.

The Effects of Posture on Hand Preference

The first systematic assessment of hand preference in a prosimian species was incidental to a study of the visual discrimination of mirror images. In this study, eight lesser bushbabies (*Galago senegalensis*) were trained to discriminate between pairs of mirror-image stimuli and pairs of nonmirror-image stimuli with the order of testing counterbalanced and with stimulus pairs presented simultaneously to four animals and sequentially to the other four (Sanford & Ward, 1986). The results showed that the lesser bushbaby could master a mirror-image discrimination. Both Mach (1887, 1959) and Orton (1937) had suggested that the capacity for mirror-image discrimination should depend on lateralization of the nervous system. In the interest of evaluating this idea, hand preference was assessed as an indicator of lateralization: seven of the animals responded with the left hand more than 80% of reaches, whereas the eighth subject had no lateralized hand preference. Interestingly, this subject had the best performance on the mirror-image discrimination and, in addition, there was no correlation between discrimination performance and strength of lateralized hand preference. The finding of lateral hand preference, however, led to further research employing the entire colony of 25 lesser bushbabies. In this study (Sanford, Guin, & Ward, 1984) the same test apparatus was used initially as in the first study. This apparatus was a simple visual fields test apparatus: a semicircular cage with a solid back and roof and a wire mesh front with three openings; one opening was centered on the semicircle and located 15 cm from the floor with the other two openings located 10 cm to either side of the central opening. Mealworms (*Tenebrio* larvae) were affixed to the end of a dowel rod and presented to the subject about 4 cm from one of the three apertures. Because of the construction of this apparatus, the bushbabies always reached through the opening for the mealworm from an upright and bipedal posture. The initial test found 12 of 25 bushbabies reaching 80%-100% with the left hand whereas the other animals were distributed about equally into the remaining four percentage categories. [Subsequently, I have re-analyzed this data with z-scores ($p< 0.01$) and found 14 of these subjects to have a left hand preference, 5 a right hand preference, and 6 to be ambipreferent.] Upon replication with the visual field apparatus, the test-retest reliability was $r = 0.651$, $p<0.01$. These subjects were further tested for worm retrieval in a free-field where reaching was negotiated from a quadrupedal posture. Under these test conditions, the population was bimodal in distribution. Although the test/retest reliability for free field response was high ($r = 0.864$, $p<0.01$), there was no correlation between the two different types of tests. Thus, the use of a preferred hand seemed contingent upon reaching from a bipedal posture.

Investigation of hand use in the lesser bushbaby was extended by Larson, Dodson, and Ward (1989) in a study that varied elevation, visibility, and angle of reach in an effort to identify more completely the variables that influence use of a preferred hand. In this experiment all test behavior was videotaped and responses scored from the taped records. Ten lesser bushbabies were tested in counterbalanced order in eight conditions of food presentation designed to manipulate posture (high vs. low food cups), visibility (clear vs. opaque food cups), and angle of reach (horizontal vs. vertical cup orientation). Each subject received 60 trials in each test condition for a total of 480 trials. As evaluated across all test conditions, seven bushbabies were found to be left-hand preferent and three right- hand preferent. Of the three conditions manipulated, only elevation of the food cup was effective in increasing use of preferred hand. This served to confirm the previously observed intensification of lateral bias for bushbabies with bipedal posture.

The diet of lesser bushbabies in their African habitat is estimated to consist of about 80% flying insects (Haddow and Ellice, cited in Doyle, 1974) which they capture with a ballistic "smash and grab" movement (Bishop, 1964). Also, they are one of several prosimians that are categorized as "vertical clingers and leapers" (Napier & Walker, 1967); not only is their locomotion characterized by bipedal leaping in an upright posture but the resting posture also favors an upright trunk and head with the long hind legs flexed in a crouch. Thus, at first I considered that intensification of laterality with elevation to bipedal posture might be a species typical, perhaps even species exclusive, characteristic of the rather stereotyped prey capture habit of the lesser bushbaby. However, a subsequent study of the black and white ruffed lemur revealed that the potentiating effects of postural adjustment on lateralized hand use may be found in very different prosimian species.

Forsythe, Milliken, Stafford, and Ward (1988) examined the hand preferences of five male sibling black and white ruffed lemurs (*Varecia variegata variegata*) resident on a moated island at the Memphis Zoological Park. The black and white ruffed lemur is a large and quadrupedal native of Madagascar. The five animals were videotaped reaching under three different conditions: free foraging, discrete food presentation on land, and discrete food presentation in the moat. Reaches in free foraging were obtained by videotaping the ongoing behaviors of the animals for 40 hours. For the discrete food presentation conditions, orange slices were thrown onto the surface of the island 50 to 300 cm from the target subject and banana slices were thrown into the moat so that they floated close to the edge of the island. In the land condition, the lemurs would observe the food piece fall, move rapidly to that location, and retrieve the food. In the moat condition, it was necessary that the lemurs make a more extreme postural adjustment by resting their hindquarters on the edge of the concrete wall that bordered the moat, stretching the upper part of the body down over the edge, and reaching for the floating banana slice with one hand while bracing with the other. One hundred unimanual hand responses were scored for each lemur in each of the three conditions. The results are shown in Table 1.1.

In the free foraging condition reaches for grasses, leaves, twigs, sticks and other potentially edible objects were most frequently made when the lemur was quiescent and the occasional postural preadjustments rarely involved more than a slow and partial turning of the upper part of the body. By comparison, the reaches so strongly lateralized to the left hand in all five lemurs following the discrete presentation of a food item on the surface of the island were preceded by visual orientation to the approaching food piece, rapid locomotion to its location, and a whole-body postural adjustment prior to the discrete reach and retrieval. The retrieval behavior for the discrete moat presentation was much the same as that for the land presentation except that the whole-body postural preadjustment was much more extreme. Thus, in this more naturalistic setting with a prosimian structurally,

TABLE 1.1
Reaching Data for Individual Animals in Three Conditions

Animal	Free foraging		DFP-land		DFP-moat	
	Total	%L	Total	%L	Total	%L
Buster	101	54	102	96	100	99
Garth	100	48	116	91	101	100
Harley	113	48	109	97	104	100
Kingfish	101	71	118	99	108	100
Sparky	102	59	110	98	102	100
Average	103.4	56.0	111.0	96.2	103.0	99.8

Note: DFP = discrete food presentation. %L = percentage of left-hand use.

behaviorally, and taxonomically quite different than the lesser bushbaby, postural adjustment prior to reaching also served to intensify use of a preferred hand.

It seems appropriate to observe at this point that field studies of retrieval of thrown food by free-ranging Japanese macaques (*Macaca fuscata*) have found lateralized hand use with the majority of animals using the left hand preferentially (Itani, Tokuda, Furuya, Kano, & Shin, 1963; Kawai, 1967; Tokuda, 1969). In light of these results it seems sensible to caution that in studies of primate hand-use laterality the potential of the total test environment to influence the behavioral response needs to be considered, especially as those environmental features may affect whole body posture and postural adjustments prior to reaching.

This research demonstrates that postural adjustment prior to reaching promotes the use of a preferred hand. It may be that the behavioral expression of an inherent lateral bias can be amplified by a neural arousal system activated by postural adjustment. What I have in mind is a general systemic arousal contingent on postural adjustment. I have been encouraged in this idea by Talbott's (1979) suggestion that visceral proprioception functions to increase integration of overall postural mechanisms. Evidence to support this contention is found in the work of Ito and Sanada (1965) who demonstrated that the righting reflexes of monkeys are functionally related to changes in visceral afference from Pacinian corpuscles in response to changes in body position relative to gravity. These visceral afferents project to the cerebellum and reticular activating system (Ito & Sanada, 1965), and to the primary somatosensory (SI), secondary somatosensory (SII), and orbital areas of neocortex (Amassian, 1951a, 1951b; Downman, 1951; Korn, 1969; Newman, 1962). The provisional neural model that I am considering does not conceive of the laterality bias as residing within the arousal system; rather the arousal system serves to elevate overall brain activity and thereby enhance the endogenous lateral bias of relevant brain structures. With this model it would be predicted that other variables which systematically increase organismic arousal, perhaps as mediated by the reticular activating system, would also increase the expression of lateralization in behavior.

SUBJECT VARIABLES: SEX AND AGE

The first indication that direction of hand preference might be sex linked in a prosimian species came from study of a matriline of 13 ring-tailed lemurs (*Lemur catta*) resident on a moated island at the Memphis Zoological Gardens (Milliken, Forsythe, & Ward, 1989). The manner of study was somewhat similar to the previously discussed study of black and white lemurs (Forsythe et al., 1988) in that all behaviors were videotaped and sliced bananas were thrown across the moat onto the surface of the island. In this study complete feeding sequences were recorded for each animal and hand-use lateralization was sought in duration of food holding and manipulation of food as well as food retrieval. From the results, lateralized patterns of food handling emerged: the lemurs that were left preferent in reaching also held food longer with the left hand and engaged in less manipulation of food; lemurs right preferent or ambipreferent in reaching engaged in longer bouts of bimanual holding and more manipulation of food with the right hand. Thus, feeding behavior was congruently lateralized in three measures as two distinct patterns, one characteristic of left preferent lemurs and another for right and ambipreferent lemurs. Further, inspection of the data set suggested that the preferred direction of these lateralized patterns of food reaching and handling were related to sex in this matriline: of the seven males, six were left-hand preferent and one was ambipreferent; of the six females three were right-hand preferent, two were ambipreferent, and one was left hand preferent. This loose assortment by sex became even more interesting when it was noted that two of the three pairs of twins in the matriline seemed to contribute to the exceptions. For example, the one ambipreferent male had a female twin who was also ambipreferent. A second pair of twins, both female, were lateralized one to the right and the other to the left. For the third pair of twins, a mixed sex pair, the male was lateralized to the left and the female to the right. The observation of laterality patterns in two sets of twins that seemed atypical of the rest of the matriline raised the question of the possible effects of prenatal experience as a factor in adult lateral hand preference. Although side of nursing preference observations for twin infant ring-tailed lemurs are not yet available, five infant lesser bushbabies (*Galago senegalensis moholi*) and five infant greater bushbabies (*Galago garnettii*) in my colonies were found to have consistent side of nursing preferences; this was true of all infants of both species whether twins or singletons (Pinger, Lavallee, Hobbs, & Ward, 1988). This line of research offers a promising experimental model for the investigation of the effects of early experience on adult lateralized behaviors.

Age differences in lateralization were initially recognized in a study of simple food reaching in 33 black lemurs (*Lemur macaco*). Forsythe and Ward (1988) conducted this study to evaluate reliability of hand preference by collecting data from the same animals in two phases with about 6 months intervening. Although only 20 lemurs were available for both phases of data collection, hand preference proved to be remarkably stable in these animals in that no lemur changed hand preference from one measurement phase to the next. Of the total population of black lemurs 20 were left-hand preferent, 12 were right-hand preferent, and only 1 had no hand preference in food reaching. There was no relationship between sex and preferred hand, but there was a negative correlation between age and percentage use of the left hand [$(r(32)=-0.538, p<0.001$]. Younger animals tended to use the left hand in food retrieval, whereas older lemurs employed the right hand more often. The strength of the age effect may also be illustrated by noting that although the average age for this group was 4.8 years (range 1-18 years), seven of the nine oldest lemurs, those 6 years old or older, were right-hand preferent.

In order to assess a taxonomic group of sufficient size and composition to reflect adequately covariations of sex and age with hand use lateralization, a study of 194 individuals, 116 males and 78 females, of six species and five subspecies of Lemur resident at the Duke University Primate Center was conducted (Ward,

Milliken, Dodson, Stafford, & Wallace, in press). Lemurs were observed eating their usual daily ration of cut fruit and chow until a minimum of 100 unimanual reaches was scored for every member of the group. The animals were housed singly, in small family groups, or in larger social groups and either in large outdoor cages or in one of four natural habitat enclosures. Data were collected from the smaller groups by direct observation and from the larger groups by videotaping. Z-score analysis ($z = 3.3$ or larger, $p<.001$) was used to determine preference. It was found that 91 (46.9%) of the lemurs were left-hand preferent, 65 (33.5%) were right-hand preferent, and 38 (19.6%) had no statistically significant preference. The distribution of hand preference in this population of lemurs was different than would be expected by chance ($X^2=21.7$, $df=2$, $p<.01$). Table 1.2 shows the proportion of subjects that were left, right, or ambipreferent in the male and female populations as a function of age. In order to balance the number of subjects in each sex/age group, three age categories were selected: 1 - 2 years, juvenile; 3 - 6 years, young adult; and 7 - 30 years, fully adult. Regardless of age, most male lemurs were left hand preferent; at the same time there was an age-related increase in the number of right preferent male lemurs and a concomitant decrease in the incidence of ambipreferent males. What seems to be a modification of this pattern is seen in the female lemurs. Although juvenile females are about equally divided into the three hand preference groups, examination of left-hand preference across age categories shows this group to be only somewhat smaller proportionately than the left preferent male group. The increase with age in the proportion of lemurs that use the right hand preferentially, which is seen in the male population as a slight trend, is seen in the female population as greatly amplified especially in the full adult category where right-hand preferent females compose the largest proportion.

It had been noted that 25 of the females were carrying and/or nursing infants. In order to assess the relationship between presence of an infant and direction of hand preference, the distributions of hand use in females with infants and females without infants were examined separately. The 25 females with infants had an average age of 7 years (range 2 - 16 years); of these females 13 (52%) were right hand preferent, 9 (36%) preferred the left hand, and 3 (12%) had no preference. The very young and very old females were eliminated from the sample of females without infants in order to compose an age-adjusted sample of 40 females with a mean age of 5.6 years (range 2 - 16 years); the distribution of hand-use preference for this group was 13 (32.5%) right, 18 (45%) left, and 9 (22.5%) nonpreferent. Thus, the group of females with infants tended to be older and contained a larger proportion of right-hand preferent individuals.

In two other primate species, an association between adult female status and right-hand preference has recently been recorded. Milliken, Dodson, and Ward (in preparation) have found seven of nine adult female greater bushbabies (*Galago garnettii*) to be strongly right hand preferent in feeding. In a study of *siamang* and *gibbon* familygroups, the total sample of five adult female hylobatids were all right hand preferent (Stafford, Milliken, & Ward, in press). It is also interesting to note that it has been well-established that human females have a

TABLE 1.2

Proportion of Lemurs in Each of Three Handedness Groups as a Function of Sex and Age

	N[*]	Left	Ambi	Right
Males				
Juveniles	41	.488	.268	.244
Young Adults	48	.542	.125	.333
Full Adults	27	.482	.148	.370
Females				
Juveniles	19	.316	.316	.368
Young Adults	30	.467	.300	.233
Full Adults	29	.414	.069	.517

[*]N = Number of lemurs in each sex by age subgroup.

measurably stronger right bias than males in tests of motor lateralization (Annett, 1980; Porac & Coren, 1977; Seltzer, Forsythe, & Ward, in press).

An overview of these lemur studies suggests that two different mechanisms may underlie the left- and right-hand preferences observed. The left-hand preference exists at a high level in this group of *Lemur*. Although the proportions of left-preferent animals are somewhat higher for males, the proportions are essentially stable over age groups for both males and females. By comparison, the proportion of right handed animals in a group increases with age for both male and female groups. The left hand bias may be an enduring characteristic of the individual based on greater development of the right hemisphere of the brain in comparison to the left. Geschwind and Galaburda (1985) have proposed that the right hemisphere leads the left in human fetal development with the left hemisphere having a slower rate of development and, consequently, a longer period of vulnerability to factors that may interfere with its development. Testosterone was proposed as one endogenous factor that affects left hemisphere development and results in a comparably greater final level of development of the right hemisphere, thus accounting for the greater incidence of left handedness in male humans. I propose that a similar differential rate of hemispheric fetal development obtains for lemurs with a higher incidence of final right hemisphere advantage than is usual for humans. I further hypothesize that the fetal testosterone effect is present in lemurs and is the source of the large proportion of male lemurs that are left hand preferent.

The increase in the proportion of right-hand preferent lemurs with age has two possible explanations. Table 1.2 indicates that the increase in right-hand preferent lemurs is essentially at the expense of the ambipreferent group because increases in the proportion of right preferent lemurs is accompanied by decreases in the proportion of lemurs that have no hand preference. This suggests that the right and ambipreferent group are essentially one group the composition of which changes over time. It is possible that the apparent conversion of ambipreferent lemurs into right preferent lemurs with age could reflect the continuing development of the left hemisphere such that in the course of young adult life there is a progression from a stage with both hemispheres equally developed (the ambipreferent lemur) to a later stage wherein the left hemisphere has continued to develop slowly until it attains functional dominance (the right handed lemur). From this it would be predicted that longitudinal study would find changes with age from ambipreferent to right preferent. In consideration of the cross-sectional data reported here, I hypothesize that there are two subpopulations: one established in left-hand preference (i.e., with stable right hemisphere dominance) and a second that is composed of ambipreferent lemurs (equal hemisphere development) that with age develop a preferential use of the right hand. Whereas the development of right- hand preference might be based on continuing anatomical development,   alternatively, it might reflect a quite different type of mechanism that can be manifested when there is equal development of the two hemispheres: a physiological effect based in a functional specialization of the left hemisphere that may be activated by social competition in the feeding situation. Tucker and Williamson (1984) have expounded a model of hemispheric specialization that assigns to the left hemisphere the role of activation as "integral to motor operations, supporting postural readiness and motivationally directed action" (p. 188). Several of the species of lemur studied are matriarchal and the adult females, especially those with infants, are very assertive at the discrete daily feeding sessions and literally take command of the feeding area. Generally, fully adult lemurs, both male and female in social groups tend to be more quickly successful during feeding competition.   The proximity of very young lemurs during feeding is tolerated by the older lemurs; juveniles and young adults, however, typically take second place at the "table", as might the older males depending on the degree of matriarchy of the species and whether the adult female has an infant. It is possible that the confidence of fully adult males in socially favorable circumstances and the matriarchal and/or maternal status of some adult females resulted in greater involvement of the activation system of the left hemisphere with consequent use of the right hand.

If it is true that the left-hand preferent animals constitute a single subpopulation composed of lemurs that have a greater development of the right hemisphere that remains unchanged throughout adult life, then these animals should have a left hand preference that is stable with aging. By contrast, if the ambipreferent and right-hand preferent animals constitute a second subpopulation composed of lemurs that have more equal development of the two hemispheres permitting the manifestation of a functional specialization of the left hemisphere when the lemur is in a behavioral state of confidence and assertiveness in feeding, then changes in variables that affect this behavioral state such as age, maternal or other social status, conditions of housing, and so forth, should be reflected in greater or lesser use of the right hand. Longitudinal studies and studies of lemurs in situations promoting different behavioral states such as with or without an infant present will permit evaluation of this model and its alternatives.

WHOLE-BODY TURNING

Rotational movement has been related to imbalances of dopaminergic activity in the basal ganglia in several mammalian species (Glick & Cox, 1978; Glick & Shapiro, 1985; Glick, Weaver, & Meibach, 1981; Zimmerberg, Glick, & Jerussi, 1974). In humans asymmetries of both size (Kooistra & Heilman, 1988) and dopamine levels (Glick, Ross, & Hough, 1982) have been reported for the *globus pallidus* of the basal ganglia. Adult humans have rotational biases that are somewhat related to sex and to other behavioral measures of laterality: males who are left-hemisphere dominant as measured by congruence of right eye, hand, and foot bias more often show a rotational bias to the right; whereas, males of mixed dominance and left-hemisphere dominant females have biases to circle to the left (Bracha, Seitz, Otemaa, & Glick, 1987). Both male and female children have rotational biases that are in most cases toward the left (Glick, in press). The lesser bushbaby also has a strong lateral bias in whole-body turning and for most individuals this bias is to the left. Larson et al. (1989) employed videotaped retrieval of mealworms from different types of food cups to determine the effect of various conditions on use of preferred hand. Because each of the 480 trials was a discrete trial initiated from a start box and concluded by the subject making a 180 degree turn to return to the start box, it was possible to score turning behavior for evidence of lateral bias. Whole-body turns were lateralized in 9 of 10 animals as determined by z scores ($p<0.001$): 8 turned consistently to the left (group mean = 83.4%, range from 59% to 99%) and 1 to the right (96%). Although the animal that preferred to turn to his right was also right-hand preferent and the animal that had no turning bias was also the least strongly handed of the 10 subjects, 2 of the right-hand preferent animals were left turning, and there was no correlation between turning and hand use. Thus, although 7 of 10 subjects used the left-hand preferentially and 8 of 10 turned left preferentially, these two response systems seemed to be unrelated in lateralization.

I have recently acquired additional evidence that the whole-body left turning bias is indeed a strong one. A breeding population of a subspecies of the lesser bushbaby (*Galago senegalensis moholi*) was tested for hand preference and turning bias in a subset of the tests employed in the Larson et al. (1989) study in order to characterize individuals of this population for the study of heritability of lateralized traits. Of the 17 animals tested, 1 had a right turning bias, 2 had no lateral bias, and the remaining 14 animals made turns reliably to the left. The average strength of the left turn bias was 88.4% (range 62% to 99%) with a response sample of 240 for each subject. Although this turning measure is not strictly comparable to the rotational measure used for rats, the turning bias of the bushbabies was much stronger than that reported for rats (Glick & Cox, 1978;

Glick & Shapiro, 1985). In my laboratory, a comparable rotational measure was recently used to collect evidence of turning bias for eight mouse lemurs (*Microcebus murinus*). The mouse lemurs were videotaped from above during a period of confinement in a circular enclosure. The average number of turns scored was 466 (range 225 - 1,271). Seven of eight mouse lemurs had a simple majority bias for left turning. The eight lemurs had an average left bias of 58.7% (range 48.4% - 73.5%), which is comparable in strength to the rotational biases of rats. The marked left whole body turning bias in the lesser bushbaby and the somewhat weaker left rotational bias in the mouse lemur suggest that prosimians may serve as a useful bridge between nonprimate mammals and human primates in further exploring the relationships between the dopaminergic system of the basal ganglia, whole-body turning biases, and other lateralized response systems.

OVERVIEW

It has only been a few years since study of prosimian lateralized behaviors began. However, in this short time it has become evident that these primitive species offer unique opportunities in the study of primate laterality. In behavior and brain structure, prosimians are less complex than anthropoid primates, yet they are primates and as such should be more adequate models of human laterality than nonprimate mammals. At the same time, prosimians can serve as appropriate links between nonprimate mammals and the anthropoid primates, including humans, in the study of the biological basis of laterality phenomena.

   In the research discussed here and in other work not treated here, I have hardly begun to evaluate prosimian lateralization; yet every prosimian study has found convincing evidence of laterality and in multiple response systems. The lateralization of prosimian behavior is a large magnitude effect both in the strength of the lateral biases and in the percentage of animals in the prosimian populations that have lateral biases in behavior. As to whether some or all prosimian species should be characterized as preferring use of the left hand in feeding becomes less clear with the finding of a relationship between direction of hand bias and sex and age variables. The interpretation of left- or right-hand preference as characteristic of any prosimian group must now be made in consideration of the sex and age composition of the group. Certainly, it is true that for the species studied to date a majority left hand preference in food reaching has been the consistent finding. However, from the perspective of the research reported here, the question of dominant direction of lateral bias in prosimian hand use seems of less immediate heuristic value than the many other questions that this research has raised.

ACKNOWLEDGMENT

Preparation of this chapter was supported in part by National Science Foundation Grant BNS-8707754 awarded to J. P. Ward.

REFERENCES

Amassian, V.D. (1951a). Cortical representations of visceral efferents. *Journal of Neurophysiology, 14,* 433-444.

Amassian, V.D. (1951b). Fiber groups and spinal pathways of cortically represented visceral afferents. *Journal of Neurophysiology, 14,* 445-460.

Annett, M. (1980). Sex differences in laterality -meaningfulness versus reliability. *Behavioral and Brain Sciences, 3,* 227-228.

Bishop, A. (1964). Use of the hand in lower primates. In J. Buettner-Janush (Ed.), *Evolutionary and genetic biology of primates* (Vol. 2, pp.133-225). New York: Academic Press.

Bracha, H.S., Seitz, D.J., Otemaa, J., & Glick, S.D. (1987). Rotational movement (circling) in normal humans: Sex difference and relationship to hand, foot and eye preference. *Brain Research, 411,* 231-235.

Collins, R.L. (1985). On the inheritance of direction and degree of asymmetry. In S.D. Glick (Ed.), *Cerebral lateralization in nonhuman species* (pp.41-71). New York: Academic Press.

Denenberg, V.H. (1981). Hemispheric laterality in animals and the effects of early experience. *The Behavioral and Brain Sciences, 4,* 1-49.

Downman, C.B.B. (1951). Cerebral destination of splanchnic afferent impulses. *Journal of Physiology, 113,* 434-441.

Doyle, G.A. (1974). Behavior of prosimians. In A.M. Schrier and F. Stollnitz (Eds.), *Behavior of nonhuman primates* (Vol. 5, pp.155-353). New York: Academic Press.

Forsythe, C., Milliken, G.W., Stafford, D.K., & Ward, J.P. (1988). Posturally related variations in the hand preferences of the ruffed lemur (Varecia variegata variegata). *Journal of Comparative Psychology, 102,* 248-250.

Forsythe, C., & Ward, J.P. (1988). Black lemur (Lemur macaco) hand preference in food reaching. *Primates, 29,* 369-374.

Galaburda, A.M., Sherman, G., & Geschwind, N. (1985). Cerebral lateralization: Historical note on animal studies. In S.D.Glick (Ed.), *Cerebral lateralization in nonhuman species* (pp. 1-10). New York: Academic Press.

Geschwind, N. (1985). Implications for evolution, genetics, and clinical syndromes. In S.D.Glick (Ed.), *Cerebral lateralization in nonhuman species* (pp. 247-278). New York: Academic Press.

Geschwind, N., & Galaburda, A.M. (1984). *Cerebral dominance.* Cambridge: Harvard University Press.

Geschwind, N., & Galaburda, A.M. (1985). Cerebral lateralization: Biological mechanisms, hypothesis and a program for research. *Archives of Neurology, 42,* 428-459, 521-552, 634-654.

Glick, S.D. (In press). Rotational behavior in children and adults. In J.P. Ward (Ed.), *Current behavioral evidence of primate asymmetries.* New York: Springer-Verlag.

Glick, S.D., & Cox, R.D. (1978). Nocturnal rotation in normal rats: correlation with amphetamine-induced rotation and effects of nigrostriatal lesions. *Brain Research, 150,* 149-161.

Glick, S.D., Ross, D.A., & Hough, L.B. (1982). Lateral asymmetry of neurotransmitters in human brain. *Brain Research, 234,* 53-63.

Glick, S.D., & Shapiro, R.M. (1985). Functional and neurochemical mechanisms of cerebral lateralization in rats. In S.D. Glick (Ed.), *Cerebral lateralization in nonhuman species* (pp.157-183). New York: Academic Press.

Glick, S.D., Weaver, L.M., & Meibach, R.C. (1981). Amphetamine induced rotation in normal cats. *Brain Research, 208,* 227-229.

Itani, J., Tokuda, K., Furuya, Y., Kano, K., & Shin, Y. (1963). The social construction of natural troops of Japanese monkeys in Takasakiyama. *Primates, 4,* 1-42.

Ito, T., & Sanada, Y. (1965). Location of receptors for righting reflexes acting upon the body in primates. *Japanese Journal of Physiology, 15,* 235-242.

Kawai, M. (1967). Catching behavior observed in the Koshima troop - a case of newly acquired behavior. *Primates, 8,* 181-186.

Kooistra, C.A., & Heilman, K.M. (1988). Motor dominance and lateral asymmetry of the globus pallidus. *Neurology, 38,* 388-390.

Korn, H. (1969). Splanchnic projection to the orbital cortex of the cat. *Brain Research, 16,* 23-38.

Larson, C.F., Dodson, D.L., & Ward, J.P. (1989). Hand preferences and whole-body turning biases of lesser bushbabies (*Galago senegalensis*). *Brain, Behavior and Evolution, 33,* 261-267.

Mach, E. (1959). *The analysis of sensations.* Chicago: Open Court. (Originally published 1887).

MacNeilage, P.F. (in press). The "Postural Origins" theory of primate neurobiological asymmetries. In N. Krasnegor (Ed.), *Biobehavioral foundations of language development.* Lawrence Erlbaum Associates, Inc. Hillsdale, N.J.

MacNeilage, P.F., Studdert-Kennedy, M.G., & Lindblom, B. (1987a). Primate handedness reconsidered. *The Behavioral and Brain Sciences, 10,* 247-263.

MacNeilage, P.F., Studdert-Kennedy, M.G., & Lindblom, B. (1987b). Primate predatory, postural, and prehensile proclivities and professional peer pressures: Postscripts. *The Behavioral and Brain Sciences, 10,* 289-303.

MacNeilage, P.F., Studdert-Kennedy, M.G., & Lindblom, B. (1988). Primate handedness: A foot in the door. *The Behavioral and Brain Sciences, 11,* 748-758.

Milliken, G. W., Dodson, D. L. & Ward, J. P. (in preparation). Lateralized patterns of hand use in feeding by the bushbaby (*Otolemur garnettii*).

Milliken, G.W., Forsythe, C., & Ward, J.P. (1989). Multiple measures of hand use lateralization in the ring-tailed lemur (Lemur catta). *Journal of Comparative Psychology, 103,* 262-268.

Napier, J.R., & Walker, A.C. (1967). Vertical clinging and leaping. *Folia*

Primatologica, 6, 204-219.

Newman, P.P. (1962). Single unit activity in the viscero-sensory areas of the cerebral cortex. *Journal of Physiology, 160,* 284-297.

Nottebohm, F. (1979). Origins and mechanisms in the establishment of cerebral dominance. In M.S. Gazzaniga (Ed.), *Handbook of behavioral neurobiology, Vol.2, Neuropsychology,* (pp. 295-344). New York: Plenum Press.

Orton, S.T. (1937). *Reading, writing and speech problems in children.* New York: W.W.Norton.

Pinger, C., Lavallee, K., Hobbs, F., & Ward, J.P. (1988, November). *An evaluation of possible indicators of later lateralization in infant prosimian primates.* Poster presentation to the SQEBC/NEABS Conference, Montreal, Canada.

Porac, C., & Coren, S. (1977). *Lateral preferences and human behavior.* New York: Springer-Verlag.

Rogers, L.J. (1980). Lateralization in the avian brain. *Bird Behaviour, 2,* 1-12.

Rogers, L.J. (1986). Lateralization of learning in chicks. *Advances in the Study of Behavior, 16,* 147-189.

Sanford, C., Guin, K., & Ward, J.P. (1984). Posture and laterality in the bushbaby (Galago senegalensis). *Brain, Behavior and Evolution, 25,* 217-224.

Sanford, C.G., & Ward, J.P. (1986). Mirror image discrimination and hand preference in the bushbaby (Galago senegalensis). *The Psychological Record, 36, 439-*449.

Seltzer, C., Forsythe, C., & Ward, J. P. (in press). Multiple measures of motor lateralization in human primates (*Homo sapiens*). *Journal of Comparative Psychology.*

Stafford, D. K., Milliken, G. W., & Ward, J. P. (in press). Lateral bias in feeding and brachiation in Hylobatids. *Primates.*

Talbott, R.E. (1979). Ferrier, the synergy concept, and the study of posture and movement. In R.E. Talbott and D.R. Humphrey (Eds.), *Posture and movement* (pp.1-12). New York: Raven.

Tokuda, K. (1969). On the handedness of Japanese monkeys. *Primates, 10,* 41-46.

Tucker, D. M., & Williamson. P. A. (1984). Asymmetric neural control systems in human self-regulation. *Psychological Review, 91,* 185-215.

Ward, J.P. (1988). Left hand reaching preferences in prosimians. *The Behavioral and Brain Sciences, 11,* 744-745.

Ward, J. P. (Ed.) (in press)_ *Current behavioral evidence of primate asymmetries.* New York: Springer-Verlag.

Ward, J.P., Milliken, G.W., Dodson, D.L., Stafford, D.K., & Wallace, M. (in press). Handedness as a function of sex and age in a large population of Lemur. *Journal of Comparative Psychology.*

Warren, J.M. (1953). Handedness in the rhesus monkey. *Science, 118,* 622-623.

Warren, J.M. (1958). The development of paw preferences in cats and monkeys. *Journal of Genetic Psychology, 93,* 229-236.

Warren, J.M. (1977). Handedness and cerebral dominance in monkeys. In S.

Harnad, R. W .Doty, L. Goldstein, J. Jaynes, & G. Krauthamer (Eds.), *Lateralization in the nervous system* (pp. 151-172). New York: Academic Press.

Warren, J.M. (1980). Handedness and laterality in humans and other animals. *Physiological Psychology, 8,* 351-359.

Zimmerberg, B., Glick, S.D., & Jerussi, T.P. (1974). Neurochemical correlate of a spatial preference in rats. *Science, 185,* 623-625.

2 Functional Lateralization in Monkeys

Charles R. Hamilton
Betty A. Vermeire
California Institute of Technology

The investigation of hemispheric specialization in human beings has so thoroughly captured the interests of researchers that many books, journals, and conferences are largely devoted to reporting and interpreting the findings. Historically, these interests first centered on clinical reports of lateralization of language, then on asymmetries in performing visuospatial tests, and, following the dramatic studies of split-brain patients and the development of methods for testing normal subjects in the 1960s, on the proposition that dichotomies such as analytic/holistic or local/global characterize the functioning of the two cerebral hemispheres. Although there is lively debate over the nature, or even the relevance, of such dichotomies, the notion that the two hemispheres differ in some basic way is now widely accepted. We use the term *hemispheric specialization* to imply a fundamental hemispheric difference in processing information, a theoretical interpretation of the more specific and less controversial findings of asymmetric performance on particular tasks, for which we use the term *lateralization*. The consequences of hemispheric specialization are probably never absolute, and certainly there is no implication that one side of the brain is unable to process particular types of information. Because the mechanisms on the two sides differ, however, differential efficiencies in performance often result. It is this concept of hemispheric specialization, not just lateralization of various functions, that excites most investigators.

It is important to know whether hemispheric specialization exists in animals. Investigating the underlying neural mechanisms will likely require sophisticated, invasive procedures that can best be performed with appropriate animal models. Understanding the evolution of hemispheric specialization and whether its presence correlates with our uniquely human modes of thought will also require comparative studies. For these reasons, and others, many investigators have begun to look for laterality in animals. As Geschwind (1985) described this enterprise "we are on the threshold of what can be described without hyperbole as a major revolution in biology" (p. 276). "What was only recently an apparently special feature of the human brain has come to be important in the study of evolution and embryology, in comparative zoology, in anatomy, pharmacology, physiology, endocrinology, and immunology indeed, probably in every branch of biology and medicine" (Geschwind & Behan, 1984, p. 222).

A BRIEF REVIEW

Examples of structural and behavioral lateralization in animals have been known for a long time (summarized in Dimond & Blizard, 1977; Harnad, Doty, Goldstein, Jaynes, & Krauthamer, 1977) although reports of human-like, cognitive lateralization did not begin to appear until the 1970s (Hamilton & Lund, 1970; Nottebohm, 1970). Since then, numerous structural, biochemical, and behavioral asymmetries have been described (Geschwind & Galaburda, 1984; Glick, 1985; Harnad et al., 1977).

The impressive work with bird song provides the best evidence of functional laterality at the population level (Nottebohm, 1980). In many respects it resembles language in human beings. However, the distant phylogenetic relationship without good intervening examples of similar laterality, and some problems of interpretation (McCasland, 1987), suggest caution in assuming that the basic mechanisms are similar in humans and birds. Similarly intriguing, and remote, is the lateralization of visual discrimination in chicks (e.g., Howard, Rogers, & Boura, 1980; Mench & Andrew, 1986).

Studies with rodents seem to indicate that lateralization of structure and function may be commonplace (summarized in Glick, 1985). However, most examples are difficult to interpret in terms of hemispheric specialization as described for human beings. In particular, the direction of lateralization in many studies varies with the individual rather than the species, and is strongly influenced by a host of variables such as environmental manipulations and the sex, age, strain, or even breeder of the animal. Usually, the lateralized function studied has been motoric or emotional rather than cognitive. Although fascinating, such examples may not provide appropriate models for studying human-like mechanisms. We should remember that every asymmetric feature in biology does not have to be relevant to hemispheric specialization!

Some experiments with nonhuman primates, on the other hand, demonstrate lateralized behaviors that more closely resemble those found in human beings and may therefore be particularly useful for investigating hemispheric specialization. The first significant findings of laterality in monkeys showed a left- hemispheric superiority for discriminating the direction of movement of a field of dots (Hamilton & Lund, 1970). Since then, left-hemispheric advantages have been found when split- brain rhesus monkeys discriminate other stimuli differing by spatial cues (reviewed in Hamilton, 1990) such as oriented gratings (Hamilton, Tieman, & Farrell, 1974) and oriented lines (Hamilton, 1983). The most convincing of these experiments are summarized in Fig. 2.1. Jason, Cowey, and Weiskrantz (1984) have found in monkeys with lateralized lesions a similar left hemispheric advantage for discriminating the position of a dot within an outline frame. The general acceptance of these positive findings has been tempered by the relatively small number of monkeys tested, the existence of nonsignificant results for other seemingly similar discriminations (Hamilton, 1990), and the fact that the direction of lateralization is opposite to that usually reported for most aspects of spatial processing in human subjects (Bryden, 1982). However, a thorough examination of lateralization for discriminating oriented lines, described here, strongly supports the conclusion that in monkeys a left hemispheric superiority does exist for distinguishing stimuli that differ by spatial cues.

Discrimination of facial characteristics, a task often associated with better performance by the right hemisphere of human subjects, seems particularly well suited to investigations of laterality in monkeys. Although the earlier studies of this type were negative (Hamilton et al., 1974; Overman & Doty, 1982) or inconclusive (Hamilton & Vermeire, 1983), more recent experiments indicate a reliable right-hemispheric advantage for discriminating facial identity or expression (Hamilton & Vermeire, 1985, 1988a; Vermeire, Erdmann, & Hamilton, 1983). The recent tests may show more sensitivity, in part, because of greater reliance on memory and categorization as discussed here.

A third group of experiments that indicate human-like laterality used

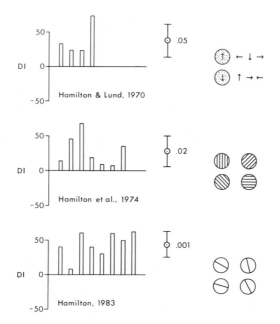

FIGURE 2.1. Laterality for discriminating three types of stimuli that differ spatially. The stimuli are pictured with the positive examples above the negative ones for direction of movement of a field of dots (top), orientation of gratings (middle), and orientation of a line (bottom). Each bar represents the dominance index for a monkey averaged across problems. The mean, standard deviation, and significance are shown; positive values of DI indicates better performance by the left hemisphere.

auditory stimuli. Discrimination of species-specific calls by Japanese macaques was better with the right ear than with the left, suggesting a left-hemispheric advantage for distinguishing speech-like sounds (Beecher, Petersen, Zoloth, Moody, & Stebbins, 1979; Petersen, Beecher, Zoloth, Moody, & Stebbins, 1978). Placing unilateral lesions in the left or right temporal lobe confirmed this suggestion beautifully (Heffner & Heffner, 1984, 1986), although the resulting deficits were rather transient. Other studies of lateralization for sounds are less conclusive because of procedural asymmetries (Dewson, 1977, 1978) or inconsistent lateralization and small sample size (Pohl, 1983).

Finally, many of the experiments that have looked for lateralization in monkeys have investigated handedness or postural asymmetries. Based on earlier studies, handedness in nonhuman primates has usually been considered idiosyncratic and not obviously related to human handedness (Hamilton, 1977; Lehman, 1978; Warren, 1977). A reconsideration by MacNeilage, Studdert-Kennedy, and Lindblom (1987), however, suggests that some aspects of visually guided reaching show left-handed preferences in prosimians and monkeys, whereas more complex manipulative tasks may show right-handed preferences. As judged from the commentaries appended to that article, most investigators are not convinced, and still do not view handedness in monkeys as similar to that in human beings. Our own data also reflect this negative opinion (Hamilton & Vermeire, 1988b). On the other hand, recent studies by several groups (e.g., Fagot & Vauclair, 1988, in preparation; MacNeilage, Studdert-Kennedy, & Lindblom, 1988; Ward, Chapter 1, this volume) provide tantalizing indications that consistent handedness may characterize some aspects of hand use in nonhuman primates. Although the newer evidence for hand preferences is impressive, it seems that the choice of hand results from the engagement of cognitive specializations in the hemisphere contralateral to the responding hand rather than from a dominant hand *per se*. Perhaps a lack of human-like consistent handedness permits the observation of more subtle types of hand preferences that change sides according to the cognitive demands of the tasks (cf. Fagot & Vauclair, in preparation). Clearly, it remains important to continue studying handedness and to investigate its relationship to other forms of lateralized behavior.

RECENT EXPERIMENTS

Several years ago we began an extensive series of experiments to determine whether the differences in lateralization that we had found for spatial and facial discriminations were reliable. Twenty-eight of our split-brain monkeys learned many discriminations with each hemisphere in experimental designs largely balanced for sex, handedness, and side of surgical retraction. The two surgically separated hemispheres (Sperry, 1968) were trained sequentially on each problem to a criterion of 90% correct over 40 trials. The errors-through-criterion for the two hemispheres were compared by a dominance index (DI) of the form 100 (R-L)/(R+L) where R and L represent the errors made by each side. Thus a DI of

100 represents complete dominance by the left hemisphere, 0 represents equal ability, and -100 represents complete dominance by the right hemisphere. When hemispheric differences in initial or maintained performance levels were of interest, the difference (L-R) in percentage of correct responses over 20 trials was used to estimate the degree of lateralization for each discrimination. The stimuli used included patterns, which do not usually reveal lateralized processing in human subjects (Davidoff, 1982); oriented lines, which usually are differentiated better by the right hemisphere of humans (Bryden, 1982); and facial expression and identity, also usually processed better by the human right hemisphere (Bradshaw & Nettleton, 1983; Bryden, 1982).

Patterns. Discriminations of geometric patterns were learned, on the average, equally well by either hemisphere. Twenty-eight monkeys learned 4 to 18 problems and the average of the DIs for the problems was calculated for each monkey. The distribution of these average DIs is shown in Fig. 2.2a. The problems were presented either as simultaneous or successive two-choice discriminations. Because there was no difference in the two methods, the results were combined and the average DI tested for significance [DI = -1.55, $t(27)$ = -.41, ns]. Of these monkeys 19 also learned 6 additional discriminations in a Go/No-Go paradigm with similar nonsignificant results [DI = -2.43, $t(18)$ = -.36].

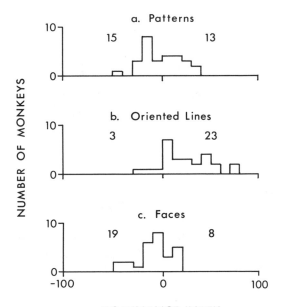

FIGURE 2.2. Laterality for discriminating patterns, oriented lines, and faces. The distributions of monkeys according to their average dominance indices indicate no laterality for patterns, left-sided laterality for oriented lines, and right-sided laterality for faces.

Thus, regardless of the method of training there is no evidence of hemispheric differences for discriminating geometric patterns. This result conforms with our 25 years of experience testing split-brain animals on similar problems (Hamilton, 1990).

Oriented Lines. Spatial discriminations, however, were processed significantly better by the left hemisphere. Of the 18 monkeys, 26 learned to discriminate one line from another that differed in orientation by 15 deg. Four problems (150 deg vs 165 deg, 105 deg vs 120 deg, 75 deg vs 60 deg, 30 deg vs 15 deg) were trained as successively presented two choice discriminations. The average DI for each monkey across the four problems was calculated and the distribution plotted in Fig. 2.2b. The overall DI was positive and significantly different from zero [DI = 23.97, $t(25) = 4.91$, $p<.001$]. Thus, the preliminary conclusions from several earlier experiments using spatial stimuli were confirmed with a much larger sample of monkeys, under more stringent and balanced conditions.

Faces. Discriminations of faces, by contrast, were learned more readily by the right hemisphere. Twenty-seven monkeys learned eight discriminations based on facial characteristics of monkeys. Different monkeys were photographed for each discrimination. Four discriminations required differentiating photographs of one individual from another, both portraying the same expression, and four discriminations required telling one facial expression from another, both performed by the same monkey. There were no significant differences in lateralization for these two types of tests, which are here combined. The distribution for the average DIs across the eight problems is shown in Fig. 2.2c. The overall DI is negative and significantly different from zero [DI = -7.18, $t(26) = -2.22$, $p<.05$], which shows that these discriminations were learned faster by the right hemisphere. Although the right-hemispheric advantage is not very large for learning these faces, it is observed consistently, and persists in tests of facial memory and categorization that are described later.

Complementary Specialization. In an earlier analysis, completed six years ago when almost all examples of lateralization from our laboratory and others showed the left hemisphere to be superior regardless of the type of stimuli tested (Hamilton, 1990), we found a significant correlation between DI and problem difficulty. The left-sided superiority was greater when the problems required more trials to reach criterion. It was as if the classic concept of left cerebral dominance, originally invoked to explain human laterality, described laterality in monkeys better than did complementary hemispheric specialization. However, we now favor an interpretation of complementary specialization over left dominance because of two aspects of our newer results (Hamilton & Vermeire, 1988a).

First, there is no significant correlation within any one type of discrimination between problem difficulty and DIs. This is most adequately demonstrated for facial discriminations, for which we now have 16 problems ($r = .06$), and less so for the orientational discriminations ($r = .08$) for which there are just 4 problems. The earlier evidence of a significant correlation between left dominance and problem difficulty was based on correlating DIs and errors across different types of discriminations rather than within each type. We now believe that the previous correlation is best interpreted as reflecting variations in the magnitude of the dominance indices associated with the types of discriminations rather than with the difficulty of the problems per se.

Second, the number of monkeys having each of the 4 possible patterns of hemispheric superiorities for the 2 types of problems (Table 2.1) differs significantly from the equal distribution predicted from chance (6:16:1:2, $X^2 = 22.52$, $p<.005$). In particular, of the 25 monkeys that learned both types of problems, 16 discriminated oriented lines better with the left hemisphere *and* faces better with the right hemisphere. This shows a specific complementary organization for these two types of problems. Furthermore, the correlation between the DIs for faces and orientations ($r = .01$) is not significant. The particular distribution and negligible correlation are just what would be expected if the four frequencies (Table 2.1) were determined only from the proportion of monkeys with left dominance for orientation (22/25) and the proportion with right dominance for faces (18/25). Bryden (1982; Bryden, Hécaen, & DeAgostini, 1983) has referred to this type of result as statistical complementarity, in contrast to causal complementarity for which lateralization of certain functions to one hemisphere would force complementary functions to be lateralized to the other hemisphere.

TABLE 2.1.
Number of Monkeys with each Combination of Superior Hemispheres for Discriminating Orientation and Faces

Superior side for orientations	L		R	
Superior side for faces	L	R	L	R
Number found	6	16	1	2
Number predicted from independent lateralization	6.16	15.84	0.84	2.16

Higher Processes. After learning the facial discriminations, the split-brain monkeys were tested for retention and for the ability to correctly respond to new examples of the discriminations. The memories of 26 monkeys were tested for the original 8 facial discriminations approximately 6 months after learning them. The distribution of results is shown in Fig. 2.3a. The initial performance on the first 20 retention trials was significantly better with the right hemisphere than with the left [L-R = -4.81, $t(25) = -3.25$, $p<.01$], showing that a right hemispheric

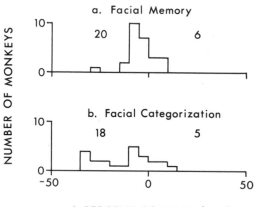

FIGURE 2.3. Laterality for facial memory and categorization. The distributions of dominance indices indicate a right hemispheric advantage for remembering and generalizing facial discriminations.

advantage is present immediately for recalling the facial discriminations learned months earlier.

Twenty-three of the monkeys were then tested for their ability to correctly categorize 20 new examples of each of 4 facial discriminations, two of individuals and two of expressions (Fig. 2.3b). For discriminating individuals, these tests of generalization used (a) new photographs of the same 2 monkeys making the original expression, and (b) photographs of the same 2 monkeys making a different expression. For discriminating expressions, the generalization tests used (a) new photographs of the original monkey making the same two expressions, and (b) photographs of a different monkey making the same two expressions. The monkeys categorized the novel photographs significantly better than chance on all 8 of the generalization tests [overall % correct = 68.94, $t(22) = 13.32$, $p<.001$], proving that they had been responding to the facial concepts we wanted them to learn rather than to various uncontrolled details in the photographs. The difference between the hemispheres in percentage of correct responses is negative and significantly different from zero [L-R = -11.68, $t(22) = -3.88$, $p<.001$], which indicates that the right hemisphere excels over the left in generalizing the learned facial differences to new examples of the same categories.

The laterality for faces becomes less variable relative to the mean, and therefore more significant, with the progression from learning to memory to categorization. This shows that in monkeys as in human beings (Bertelson, Vanhaelen, & Morais, 1979; Moscovitch, 1979) laterality is more evident at higher levels of cognitive processing.

Inverted Faces. Inverting facial stimuli disrupts recognition in human subjects more severely than does inversion of other objects normally seen upright (Leehey, Carey, Diamond, & Cahn, 1978; Yin, 1970). Furthermore, this disruption seems to affect mechanisms in the right hemisphere more than those in the left. To see whether similar effects would be present in monkeys (Vermeire & Hamilton, 1988) we first retrained each hemisphere of 16 of our monkeys to criterion on the 8 facial discriminations they had previously learned (Fig. 2.4a). Most monkeys remembered the faces well, and again showed the typical right-hemispheric advantage [DI = -21.32, $t(15)$ = -2.96, $p<.01$]. As soon as a particular discrimination was relearned to criterion with one hemisphere, we immediately presented the same discrimination with the faces inverted (Fig. 2.4b). The monkeys readily learned the inverted faces with each hemisphere but no longer showed a significant hemispheric advantage [DI = -1.22, $t(15)$ = -.15, ns]. Thus, with respect to lateralization, inverted faces appear to be treated more like geometric patterns than like upright faces. This is consistent with the suggestion based on human data that upright faces are processed by specialized mechanisms in the right hemisphere.

Facial Expression and Identity. Although the degree of lateralization was very similar for discriminating facial expression and identity, learning the expressions was significantly more difficult for the monkeys than learning the

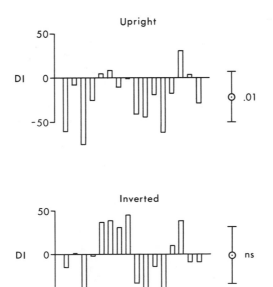

FIGURE 2.4. Laterality for discriminating upright and inverted faces. The data, plotted as in Fig. 1, again show a right hemispheric advantage for discriminating upright faces but indicate a loss of lateralized processing for inverted faces.

individuals (Vermeire, in preparation). A similar difference was also observed in the tests of memory and of categorization. For quantitative evaluation of these differences it was convenient to calculate an index (EI) of the form 100 (E-I)/(E+I) to express the relative ease of discriminating expressions (E) and individuals (I). For learning and memory we used the errors-through-criterion in the calculations and for categorization we used the percentage of correct responses, with the sign reversed for comparability. The average indices showed a significant advantage for discriminating individuals over expressions during learning [EI = 21.19, $t(25) = 4.78$, $p<.001$], remembering [EI = 16.12, $t(25) = 2.89$, $p<.01$], and categorizing [EI = 10.02, $t(22) = 8.80$, $p<.001$] the facial stimuli.

Most human subjects, by contrast, found the expressions of monkeys much easier to distinguish than the individuals. Twenty subjects sorted the same stimuli according to perceived differences in expression or identity. An analogous index showed that the human subjects made more errors discriminating individual monkeys than they did with expressions (EI = -43.17, $t(19) = -3.28$, $p<.01$). The fact that human beings and monkeys yield the opposite result is important because it rules out simple physical differences in the stimuli as the basis of the difference in discriminability, for physical differences would be the same for both species. Thus, some species-specific differences in processing the faces of monkeys, either innate or learned, must underlie these behavioral findings.

SPECULATIVE CONCLUSIONS

Two conclusions of a more general nature may be proposed tentatively at this stage of the research. The arguments assume that our findings of lateralization for spatial and facial processing in monkeys are valid.

Homology With Human Laterality. Concluding that human laterality can be described by the concept of hemispheric specialization ultimately depends on whether conceptual dichotomies such as analytic/holistic are successful in specifying the characteristics that differentiate tasks performed better by one hemisphere or the other. The conclusion is warranted if a number of tasks lateralized to the same side can be convincingly classified together according to these common characteristics. Even though the precise nature of the hypothetical dichotomy is still debated, there do seem to be enough similarities between tasks done better by a given hemisphere of human subjects to support a theory of hemispheric specialization. To reach an equivalent level of confidence concerning hemispheric specialization in monkeys will take a much longer time because of the difficulty in obtaining the relevant data. However, some confidence can be gained by analogy if the tasks that are thought to be lateralized in monkeys show strong resemblances to the better studied ones that are lateralized in human beings. We have observed five types of similarities in the experiments just described.

First, the finding that oriented lines and faces show significant lateralization whereas geometric patterns do not is common to both monkeys and human beings. This indicates an overall similarity in the types of processing that are lateralized in each species. Although faces are lateralized to the right hemisphere in both species, oriented lines appear lateralized to opposite sides in humans and monkeys, which invites some comment. This contrast would argue against the proposed homology if the species difference resulted from moving a structural mechanism for spatial processing to the opposite hemisphere in one species because, if homologous, structural mechanisms should maintain their lateralized relationships across species. If the species difference resulted from behavioral strategies the problem is less severe because dynamic mechanisms seem less constrained by structural considerations. For example, different individuals of the same species may use opposite hemispheres to tackle certain tasks. Alternatively, the apparent reversal in spatial laterality between species may represent a pseudoproblem because human subjects may, in fact, also be lateralized more to the left for the particular tests of line orientation that we used. We will be better able to evaluate this possibility after testing these orientation discriminations in human split-brain patients.

Second, finding laterality for faces and orientation in monkeys to be statistically independent resembles finding laterality for aphasia and spatial disorder in human patients (Bryden et al., 1983) to be statistically independent. This indicates that the assignment of lateralized processes to a particular hemisphere may be governed by the same principles in each species. Of additional interest, the statistical independence of lateralized mechanisms places important constraints on models of hemispheric specialization. For example, how could a model that explains hemispheric specialization by structural differences between the hemispheres account for those individuals who turn out to have complementary functions, implying complementary structures, in the same hemisphere? Of course, considerably more data must be evaluated before reaching the general conclusion that the allocation of complementary functions to the two hemispheres in each species is statistically determined rather than causally related.

Third, it appears that cognitive mechanisms deeper in the processing hierarchy of each hemisphere are more clearly lateralized than mechanisms based on more peripheral, perceptual processes. Moscovitch (1979) has argued this point for human subjects most emphatically, although the idea is also favored by others (Bertelson et al. 1979). Our limited data with facial processing in monkeys also support this notion. We are now testing memory and, especially, categorization of oriented lines to see if they too will reveal laterality more strongly than does learning.

Fourth, inversion of facial stimuli removes the right- hemispheric advantage for facial processing both in monkeys and in human beings. This effect in humans is usually taken as support for specialized mechanisms in the right hemisphere (Leehey et al., 1978; Yin, 1970). Regardless of the interpretation, however, the effects of manipulating this variable are similar in both species, which supports the proposed homology.

Fifth, the relative ease of discriminating conspecific individuals and expressions appears similar for the two species. Human subjects find individuals of their species easier to tell apart than expressions (Etcoff, 1984; Ley & Bryden, 1979; Strauss & Moscovitch, 1981), as do our monkeys (Vermeire, in preparation). By contrast, human subjects find discriminating photographs of individual monkeys more difficult than discriminating expressions of monkeys. Perhaps monkeys will show a similar effect when tested with photographs of human beings.

In conclusion, the parallels in lateralized mechanisms of monkeys and of human beings are quite striking. Unless new evidence negates these similarities, it seems reasonable to conclude that monkeys possess hemispheric specialization with human-like characteristics.

Evolutionary Implications. Several scenarios for the evolution of hemispheric specialization in human beings have been thoughtfully discussed by Corballis (1983; 1989). The most compelling and popular of these envisions first the adoption of bipedal posture by early hominids, followed by left hemispheric control of praxic function associated primarily with the use of tools and gestural communication, and then by the lateralization of language to the left hemisphere. Whether the complementary right-sided specializations were acquired by default or were actively selected is less clear. Regardless, the inference that specialized cognitive differences between the hemispheres emerged as a result of the lateralization of specific functions such as praxis and language characterizes these scenarios.

If the complementary hemispheric superiorities found in rhesus monkeys reflect human-like hemispheric specialization, then prior lateralization of handedness or language cannot be a requirement for the development of cognitive hemispheric specialization, for human-like handedness and language are not found in monkeys. Furthermore, if the simian and human specializations result from the same evolutionary events, as would be likely for animals within the same order, then the development of human hemispheric specialization must have preceded the more specialized development of lateralization of handedness and language. This possible evolutionary sequence, already favored by some (e.g., Bogen & Bogen, 1969), is particularly appealing if hemispheric specialization follows from fundamental, although likely modest, structural differences between the hemispheres (Hamilton & Vermeire, 1988b), for such differences must arise before the functional consequences they enable. On the other hand, if lateralization in monkeys only represents the parallel evolution of functional asymmetry, then only the weaker conclusion that cognitive lateralization can occur independently of lateralization of handedness or language should be drawn.

In a more general vein, these results negate the argument that human beings are unique in having consciousness, exceptional creative abilities, and superior intelligence because of their unique development of hemispheric specialization. If hemispheric specialization is present both in human beings and in monkeys, then the strong form of the argument, as expressed earlier, clearly is not tenable. However, a weaker form that envisions a quantitative relationship between the degree of hemispheric specialization and the extent of consciousness, creative abilities, and intelligence is plausible. Monkeys, accordingly, would have less conspicuous capabilities than human beings because they were less lateralized. In either event, the extreme position that the uniqueness of human mental abilities is explainable by the unique possession of cognitively specialized hemispheres is contradicted.

ACKNOWLEDGMENTS

This research was supported in part by USPHS grants MH-34770 and BRSG RR-07003.

REFERENCES

Beecher, M.D., Petersen, M.R., Zoloth, S.R., Moody, D.B., & Stebbins, W.C. (1979). Perception of conspecific vocalizations by Japanese macaques. *Brain, Behavior and Evolution, 16*, 443-460.

Bertelson, P., Vanhaelen, H., & Morais, J. (1979). Left hemifield superiority and the extraction of physiognomic invariants. In I. Steele Russell, M. Van Hof, & G. Berlucchi (Eds.), *Structure and function of the cerebral commissures* (pp. 400-410). London: Macmillan.

Bogen, J.E., & Bogen, G.M. (1969). The other side of the brain III: The corpus callosum and creativity. *Bulletin of the Los Angeles Neurological Society, 34*, 191-220.

Bradshaw, J.L., & Nettleton, N.C. (1983). *Human cerebral asymmetry.* Englewood Cliffs, NJ: Prentice-Hall.

Bryden, M.P. (1982). *Laterality: Functional asymmetry in the intact brain.* New York: Academic Press.

Bryden, M.P., Hecaen, H., & DeAgostini, M. (1983). Patterns of cerebral organization. *Brain and Language, 20*, 249-262.

Corballis, M.C. (1983). *Human Laterality.* New York: Academic Press.

Corballis, M.C. (1989). Laterality and human evolution. *Psychological Review, 96*, 492-505.

Davidoff, J. (1982). Studies with non-verbal stimuli. In J. G. Beaumont (Ed.), *Divided visual field studies of cerebral organization* (pp. 29-55). New York: Academic Press.

Dewson, J.H., III. (1977). Preliminary evidence of hemispheric asymmetry of auditory function in monkeys. In S. Harnad, R.W. Doty, L. Goldstein, J. Jaynes, & G. Krauthamer (Eds.), *Lateralization in the nervous system* (pp. 63-71). New York: Academic Press.

Dewson, J.H., III. (1978). Some behavioral effects of removal of superior temporal cortex in the monkey. In D. Chivers & J. Herbert (Eds.), *Recent advances in primatology: Behavior.* (Vol., pp. 763-768). London: Academic Press.

Dimond, S. J., & Blizard, D.A. (Eds.). (1977). Evolution and   lateralization of the brain. *Annals of the New York Academy of Sciences, 299*, 1-501.

Etcoff, N.L. (1984). Selective attention to facial identity and facial emotion. *Neuropsychologia, 22*, 281-295.

Fagot, J., & Vauclair, J. (in preparation). The necessity of distinguishing manual specialization from handedness in nonhuman primates.

Fagot, J., & Vauclair, J. (1988). Handedness and manual   specialization in the baboon. *Neuropsychologia, 26*, 795-804.

Geschwind, N.(1985).   Implications for evolution, genetics, and   clinical syndromes. In S.D. Glick (Ed.), *Cerebral   lateralization in nonhuman species* (pp. 247-278). New York: Academic Press.

Geschwind, N., & Behan, P.O. (1984). Laterality, hormones, and immunity. In N. Geschwind & A.M. Galaburda (Eds.), *Cerebral   dominance: The biological foundations* (pp. 211-224). Cambridge, MA: Harvard University Press.

Geschwind, N., & Galaburda, A.M. (Eds.). (1984). *Cerebral dominance: The biological foundations.* Cambridge, MA: Harvard University Press.

Glick, S.D. (Ed.)(1985). *Cerebral lateralization in nonhuman species.* New York: Academic Press.

Hamilton, C.R. (1977). An assessment of hemispheric specialization in monkeys. *Annals of the New York Academy of Sciences, 299*, 222-232.

Hamilton, C.R. (1983). Lateralization for orientation in split-brain monkeys. *Behavioural Brain Research, 10*, 399-403.

Hamilton, C.R. (1990). Hemispheric specialization in monkeys. In C.B. Trevarthen (Eds.), *Brain circuits and functions of the mind.* Cambridge, U.K: Cambridge University Press.

Hamilton, C.R., & Lund, J.S. (1970). Visual discrimination of movement: Midbrain or forebrain? *Science, 170*, 1428-1430.

Hamilton, C.R., Tieman, S.B., & Farrell, W.S., Jr. (1974). Cerebral dominance in monkeys? *Neuropsychologia, 12*, 193-198.

Hamilton, C.R., & Vermeire, B.A. (1983). Discrimination of monkey faces by split-brain monkeys. *Behavioural Brain Research, 9*, 263-275.

Hamilton, C.R., & Vermeire, B.A. (1985). Complementary   hemispheric superiorities in monkeys. *Neuroscience Abstracts, 11*, 869.

Hamilton, C.R., & Vermeire, B.A. (1988a). Complementary   hemispheric specialization in monkeys. *Science, 242*, 1691-1694.

Hamilton, C.R., & Vermeire, B.A. (1988b). Cognition, not   handedness, is lateralized in monkeys. *The Behavioral and Brain Sciences, 11*, 723-725.

Harnad, S., Doty, R.W., Goldstein, L., Jaynes, J., & Krauthamer, G. (Eds.). (1977). *Lateralization in the nervous system.* New York: Academic Press.

Heffner, H.E., & Heffner, R.S. (1984). Temporal lobe lesions and perception of species-specific vocalizations by macaques. *Science, 226*, 75-76.

Heffner, H.E., & Heffner, R.S. (1986). Effect of unilateral and bilateral auditory cortex lesions on the discrimination of vocalizations by Japanese macaques. *Journal of Neurophysiology, 56,* 683-701.

Howard, K.J., Rogers, L.J., & Boura, A.L.A. (1980). Functional lateralization of the chicken forebrain revealed by use of intracranial glutamate. *Brain Research, 188,* 369-382.

Jason, G.W., Cowey, A., & Weiskrantz, L. (1984). Hemispheric asymmetry for a visuospatial task in monkeys. *Neuropsychologia, 22,* 777-784.

Leehey, S.C., Carey, S., Diamond, R., & Cahn, A. (1978). Upright and inverted faces: The right hemisphere knows the difference. *Cortex, 14,* 411-419.

Lehman, R.A.W. (1978). The handedness of rhesus monkeys: I. Distribution. *Neuropsychologia, 16,* 33-42.

Ley, R.G., & Bryden, M.P. (1979). Hemispheric differences in processing emotions and faces. *Brain and Language, 7,* 127-138.

MacNeilage, P.F., Studdert-Kennedy, M.G., & Lindblom, B. (1987). Primate handedness reconsidered. *The Behavioral and Brain Sciences, 10,* 247-303.

MacNeilage, P.F., Studdert Kennedy, M.G., & Lundblom, B. (1988). Primate handedness: A foot in the door. *The Behavioral and Brain Sciences, 11,* 737-746.

McCasland, J.S. (1987). Neuronal control of bird song production. *Journal of Neuroscience, 7,* 23-39.

Mench, J.A., & Andrew, R.J. (1986). Lateralization of a food search task in the domestic chick. *Behavioral and Neural Biology, 46,* 107-114.

Moscovitch, M. (1979). Information processing and the cerebral hemispheres. In M.S. Gazzaniga (Ed.), *Handbook of behavioral neurobiology,* (Vol. 2, pp. 379-446). New York: Plenum.

Nottebohm, F. (1970). Ontogeny of bird song. *Science, 167,* 950-956.

Nottebohm, F. (1980). Brain pathways for vocal learning in birds: A review of the first 10 years. In J.M. Sprague & A.N. Epstein (Eds.), *Progress in psychobiology and physiological psychology,* (Vol. 9, pp. 85-124). New York: Academic Press.

Overman, W. H., Jr., & Doty, R.W. (1982). Hemispheric specialization displayed by man but not macaques for analysis of faces. *Neuropsychologia, 20,* 113-128.

Petersen, M.R., Beecher, M.D., Zoloth, S.R., Moody, D.B., & Stebbins, W.C. (1978). Neural lateralization of species-specific vocalizations by Japanese macaques. *Science, 202,* 324-326.

Pohl, P. (1983). Central auditory processing. V. Ear advantages for acoustic stimuli in baboons. *Brain and Language, 20,* 44-53.

Sperry, R. W. (1968). Mental unity following surgical disconnection of the cerebral hemispheres. *Harvey Lectures, 62,* 293-323.

Strauss, E., & Moscovitch, M. (1981). Perception of facial expressions. *Brain and Language, 13,* 308-333.

Vermeire, B. A. (in preparation). Differential discriminability of monkey facial identity and expression in monkeys (*Macaca mulatta*) and people (*Homo sapiens*).

Vermeire, B. A., Erdmann, A.L., & Hamilton, C.R. (1983).   Laterality in monkeys for discriminating facial expression and identity. *Neuroscience Abstracts, 9,* 651.

Vermeire, B.A., & Hamilton, C.R. (1988). Laterality in monkeys discriminating inverted faces. *Neuroscience Abstracts, 14,* 1139.

Warren, J.M. (1977). Handedness and cerebral dominance in monkeys. In S. Harnad, R.W. Doty, L. Goldstein, J. Jaynes, & G. Krauthamer (Eds.), *Lateralization in the Nervous System* (pp. 151-172).   New York: Academic Press.

Yin, R.K. (1970). Face recognition by brain injured patients: A dissociable ability? *Neuropsychologia, 8,* 395-402.

3 Issues in the Assessment of Handedness

M. P. Bryden
University of Waterloo

R.E Steenhuis
University Hospital, Ontario

If one examines the literature on cerebral specialization, it is evident that most people consider handedness to be a critical variable. However, the relationship between handedness and cerebral specialization is not clearly understood. Furthermore, much of the experimental research is based on samples of right-handed undergraduates: in the truly compulsive, in right-handed males without a familial history of sinistrality. Even when supposed "left-handers" are the object of investigation, the actual classification is often one of right-handed versus non-right-handed. In the rare event that handedness is measured and different categories of handedness are employed, the specific measures vary from study to study. We argue that there are theoretical assumptions being made in all of these habits, and that these assumptions may not be valid.

Such practices actually prejudge the task under investigation as being related to cerebral specialization, assume effects of sex and familial sinistrality (FS) that are not all that well documented, and may also assume a conception of complementary specialization that lacks strong support. In this chapter, we examine the basis for these practices and offer some suggestions for improving the measurement of handedness.

First of all, many studies of cerebral specialization, especially those involving normal subjects, are limited to male subjects without a history of familial sinistrality. By selecting right-handers, one is presumably paying attention to the literature on cerebral speech lateralization, and recognizing the fact that virtually all right-handers are left hemispheric for speech (Rasmussen & Milner, 1977; Segalowitz & Bryden, 1983). Males are often selected in preference to females in the common belief that males are more strongly lateralized than females (McGlone, 1980), and that by selecting only right-handed males the probability of sampling only people with left hemisphere speech will be further enhanced. Finally, the grounds for limiting the study to those individuals with no familial history of left-handedness (FS-) seems to involve the belief that those with a familial history of left-handedness (FS+) may well have some genetic predilection to left-handedness and therefore have an increased likelihood of abnormal speech language lateralization (Annett, 1985).

ON EMPLOYING A RESTRICTED SAMPLE

The major reasons for limiting one's sample are to save time and effort. Because only about 10% of the population is left-handed, it is often difficult to find a reasonable number of left-handed subjects. Right-handers are easy to come by, and some studies are restricted to males and/or FS- subjects to increase the likelihood of obtaining a convincing laterality effect. There are two major problems with employing a restricted sample. First of all, such a procedure presumes that the task being used has something to do with cerebral lateralization. In many cases, further inquiry would lead to evidence that more peripheral factors, at least in part, determined the magnitude of observed laterality effects.

For example, Orsini, Satz, Soper, and Light (1985), in a study employing both right-handed and left-handed subjects, have demonstrated that the interfering effect of speaking or reading on tapping, a time-sharing task, is greater on the dominant hand than on the nondominant hand. If one accepted the conventional view that interference in time-sharing resulted from speech and manual performance being controlled by the same hemisphere, one would have to conclude that left-handers were the mirror image of right-handers, and therefore that the majority had right hemispheric language. Yet a great deal of data (e.g., Rasmussen & Milner, 1977; Segalowitz & Bryden, 1983) claims that this is not so. Without this large-scale study of left-handers on a time-sharing task, we would not appreciate that other factors had to be taken into consideration.

From studies with right-handed subjects, Kirsner and Schwartz (1986) have recently argued that many of the visual field differences observed in word recognition and lexical decision studies can be attributed to peripheral effects, involving the interaction of the locus of information in words with a very sharp acuity gradient. They argue that people are more accurate in the right visual field largely because the beginning of words is more important than the end, and the beginning of a word is closer to fixation and therefore more visible when it appears in the right visual field. Although there are obviously many studies to which this criticism does not apply, such effects may well exaggerate right visual field (RVF) superiorities in some experiments. Rather than assuming that all RVF superiorities are related to cerebral specialization for language, it may be important to demonstrate that left- and right-handers differ in appropriate ways, and one can hardly do this without testing the left-handers.

A second problem is that confining our research to males, or to FS- people limits the possibility of our understanding of the effects of gender and FS. If one does not investigate a particular variable, it is difficult to evaluate its effect. Current evidence indicates that it is premature to assume that we fully understand the role of either gender or of familial sinistrality in determining cerebral organization.

Consider the existing data relating handedness to cerebral function (Table 3.1). The data presented here for the lateralization of language functions are based on Rasmussen and Milner's (1977) study of patients administered sodium amytal and on Segalowitz and Bryden's (1983) survey of the literature concerning the incidence of aphasia following unilateral brain damage. Data for the lateralization of visuospatial function are derived from the Bryden, Hécaen, and DeAgostini (1983) investigation of visuospatial deficits following unilateral brain damage. It is clear from the data in Table 3.1 that, although handedness is certainly associated with the lateralization of cerebral function, it is not a very good predictor. Even in left-handers, the safest bet is that language functions are lateralized to the left hemisphere and visuospatial functions to the right hemisphere. An improved understanding of the lateralization of cerebral function depends on our better understanding of this rather weak relationship between handedness and lateralization.

TABLE 3.1
Relationship Between Handedness and Lateralization of Cerebral Function

		Dominant Hemisphere	
Language Functions	Left	Bilateral	Right
Right-handers	96%	0%	4%
Left-handers	66%	17%	17%
Visuospatial Abilities			
Right-handers	32%	0%	68%
Left-handers	30%	32%	38%

Of all non-invasive procedures for investigating cerebral speech lateralization, the dichotic listening task has provided the most compelling evidence. One of us has recently reviewed the literature on sex, handedness, and FS effects on verbal dichotic listening performance in normals (Bryden, 1988). To the extent that this technique is effective, differences in large samples of normal subjects should tell us something about the relation between speech lateralization and various demographic variables. The effects of handedness on dichotic listening performance are clearly robust, with a much higher proportion of right-handers (81%) showing the conventional right-ear effect (REA) than left-handers (64%). However, among the right-handers, sex differences are only of borderline significance, with an REA being observed slightly more often in men than in women. Familial sinistrality, on the other hand, has no clear effect: In both left-handed and right-handed samples, FS effects are small and inconsistent. Thus, some of the effects one is trying to guard against by selecting only right-handed FS- males are so small that they are hardly worth the effort. The probability of sampling people with left hemisphere speech is not increased by using FS- subjects rather than FS+ subjects, and is only marginally changed by selecting males (but see McKeever, Seitz, Hoff, Marino, & Diehl, 1983).

To understand the way in which such variables as gender and FS influence cerebral lateralization, we need to investigate these variables in fairly large samples. Restricting the sample to males or FS- subjects on the basis of the present evidence simply avoids the issue.

Furthermore, without investigating women, for instance, we will not understand whether or not differing patterns of cerebral organization have any effect on cognitive ability. It has been argued that the poor spatial ability found in women is a consequence of the greater incidence of bilateral language representation found in women (Levy, 1972). There is also some evidence to suggest that sex differences in spatial ability vary with handedness (Sanders, Wilson, & Vandenberg, 1982). However, a recent study of laterality effects on one spatial task, mental rotation, was confined to right-handed FS- male subjects (Fischer & Pellgrino, 1988). Again, such an approach makes it impossible to determine the effects of sex, handedness, or familial sinistrality.

LEFT-HANDERS OR NON-RIGHT-HANDERS?

There are many ways of classifying people with respect to handedness. At present, it is commonplace to employ some kind of questionnaire, such as the Edinburgh Handedness Inventory (Oldfield, 1971) or the index developed by Porac and Coren (1981). By convention, positive scores are assigned to the right-handed responses, negative scores to left hand responses, and the scores summed across all items employed. The distribution is then divided in some way. In the experimental literature, it is most common to classify those subjects with positive totals as "right-handed" and those with negative totals as "left-handed" (e.g., Bryden, 1986). However, this is not the only logical subdivision. Some have argued that one should differentiate between pure right- or left-handers (e.g., those who perform virtually all activities with the dominant hand) and "mixed" or "weak" handers (those who are less certain or less consistent in their preferences; cf. Annett, 1985).

In the clinical literature, it is common practice to classify subjects as either right-handed (RH) or "not-right-handed" (NRH) (e.g., Kimura, 1983; Rasmussen & Milner, 1977; Witelson, 1985). This practice, although increasing the size of the smaller group, provides a strong hidden statement about the nature of handedness. There are at least three views one can take about this practice. Handedness can be considered to be a unidimensional continuum on which a division can be made at any arbitrarily chosen point. Alternatively, it may be that Annett (1985) is right, and that the true distinction is between those who bear a postulated right-shift (RS) gene and those who do not. Finally, one may have to consider handedness as multidimensional, and to consider degree and direction of hand preference as distinct factors, as well as being concerned with the consistency of preference on the various dimensions.

It is certainly possible to imagine handedness as a single dimension, with people varying only in degree. In this case, people are simply arrayed along a continuum, and the RH-NRH distinction makes some sense. This certainly has statistical advantages; by classifying more people in the smaller category (NRH), the observed proportions become more stable and increase the likelihood of formal significance. Further, subjects are easier to find than if one requires truly left-handed people. There are several problems with this approach. First, it is too easy to slip from describing the subjects as "non-right-handers" to remembering them as "left-handers." Second, handedness may not be unidimensional (cf. Healey, Liederman, & Geschwind, 1986), and therefore the two groups may differ in ways that are not fully captured by the RH-NRH distinction. Finally, if there is a valid distinction between direction of handedness (left or right) and degree of handedness (strong or weak), the NRH group differs from the RH group in both degree and direction, and one does not know which of these factors is important.

Another possibility is that Annett (1985) is right, and there are two distinct phenotypes, those manifesting a right shift (RS+) and those not manifesting this shift (RS-). According to one simple form of Annett's model (see Annett, 1985, p. 263), the RS- group has a handedness distribution on a peg-moving task that is centered at zero, whereas the RS+ group has one with a positive (right-handed) mean at +1.5 standard deviations. Given such data, the only really logical way to divide the handedness continuum is to use a likelihood ratio, and split it at the point where the two distributions intersect. That is, one group should consist of all of those people showing handedness scores that make it *more likely* that they are RS+ than RS-, and the other group should consist of those whose scores make them *more likely* to be RS- than RS+. By Annett's (1985) Figure 14.1, the cut point should be placed at approximately -0.2 standard deviations (somewhat to the left of the null point). The Rasmussen and Milner (1977) split into "RH" and "NRH" is nowhere near this point, and therefore their division compares one group that is almost certainly RS+ with a second group that includes a mixture of RS+ and RS- in some uncertain proportion. Clearly, this is not the best way to find out the difference between RS+ and RS- people. Even people who are slightly better at peg moving with their left hand are more likely to be RS+ than RS-, and the dividing point should reflect this. Annett herself, however, does not use this procedure, but divides people into right-handers and left-handers on the basis of writing hand (Annett, 1970, 1985).

The third possibility is that the real distinction is between those that can be called left-handers and those that can be called right-handers, with people in each group differing in their degree of handedness, and possibly in the specific patterns of hand preference. By this argument, the cut point should be at zero on some continuous distribution of hand preference or hand performance scores. Those divisions that compare pure right-handers to a mixture of right-handers and left-handers (NRH) hopelessly confound degree and direction. The NRH group is not only more left-handed, but also less strongly handed than the RH group. Collins (1985), in mouse work, has shown that he can breed animals for degree of paw preference, but not for direction. In the mouse, this implies that degree is under genetic control but direction is not. Generalizing to the human, it suggests at the very least that degree and direction should be considered to be separate factors (see Bryden, 1987).

Let us examine the often-cited work by Rasmussen and Milner (1977) on handedness and cerebral speech lateralization more carefully, as one example of the possible problems created by using a RH-NRH distinction. In this study, Rasmussen and Milner used an 18-item hand-preference inventory to assess handedness, with scores ranging from 18 (right-handed) to 90 (left-handed) (the mean, if one answered all questions as "use both hands equally," was 54). They then state that people with scores of 55 or greater were considered to be *strongly left-handed,* and eventually used a score of 30 to cut the group into RH and Non-RH. On the basis of our work with similar questionnaires (Steenhuis & Bryden, 1987), their RH-NRH split would divide the population roughly at the median, whereas more conventional categorization would suggest that only about 10% of the population is "left-handed" (Bryden, 1977; Porac & Coren, 1981). Furthermore, all people whose scores were to the left of the null point were termed *strongly left-handed*! A person who preferred the left hand for nine activities and the right for eight would be called strongly left-handed. Our own data would suggest that about 80% of the Rasmussen and Milner NRH group would claim to be right-handed. For instance, a person who answered *every* question as "usually use right hand" (rather than "always use right hand") would obtain a score of 36 and would be classified as NRH. Worse yet, the mean absolute deviation from the center of this distribution is about 30 in the RH group, and about 13 in the NRH group. Thus, at least in this sample, the contrast is between a group of people who are strongly lateralized right-handers and a second group that is only about 20% truly left-handed and about 90% relatively weakly lateralized. It is really impossible to tell whether it is degree or direction or both that is related to speech lateralization in such a sample. It should be emphasized that the Rasmussen and Milner data are only used because they are readily accessible; they are certainly not the only ones guilty of such a practice; it is quite commonplace in the clinical literature (cf. Kimura, 1983; Witelson, 1985).

In contrast to the situation with clinical populations, most experimental studies in normal subjects of the relation between handedness and cerebral lateralization have employed consistent and objective definitions of handedness, albeit they do not all use the same definitions. Lake and Bryden (1976), for example, classified their subjects on the basis of the Oldfield (1971) handedness questionnaire: Subjects with positive scores were considered to be right-handed and those with negative scores were classified as left-handed. Similar procedures have been employed in other large-scale studies of the effects of handedness on dichotic listening or lateralized tachistoscopic performance (e.g., McKeever, Nolan, Diehl, & Seitz, 1984; Piazza, 1980; Orsini et al., 1985). Rarely, however, is any distinction made between strong and weak handedness. Consequently, most right-handers are strong and consistent in their preferences, whereas the left-handed sample includes many people who perform some activities with the right hand. As a result, the left-handed group is almost certainly less strongly handed than the right-handed group. Likewise, the left-handed group is likely to be less consistent in its preferences than the right-handed group. Some of these differences may well arise from the societal pressures to be right-handed (cf. Dawson, 1977; Porac & Coren, 1981), leading us to expect left-handers to be less consistently handed than right-handers.   As a consequence, we accept the differences in performance without questioning their origins.

IMPROVING THE PREDICTION OF CEREBRAL FUNCTION

The fact that there are varying definitions of handedness employed in the literature leads to many problems, and makes it very difficult to generalize from the clinical literature to the experimental literature.   In particular, it becomes almost impossible to make a clear statement about the relation of handedness to cerebral organization. How can we improve this state of affairs? There seem to be three solutions: we can improve the definition of lateralization of function; we can improve the definition of handedness; or we can find some other measure to replace handedness or to act in conjunction with it.

Snyder and Novelly (1988) pointed out that there are vast differences between hospitals in their criteria for claiming bilateral language representation following unilateral sodium amytal administration (Wada testing), with percentages ranging from 0% to 60% bilateral language. Similar problems exist in the aphasia literature, in that different institutions vary in their criteria for deciding that a particular individual exhibits an aphasic disturbance. In particular, different criteria may be employed for deciding that aphasia follows upon left hemisphere damage, when it might be expected, and upon right hemisphere damage, when it might not. Furthermore, unilateral brain damage studies cannot provide anything more than a crude estimate of the incidence of bilateral language representation, and the failure to observe aphasic symptoms following unilateral brain damage does not necessarily imply that the language hemisphere has not been damaged. Thus, estimates of the incidence of left and right hemispheric language representation provided by surveys such as that of Segalowitz and Bryden (1983) may be subject to major errors. Similar problems exist in attempts to determine the relative frequency of visuospatial representation in the two hemispheres (cf. Bryden et al., 1983). Thus, prediction of cerebral function from handedness could be improved by strengthening the definition of aphasic disturbance or of visuospatial disturbance.

Alternatively, we may need to find another measure of lateral asymmetry that is more closely related to language. Ideally, such a measure should divide the right-handed group into a small subgroup (those with right-hemisphere language) and a very large one (those with left-hemisphere language), and the left-handed group into more equal portions. Dissatisfaction with handedness as a predictor is one reason why some people have suggested eye dominance as a measure of lateralization that is presumably less contaminated by cultural factors (cf. Porac & Coren, 1976), why Luria (1970) was interested in measures of "latent left-handedness" such as arm crossing and hand clasping (see also Bryden, 1989), why Chapman, Chapman, and Allen (1987) and Peters (1988) have been interested in footedness, and why Levy (Levy & Nagylaki, 1972; Levy & Reid,

1978) offered handwriting posture as a potential predictor variable. Of all of these variables, handwriting posture has about the right distribution, but it has not been found to be related to speech lateralization as assessed through sodium amytal procedures (Ajersch & Milner, 1983; Weber & Bradshaw, 1981). Although the application of more sophisticated statistical techniques, such as log-linear modeling (Fienberg, 1980), may reveal that some of these variables interact with handedness to improve the prediction of language lateralization (or some other function), a proper classification study requires far larger samples than are presently available.

As a third alternative, it may be wise to refine our measure of handedness, so that we better understand what we are measuring. It is this final point that pursue here. In effect, we want to argue that there are three and perhaps four more or less independent factors that should be considered relevant in determining the relation between handedness and cerebral organization, and in particular language lateralization.

One of these is the anatomical asymmetry in the temporal planum. Geschwind and Galaburda's (1987) summary of the literature (Table 5.1, pp. 22-27) leads to the conclusion that about 70% of the population has a larger left temporal planum, 15% a larger right temporal planum, and 15% exhibit anatomical asymmetry. Because about 92% of the population has left-hemispheric language, and 90% is right-handed, anatomical asymmetries alone cannot account for the lateral distribution of language processes. Nevertheless, there are now studies beginning to appear that demonstrate a relation between temporal planum asymmetry and language lateralization (Strauss, Lapointe, Wada, Gaddes, & Kosaka, 1985; Witelson, 1983).

A second factor is handedness. Geschwind and Galaburda (1987) showed that temporal planum asymmetry varies somewhat with handedness, and we know that there is a weak association of handedness with speech lateralization (cf. Segalowitz & Bryden, 1983). Obviously, we have to consider handedness as relevant, but how? We argue that handedness is not a unidimensional trait, but that we need to consider at least two distinct dimensions. It is possible that most of the existing research has concentrated on the wrong one.

A third factor is what I term *environmental flexibility*. Recently, one of us reported preliminary data from a three-generational study of handedness that indicated that degree of hand preference was more heritable than direction of hand preference (Bryden, 1987). This is in line with Collins' (1985) observation in mice that degree and direction are separate factors. In actual fact, *degree of handedness* is perhaps a poor term, in that what Collins has shown is that some animals will readily shift their paw preference, and we should like to postulate the same thing in people. That is, that some people are highly responsive to environmental situations, and alter their hand preference easily, whereas others are not so responsive. Thus, we might speak of people as Rigid and Plastic, for lack of a better set of terms. Although some people may start out with an inclination to be left-handed, environmental pressures drive them to be right handed.

IMPROVING THE MEASUREMENT OF HANDEDNESS

Let us now consider the handedness variable in greater detail. For a long time three general principles about handedness seemed to be self-evident. Because of training practices in the home and school, one should assess more than writing hand. At the same time, handedness was considered to be a unidimensional variable, and hand preference and hand performance were seen as closely related. These principles have guided both the choice of test items and the conceptualization of handedness in the neuropsychological literature.

Many of us have felt that writing hand alone was not sufficient information to assess handedness, for cultural pressures made us be right-handed for writing if not for other things. Others have not seen this as so self-evident; the ultimate criterion for division into left and right employed by both Annett (1985) and McManus (1985), for example, is writing hand. A report by Beukelaar and Kroonenberg (1986) is fine evidence that handwriting pressures changed in Holland shortly after World War II. Payne (1987) has compared Muslim and Christian samples in Nigeria, and has shown very large differences between the groups in terms of their belief as to which hand should be used, although only small differences in actual preferences.

Second, it has seemed clear that handedness was unidimensional and that we wanted to string people out along a single dimension of "handedness." This assumption led one of us (Bryden, 1977) to analyze the data from the Oldfield (1971) and Crovitz and Zener (1962) hand-preference questionnaires, and to arrive at a suggested list of five (or eight) items for a preference inventory; items that are now in fairly common use.

It is further assumed that hand preference and hand performance are related to one another, such that strongly handed people on a preference inventory show a strong performance difference between the hands, and weakly handed people would show a small performance difference. This implies that one can use either preference inventories or performance tasks to assess handedness, and that they are to a large extent interchangeable. This assumption also led to the development of a group performance test, in which people are asked to place dots in circles rapidly (Tapley & Bryden, 1985). The data from this test indicated two normally distributed subgroups, one right-handed with a positive mean, and one left-handed with a negative mean.

Each of these points have led to some difficulties. There is a continuing debate as to just what activities should be sampled in a handedness inventory, with some preferring short questionnaires (e.g., Bryden, 1977; Porac & Coren, 1981), and others arguing for many items sampling a broad range of activities (e.g., Provins, Milner, & Kerr, 1982). Healey et al. 1986) have published data that have suggested that handedness is multifactorial. Likewise, the primate data reported by McNeilage, Studdert-Kennedy, and Lindblom (1987) suggest separate reaching and manipulation factors. Thus, handedness may not be unidimensional after all. Finally, there are those who argue that preference and performance are only poorly related (e.g., Porac & Coren, 1981). Annett (1985), however, has shown that performance and preference measures are fairly closely related.   As one instance, Annett and Kilshaw (1983), using a peg moving task, reported data on performance differences between the hands that suggested two normally distributed subgroups, one with a positive (RH) mean, and one with a zero mean. This is consistent with her division into right-shift (RS+) and nonright-shift (RS-) people, but inconsistent with the Tapley and Bryden (1985) data.

Steenhuis and Bryden (1989) have recently been testing a large number of self-professed left-handers and right-handers on both Annett and Kilshaw's (1983) peg-moving test   and Tapley and Bryden's (1985) dot-filling task.   Interestingly, we find that both groups are correct, in the sense that right-handers show a positive mean and left-handers a negative mean on the dot-filling task, whereas right-handers show a positive mean and left-handers a zero mean on the peg-moving task. Thus, it is possible to replicate both studies with the same sample of subjects.   Furthermore, because the categorization was of self-professed left-handers and self-professed right-handers, it suggests that the Tapley-Bryden task provides a better discrimination of groups.   Furthermore, Steenhuis and Bryden (1988b) showed that preference and performance measures are best related when the preference questions asked are relevant to the skill examined.

With respect to hand-preference inventories, we found that the 8-item (Bryden, 1977) version of the Oldfield that we had been using for years was strongly unifactorial. Adding the dot-filling task did not alter this. However, the suggestion by Healey et al. (1986) that handedness was not truly unifactorial led us to begin working with expanded handedness questionnaires (see also Provins et al., 1982).   We have employed a number of different versions of a preference inventory, ranging from 25 to 60 questions, and patterned after those used by Healey et al. (1986), by Dean (1978), and those surveyed by Fennell (1986).   At the present time, we have data on each of three versions of a long preference test, on samples of 600 to 1,000 undergraduate students.

Invariably, we find three factors, with sometimes the hint of a fourth (Steenhuis & Bryden, 1987, 1988a).   Factor 1 is what one would conventionally term *handedness*.   Items loading on it are moderately skilled unimanual behaviors. The typical subject claims that he or she always uses a particular hand for each of these behaviors, and thus most responses are in the extreme "1" and "5" categories, although right-handers may do some of the activities left-handed and vice-versa.   Both the factor scores and the individual items are highly reliable.

Factor 2 is what we have termed *picking and reaching*.   Items that ask about relatively simple unskilled acts of reaching and picking up load on this factor, such as picking up a pin or a penny, reaching for a glass, or pointing. They are characterized by a large number of "equal" or "usually" responses, in Categories 2-4.   The individual items do not show particularly high test-retest reliability, although the factor score does. Thus, a person may change his or her mind from one administration of the test to another, but if one asks four to six questions of this type, the average score will be highly reliable.

Factor 3 seems to isolate two items, swinging a baseball bat and using an axe. It is not, as Healey et al. (1986) suggested, a proximal or axial movement factor, for other items we have devised that inquire about axial movements, such as pushing through cabaret doors, do not load on this factor. Responses tend to be extreme in Categories 1 and 5, but it is only weakly correlated with Factor 1. Thus, many left-handers bat right-handed, and many right-handers bat left-handed, an observation that may very well be related to the bimanual nature of the task.

Factor 4, when it appears, seems to be a strength factor, with items like picking up a heavy suitcase loading on it. We are not convinced that this is a reliable factor, because it appears in only one of our three major analyses.

For this study, we are concentrating on Factors 1 and 2. We have selected three groups of subjects: left-handers, right-handers who are weak on Factor 2, and right-handers who are strong on Factor 2, and are comparing them on a variety of performance tests as well as giving them a standard verbal dichotic listening test to assess speech lateralization at least crudely. It may well turn out that Factor 2 is a better measure of "natural" handedness, and therefore is better correlated with lateral dominance than factor one, which is what most people are using.

HANDEDNESS AND CEREBRAL LATERALIZATION

Now, let us assume that there are distinct factors determining direction of initial hand bias and strength of bias, much as Collins (1985) has separated degree and direction in mice. To begin with, let us assume that the initial basis for handedness lies in an anatomical asymmetry of the brain. Basing our argument on the data presented by Geschwind and Galaburda (1987) for temporal planum asymmetry, and recognizing that the temporal planum is not the hand area, let us assume that about 75% of the population has a larger or more elaborated anatomical substrate for handedness in the left cerebral hemisphere, and about 25% a larger region in the right cerebral hemisphere. Thus, if anatomical factors were all that were important, about 25% of the population would be left-handed.

In fact, the highest figures for the incidence left-handedness are on the order of 20%, in the Alaskan Eskimos (Dawson, 1977), native-born Israelis (Kobylianski, Micle, & Arensberg, 1978), and in the mentally retarded (Satz, 1972), suggesting that this figure is about as high as one will observe. On the other hand, the cross-cultural survey by Dawson (1977) and the literature on handedness in the Chinese suggests that there are a hard-core residual of about 2% of the population who are left-handed regardless of the parental and cultural pressures to conform to the right-handed norm.   Therefore, about 10% of "natural" left-handers are sufficiently fixed in their handedness that they will not change despite strong pressure. Logically, the same is true for right-handers, and about 10% of them would not change to sinistrality even if pressured to do so. In other words, about 10% of the population are what we might call "rigid" in their handedness; they correspond to Collins' (1985) mice who show strong preferences. The remaining 90% are "flexible," and handedness is driven in part by environmental pressure. Given that the environment is strongly biased toward right-handedness, the effect of this is to shift a large proportion of those people who have more elaborate anatomical substrates for handedness in the right hemisphere to manifest right-handedness rather than left-handedness. By this argument, the high incidence of left-handedness in various pathological groups, emphasized by Paul Satz, may well be not a result of early brain damage but a consequence of the fact that their environment is relatively unbiased, because no one really seems to care whether such people are right-handed or left-handed. The whole strong-weak distinction, of course, is recognition of the fact that handedness is labile, and that varying environments can affect the observed incidence of handedness.

One should recognize that, if these arguments are correct, that many overtly weak right-handers are really weak left-handers affected by the environment, and that the original classification we objected to in the opening paragraphs of right-handers and nonright-handers may turn out to be a perfectly reasonable one. However, the NRH group would also include a small number of strong left-handers, who should differ from the weakly handed majority, and this distinction would continue to be lost.

Finally, we should like to make two brief points about degree of handedness. First, Bryden (1987) has reported evidence from a three-generational study to indicate that degree of handedness is more heritable than direction of handedness. Second, evidence such as that from the Hawaii family study, where "ambidexters" are clearly different from either left-handers or right-handers in spatial ability, suggests that degree of handedness can be at least as important a factor as direction of handedness.

HANDEDNESS AND PERSONALITY

At this point, we should also like to make one observation about the relationship of handedness to personality variables. There are frequent reports that left-handers possess certain odd or "quirky" behaviors. The very distribution of handedness means that a certain number of individuals will fall near the zero-point of our handedness scales. Of 1,000 people, suppose that 100 are left-handed, 50 borderline, and 850 clearly right-handed. Let us also suppose that a particular "quirky" behavior is observed in 6% of the population, regardless of handedness. Now, of our 1,000 people, 6 people will be both left-handed and quirky, 3 will be borderline and quirky, and 51 will be right-handed and quirky. However, if we now ask people to self-classify themselves as to handedness, and those who possess "quirky" behavior are proud to be part of a minority group, the borderline people will call themselves left-handed, while those borderline people who do not possess this behavior will align themselves with in majority and term themselves right-handed. Thus, the 3 borderline people who are quirky will call themselves left-handed, whereas the 47 who are not will call themselves right-handed. This will change the proportions of "quirky" behavior in the self-professed left-handed to $6 + 3/ 100 + 3 = 9/103 = 8.74\%$, and the proportion in the self-professed right-handed to $51/850 + 47 = 51/897 = 5.69\%$. This is certainly enough of a difference to impress some people, and may actually be the basis for some of the reports of personality differences between left-handers and right-handers (cf. Furnham, 1983; Harburg, Roeper, Ozgoren, & Feldstein, 1981).

ON FAMILIAL SINISTRALITY

There has been a lot said about familial sinistrality (FS) in recent years, and a lot of odd points have been made. Although some people seem to prefer to distinguish between FS+ and FS- left-handers, apparently feeling that FS+ left-handers are somehow "real" or "natural" left-handers, whereas FS- left-handers are "adventitious," this may not make a great deal of sense. If one works out the details of a model of handedness and cerebral lateralization, such as that of Annett (1985) or Levy and Nagylaki (1972), the difference in incidence of right-hemisphere language between FS+ and FS- right-handers is far greater than that between FS+ and FS- left-handers. Thus, one should be comparing FS+ and FS- right-handers, rather than FS+ and FS- left-handers (McKeever et al., 1983). Considering a disease model, this makes some sense: one does not compare schizophrenics with schizophrenic relatives to those without schizophrenic relatives; rather one compares relatives of schizophrenics to those who have no schizophrenic relatives. Even here, there is a definitional problem. FS is clearly contaminated by family size (Bishop, 1980). In addition, the further out you reach (to second-order relatives, for instance), the higher the likelihood that a person will be FS+. In addition, the less likely is it that the data will be meaningful: Few people know the handedness of their (deceased) grandparents. Perhaps what we should be doing is to define specific relationships and deal with them: as by comparing right-handed females who have a single left-handed brother as compared to right-handed females who have a single right-handed brother.

CONCLUSIONS

In this chapter, we have examined some of the common practices for controlling for handedness in studies of cerebral lateralization. We argue that the common practice of restricting one's studies to right-handers, or even to right-handed males without a familial history of left-handedness, prejudges the procedures as being related to cerebral lateralization and avoids the problem of coming to a fuller understanding of the relationship between cerebral lateralization and such variables as handedness, familial sinistrality, and sex.

Present data indicate only a weak relationship between handedness and cerebral lateralization. We offer some suggestions as to how to improve the measurement of handedness, and some speculations about the separability of degree and direction of handedness. Finally, we propose the beginnings of a model of handedness and cerebral lateralization that posits separate anatomical, hand, and environmental responsivity factors.

ACKNOWLEDGMENT

The work reported in this chapter was supported by Grant No. A0095 from the Natural Sciences and Engineering Research Council of Canada to M.P.B.

REFERENCES

Ajersch, M.K., & Milner, B. (1983) Handwriting posture as related to cerebral speech lateralization, sex and writing hand. *Human Neurobiology*, *2*, 143-145.

Annett, M. (1970). A classification of hand preference by association analysis. *British Journal of Psychology*, *61*, 303-321.

Annett, M. (1985). *Left, right, hand and brain: The right shift theory*. Hillsdale, NJ: Lawrence Erlbaum Associates.

Annett, M., & Kilshaw, D. (1983). Right- and left-handed skill II: Estimating the parameters of the distribution of L-R differences in males and females. *British Journal of Psychology*, *74*, 269-283.

Beukelaar, L.J., & Kroonenberg, P.M. (1986). Changes over time in the relationship between hand preference and writing hand among left-handers. *Neuropsychologia*, *24*, 301-303.

Bishop, D.V.M. (1980). Measuring familial sinistrality. *Cortex*, *16*, 311-313.

Bryden, M.P. (1977). Measuring handedness with questionnaires. *Neuropsychologia*, *15*, 617-624.

Bryden, M. P. (1986). Dichotic listening performance, cognitive ability, and cerebral organization. *Canadian Journal of Psychology*, *40*, 445-456.

Bryden, M. P. (1987). Handedness and cerebral organization: Data from clinical and normal populations. In D. Ottoson (Ed.), *Duality and unity of the brain* (pp. 55-70). Harmondsworth, UK: Macmillan.

Bryden, M.P. (1988). An overview of the dichotic listening procedure and its relation to cerebral organization. In K. S. Hugdahl (Ed.), *Handbook of dichotic listening*. Chichester, UK: John Wiley.

Bryden, M.P. (1989). Handedness, cerebral lateralization, and measures of "latent left-handedness" *International Journal of Neuroscience*, *44*, 227-233.

Bryden, M.P., Hécaen, H., & DeAgostini, M. (1983). Patterns of cerebral organization. *Brain and Language*, *20*, 249-262.

Chapman, J. P, Chapman, L.J., & Allen, J.J. (1987). The measurement of foot preference. *Neuropsychologia*, *25*, 579-584.

Collins, R.L. (1985). On the inheritance of direction and degree of asymmetry. In S.D. Glick (Ed.), *Cerebral lateralization in nonhuman species* (pp. 41-71). Orlando, FL: Academic Press.

Crovitz, H. F., & Zener, K. (1962). A group-test for assessing hand and eye dominance. *American Journal of Psychology*, *75*, 271-276.

Dawson, J.L.M.B. (1977). An anthropological perspective on the evolution and lateralization of the brain. *Annals of the New York Academy of Sciences*,

299, 424-447.

Dean, R.S. (1978). *Dean laterality preference schedule.* University of Wisconsin -- Madison, WI: Madison Press.

Fennell, E.B. (1986). Handedness in neuropsychological research. In H. J. Hannay (Ed.), *Experimental techniques in human neuropsychology* (pp. 15-44). New York: Oxford University Press.

Fienberg, S.E. (1980). *The analysis of cross-classified categorical data* (2nd ed.). Cambridge, MA: MIT Press.

Fischer, S.C., & Pellegrino, J.W. (1988). Hemisphere differences for components of mental rotation. *Brain and Cognition, 7,* 1-15.

Furnham, A. (1983). Personality and handedness. *Personality and Individual Differences, 4,* 715-716.

Geschwind, N. & Galaburda, A.S. (1987). *Cerebral lateralization.* Cambridge, MA: MIT Press.

Harburg, E., Roeper, P., Ozgoren, F., & Feldstein, A.M. (1981). Handedness and temperament. *Perceptual and Motor Skills, 52,* 283-290.

Healey, J.M., Liederman, J., & Geschwind, N. (1986). Handedness is not a unidimensional trait. *Cortex, 22,* 33-54.

Kimura, D. (1983). Speech representation in an unbiased sample of left-handers. *Human Neurobiology, 2,* 147-154.

Kirsner, K., & Schwartz, S. (1986). Word and hemifields: Do the hemispheres enjoy equal opportunity? *Brain and Cognition, 5,* 354-361.

Kobylianski, E., Micle, S., & Arensberg, A. (1978). Handedness, hand-clasping, and arm-folding in Israeli males. *Annals of Human Biology, 5,* 247-251.

Lake, D., & Bryden, M.P. (1976). Handedness and sex differences in hemispheric asymmetry. *Brain and Language, 3,* 266-282.

Levy, J. (1972). Lateral specialization of the human brain: Behavioral manifestations and possible evolutionary basis. In J.A. Kiger (Ed.), *The biology of behavior* (pp. 159-180). Corvallis, OR: Oregon State University Press.

Levy, J., & Nagylaki, T. (1972). A model for the genetics of handedness. *Genetics, 72,* 117-128.

Levy, J., & Reid, M. (1978). Variations in cerebral organization as a function of handedness, hand posture in writing and sex. *Journal of Experimental Psychology: General, 107,* 119-144.

Luria, A.R. (1970). *Traumatic aphasia.* The Hague, Netherlands: Mouton.

McGlone, J. (1980). Sex differences in human brain organization: A critical survey. *The Behavioral and Brain Sciences, 3,* 215-227.

McKeever, W.F., Nolan, D.R., Diehl, J.A., & Seitz, K.S. (1984). Handedness and language laterality: Discrimination of handedness groups on the dichotic consonant-vowel task. *Cortex, 20,* 509-523.

McKeever, W.F., Seitz, K.S., Hoff, A.L. Marino, M.F., & Diehl, J.A. (1983). Interacting sex and familial sinistrality characteristics influence both language lateralization and spatial ability in right handers. *Neuropsychologia, 21,* 661-668.

McManus, I. C. (1985). Right- and left-hand skill: Failure of the right shift model. *British Journal of Psychology, 76*, 1-16.

McNeilage, P.F., Studdert-Kennedy, M. G. & Lindblom, B. (1987). Primate handedness reconsidered. *The Behavioral and Brain Sciences, 10*, 247-303.

Oldfield, R.C. (1971). The assessment and analysis of handedness: The Edinburgh Inventory. *Neuropsychologia, 9*, 97-113.

Orsini, D.L., Satz, P., Soper, H.V., & Light, R.K. (1985). The role of familial sinistrality in cerebral organization. *Neuropsychologia, 23*, 223-232.

Payne, M. A. (1987). Impact of cultural pressures on self-reports of actual and approved hand use. *Neuropsychologia, 25*, 247-258.

Peters, M. (1988). Footedness: Asymmetries in foot preference and skill and neuropsychological assessment of foot movement. *Psychological Bulletin, 103*, 179-192.

Piazza, D.M. (1980). The influence of sex and handedness in the hemispheric specialization of verbal and nonverbal tasks. *Neuropsychologia, 18*, 163-176.

Porac, C., & Coren, S. (1976). The dominant eye. *Psychological Bulletin, 83*, 880-897.

Porac, C., & Coren, S. (1981). *Lateral preferences and human behavior.* New York: Springer-Verlag.

Provins, K.A., Milner, A.D., & Kerr, P. (1982). Asymmetry of manual preference and performance. *Perceptual and Motor Skills, 54*, 179-194.

Rasmussen, T., & Milner, B. (1977). The role of early left-brain injury in determining lateralization of cerebral speech functions. *Annals of the New York Academy of Sciences, 299*, 355-369.

Sanders, B., Wilson, J.R., & Vandenberg, S.G. (1982). Handedness and spatial ability. *Cortex, 18*, 79-90.

Satz, P. (1972). Pathological left-handedness: An explanatory model. *Cortex, 8*, 121-135.

Segalowitz, S.J., & Bryden, M.P. (1983). Individual differences in hemispheric representation of language. In S. J. Segalowitz (Ed.), *Language functions and brain organization* (pp. 341-372). New York: Academic Press.

Snyder, P.J., & Novelly, R.A. (1988, March). *Administration of the intracarotid sodium amytal procedure (ISAP) and the assessment of hemispheric lateralization of speech: A call for standards.* Paper presented at BABBLE conference, Niagara Falls, NY.

Steenhuis, R.E., & Bryden, M.P. (1987, June). Handedness is a matter of degree and direction. Paper presented at Canadian Psychological Association Meetings, Vancouver, BC.

Steenhuis, R.E., & Bryden, M.P. (1988a). Different dimensions of handedness that relate to skilled and unskilled activities. *Journal of Clinical and Experimental Neuropsychology, 10*, 40 (Abstract).

Steenhuis, R.E., & Bryden, M.P. (1988b). The relation between hand preference and hand performance. *Canadian Psychologist, 29* (2a), Abstract No.

747.

Steenhuis, R.E., & Bryden, M.P. (1989, February). *Hand preference and performance: Right-handers, left-handers, and left-handers who are not consistently left-handed.* Paper presented at International Neuropsychology Society meeting, Vancouver, BC.

Strauss, E., Lapointe, J.S., Wada, J.A., Gaddes, W., & Kosaka, B. (1985). Language dominance: Correlation of radiological and functional data. *Neuropsychologia, 23,* 415-420.

Tapley, S.M., & Bryden, M.P. (1985). A group test for the assessment of performance between the hands. *Neuropsychologia, 23,* 215-222.

Weber, A.M., & Bradshaw, J.L. (1981). Levy and Reid's neurological model in relation to writing hand/posture: An evaluation. *Psychological Bulletin, 90,* 74-88.

Witelson, S. F. (1983). Bumps on the brain: Right-left asymmetry as a key to functional lateralization. In S. J. Segalowitz (Ed.), *Language functions and brain organization.* New York: Academic Press.

Witelson, S.F. (1985). The brain connection: The corpus callosum is larger in left handers. *Science, 229,* 665-668.

4 Handedness, Language Laterality and Spatial Ability

Walter F. McKeever [1]
Northern Arizona University

Since the late 1960, we have seen the development of a diversity of techniques for assessing hemispheric specializations of function. Specializations for language functions, spatial information processing, and the processing and storage of "emotional" stimuli have been studied extensively. A number of chapters in this volume report interesting data that required the development of tachistoscopic, dichotic, evoked potential, blood flow, and other techniques that assess functional asymmetries. Differences in hemispheric specializations as a function of handedness, sex, familial sinistrality (FS), and other factors have received considerable attention. In this Chapter I focus on the question of spatial ability as a function of sex, handedness, and FS factors and express my own conclusions regarding the adequacy of some explanations of sex and handedness differences in spatial ability. Interest in this topic has followed from demonstrated or hypothesized differences in hemispheric specialization characteristics of the sexes and handedness groups. The literature relevant to this topic is very extensive and, in some areas, contradictory. A number of excellent reviews are available with respect to the question of spatial ability differences as a function of gender (e.g., Harris, 1981; McGee, 1979). No major review of the question of spatial ability differences between handedness groups, nor as a function of FS, has appeared since the late 1970s. It is not my intention to devote this chapter to a major review of these areas; but it is necessary to provide a certain amount of review as a backdrop to the data I present later.

Jerre Levy (1969) suggested that left-handers were perhaps slightly superior to right-handers in verbal abilities, but inferior to right-handers in visuo-spatial abilities. Her reasoning was based on the well-established fact that although nearly all right-handers are left-hemisphere "dominant" for language processes, left-handers are more variable with regard to language laterality. Data attesting to this fact have been reported by many investigators. Goodglass and Quadfasel (1954), employing clinical reports of aphasia frequencies following unilateral cortical damage as their data source, estimated that only 53% of left-handers possess left-hemisphere language dominance. Rasmussen and Milner (1977), basing their estimates on Wada Test data, suggested that left-hemispheric speech dominance occurs in approximately 96% of right-handed persons, but in only 70% of left-handed persons. More recently, Segalowitz and Bryden (1983) have estimated the incidence figures for left-hemisphere dominance in right- and left-handers at 95.5% and 61.4%, respectively. Both Rasmussen and Milner (1977) and Segalowitz and Bryden (1983) estimated that the non left-hemisphere dominant left-handers are essentially equally divided between those with right-hemisphere dominance and those with bilateral language representation. It has also been suggested by Levy (1974) and McGlone (1980) that women may be less left-hemisphere dominant for language or "verbal" processing than men.

Levy's hypothesis suggests that utilization of the right hemisphere for speech processing in many left-handers (and women) might be expected to expand the total neural mass available for language functions, but that it reduces, concomitantly, the neural mass available for the processing of spatial information. There is considerable evidence that the right hemisphere is more involved in spatial information processing and storage than is the left hemisphere. This modal spatial laterality pattern, however, is generally thought to be less marked than that for language functions. Bryden, Hécaen, and De Agostini (1983), for example, estimated that only about 76% of right-handed males and 59% of right-handed females are right hemisphere dominant for spatial ability. Part of the difficulty with these estimates resides in the fact that the Bryden and De Agostini figures are based on the incidence of spatial disorders following unilateral brain lesions, and may not reveal precisely the balance of lateralized information processing in the normal brain. Using blood-flow indices of hemispheric asymmetry during the performance of spatial tasks, Deutsch, Bourbon, Papanicolaou, and Eisenberg (1988) found no sex differences in the pattern of asymmetry (right- hemisphere superiority) despite the fact that females performed significantly worse than males on one of the three tasks used (a mental rotation task) and tended to perform at a lower level on the other tasks as well.

It is well-established that "spatial ability" is not a unitary trait. At least two major types of spatial ability have been identified in factor-analytic studies (McGee, 1979). One type is required when the subject must recognize an irregularly shaped configuration as the same despite differences in the aspect of the configuration presented to him or her. This type of ability is referred to as *mental- rotation ability*. A second type of spatial ability is often referred to as *spatial-relations* ability. This type of ability is needed for tasks that require an appreciation of the arrangement of elements within a stimulus configuration. Examples of items designed to test for mental-rotation ability (Stafford Identical Blocks Test) and for spatial-relations ability (Minnesota Paper Form Board) are shown in Fig. 4.1. That different types of spatial ability exist means that different cortical loci and networks must mediate them. Deutsch et al. (1988) found that, of three spatial tasks they employed, the mental-rotation task elicited the clearest hemispheric asymmetry of blood flow (right-hemisphere dominance) and that it also revealed the clearest right parietal locus of activation. Additionally, the mental rotation task was the only one to show a significant sex difference (males superior) in number of correct solutions. Similarly, in a study by Osaka (1984),

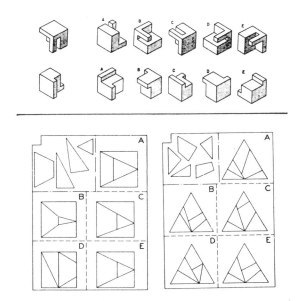

FIGURE 4.1. Examples of items from the Stafford Identical Blocks Test (I) and the Minnesota Paper Form Board (II). In the Stafford, subject chooses the lettered block which is the same shape as the test block to the left. In the Minnesota, subject chooses the lettered configuration which could be made from shapes in upper-left section. (Stafford Identical Blocks Test items reproduced by permission of the Pennsylvania State University, University Park. Copyright, 1962, Robert Stafford; Revised Minnesota Paper Form Board items reproduced by permission of The Psychological Corporation, San Antonio. Copyright 1941, Renis Likert and W. H. Quasha).

mental rotation task performances produced the clearest asymmetry of EEG activation. Linn and Petersen (1985), in a meta-analysis of studies of sex differences in spatial ability, concluded that sex differences are most consistently obtained in those studies that have employed spatial tasks that require mental rotation.

SEX AND SPATIAL ABILITY

There is a long history of reports of sex differences, favoring males, in spatial abilities (see reviews of Harris, 1981; Maccoby & Jacklin, 1974). Harris provided a thorough review of data bearing on the hypothesis that these differences are due to socialization, but concluded that the differences cannot be wholly explained in terms of sex-role training. Several lines of evidence have suggested a possible influence of gonadal hormones on the pattern of sex differences, and of within-sex differences, in abilities (Broverman, Klaiber, Kobayashi, and Vogel, 1968; Broverman, Broverman, Vogel, and Palmer, 1964;

Christiansen and Knussman, 1988; Klaiber, Broverman, and Kobayashi, 1967; Petersen, 1976; Shute, Pellegrino, Hubert, and Reynolds, 1983). For the most part, these studies suggest that spatial ability is favored by higher levels of androgens in females, but that among males, the less masculinized show higher spatial abilities than the more masculinized individuals. Christiansen and Knussman (1988), however, have presented some data that they feel argues for a positive correlation between spatial ability and "androgens" in males. Such contradictions indicate that the possible role of sex steroids in the ability pattern can be considered no more than an interesting hypothesis at present. That sex differences in the ability pattern exist, however, seems firmly established.

HANDEDNESS AND SPATIAL ABILITIES

The hypothesis that spatial ability differences exist as a function of handedness is much less firmly established. Levy (1969) provided the initial support for her hypothesis. She administered the Wechsler Adult Intelligence Scale (WAIS) to 15 right-handed and 10 left-handed graduate students at Cal Tech. She found that the left-handers had a slightly higher Verbal Scale IQ and a substantially lower Performance Scale IQ than did right-handers. Because the Performance Scale of the WAIS contains several subtests that can be described as "spatial" tests, Levy concluded that her hypothesis was supported. Miller (1971) reported similar findings, employing the Mill Hill Vocabulary Test as a verbal measure and the Raven Matrices as a spatial measure. Nebes (1971) reported that left-handers scored significantly lower than right-handers on a test requiring the matching of manually palpated to visually inspected arcs of differing degrees. Such positive findings were soon countered, however, by negative findings regarding handedness differences in abilities (Fagan-Dubin, 1974; Hardyck, Petrinovich, and Goldman, 1976; Kutas, McCarthy, and Donchin, 1975), and a major review by Hardyck and Petrinovich (1977) concluded that no demonstrable ability differences could be said to exist between left- and right- handers.

Hicks and Beveridge (1978), however, noted that the 24 studies reviewed by Hardyck and Petrinovich had all involved tests of what Cattell (1971) had called "crystallized intelligence" (i.e., tests of knowledge or automatized skills such as reading). They suggested that studies that had employed measures of the other type of ability proposed by Cattell, namely "fluid intelligence," supported Levy's hypothesis. Fluid intelligence tasks typically require active problem solving and involve spatial or figural materials. They cited three such studies not reviewed by Hardyck and Petrinovich (Flick, 1966; Orme, 1970; Wittenborn, 1946). In addition, they conducted an experiment which included a measure of cyrstallized intelligence (a vocabulary test) and a measure of fluid intelligence - the Cattell Culture Fair Test, Scale 3 (Cattell & Cattell, 1973). The tests were administered to 37 right-handed and 30 left-handed college students. Consistent with their hypothesis, the results showed the two groups to be comparable on the vocabulary test, but significantly different (right-handers superior) on the fluid intelligence measure.

Two rather large-scale studies have suggested that there is a sex by handedness interaction in spatial ability. Yen (1975) studied the performances of 2,477 high school students on a battery of spatial tests. Her results indicated that a significant handedness effect, favoring right-handers, existed for males, but no handedness differences were found for females. Sanders, Wilson, and Vandenberg (1982), however, studied the performances of 830 adolescents and adults on a battery of spatial tests, and concluded that, among females, right-handers were superior in spatial ability, whereas among males, left handers were superior to right handers. Harshman, Hampson, and Berenbaum (1983) have suggested that spatial ability may be moderated by reasoning ability, and that this factor might explain the discrepancy between the results of Yen (1975) and of Sanders et al. (1982). They propose that among high reasoning ability individuals, the sex-handedness pattern obtained by Yen may be expected, but that among low reasoning ability subjects the sex-handedness interaction pattern obtained by Sanders et al. (1982) may be typical. This is an interesting notion, derived from some retrospective spatial test data of their own, and worthy of experimental testing. With respect to the Yen (1975) and Sanders et al. (1982) findings, however, I note that both involved group testings of the subjects. Group testing with extensive batteries may not elicit the maximal effort of the subjects, and factors such as distractibility and sociability, which might well interact with handedness, sex, and abilities can distort test results. Additionally, the question of the ages of subjects in the various handedness and sex groups of the Sanders et al. study was not addressed, despite the fact that ages ranged from 14 to 60.

FAMILIAL SINISTRALITY AND ABILITIES

A number of studies conducted during the 1980s, which have typically found handedness differences favoring right-handers on spatial tasks, have attempted to identify a subgroup of left-handers who might be responsible for the handedness effect. Familial sinistrality, sometimes in combination with strength of left-hand preference, has received the most attention.

Burnett, Lane, and Dratt (1982) administered the Spatial Visualization test (a test of mental-rotation ability) from the Guilford-Zimmerman Aptitude Survey to 124 female and 229 male undergraduates at Rice University. They also administered the Edinburgh Handedness Inventory (Oldfield, 1971) as a measure of degree of hand preference for common unimanual activities and they recorded the presence or absence of left-handers in the subjects' immediate families. Five levels (quintiles) of direction and degree of hand preference were established. Results showed that males outperformed females at all levels of hand preference; generally, the highest scores were obtained by slightly to moderately, as opposed to strongly, right-handed subjects; and FS was unfavorable for spatial ability among the non right-handers, clearly favorable among right-handed males, and slightly and inconsistently favorable among right-handed females. Burnett et al. concluded that these effects probably reflected language and motor dominance differences of the groups, with less marked dominance favorable to spatial ability.

Bradshaw, Nettleton, and Taylor (1981) administered the Australian version of the WAIS to 48 left- and 48 right-handed subjects who either had or lacked left-handedness in their families. All of the subjects met the criterion of having a strong preference for their preferred hand. Results indicated that left-handed FS+ subjects had significantly lower Performance Scale IQs, but not lower Verbal Scale IQs, than did either right-handers in general or FS- left-handers. Thus, like Burnett et al. (1982), they suggested that FS+ was unfavorable for spatial ability in left-handers, but they saw no effects of FS in right-handers.

Searleman, Hermann, and Coventry (1984), studying only left-handed individuals, reported that strongly left-handed FS+ college students scored markedly lower on the combined verbal and mathematics sections of the Scholastic Aptitude Test than did strongly left handed FS- subjects or weakly left-handed subjects. The superiority of the strongly left-handed FS- subjects over all other left-handers was greatest on the verbal section of the test. It should be noted, however, that the groups involved were all quite small (only 11 subjects were strongly left handed and FS-, and only 13 subjects were strongly left handed and FS+). Searleman et al. suggested that studies finding no handedness differences or FS effects on abilities may have failed to see the negative influence of FS+ and positive effects of FS- statuses in strongly left-handed persons because they did not assess degree of left-hand preference. They cited the Burnett et al. (1982) findings as consistent with their own results and also noted that Bradshaw et al. (1981) restricted their sample to strongly right-handed and strongly left-handed subjects. It should be mentioned, however, that in the Burnett et al. study there were no strongly left-handed males according to the criteria for strength of handedness employed by Searleman et al. They also suggested that the study of Briggs, Nebes, and Kinsbourne (1976), which found only weak relationships between FS+ and poor WAIS performance among left-handers, might have shown strong relationships between FS+/strong left-handedness and poor performance had the investigators assessed strength of handedness.

These studies suggest that the combination of FS+ status and strong left-hand preference may be a marker for lessened abilities in left-handers.

STUDIES FROM OUR LABORATORY

In this section I present data from our laboratory, and I attempt to relate it to several points of view, subsequently. We have looked at the question of possible handedness and sex differences in spatial ability in a rather narrow fashion with regard to specific measures of spatial ability. With respect to subject characteristics, however, we have perhaps looked at a more diverse set of variables than is typical in the area. In addition, to handedness, sex, and FS, we have looked at "androgyny" as defined by subject ratings, hormonal characteristics, and at history (presence/absence) of immune (mostly allergy) disorders. Basically, we have used only two spatial tests. The one we have used most is the Stafford Identical Blocks Test (SIBT). The other, which we have employed only more recently, is the Minnesota Paper Form Board (MPFB). Sample items from each test were shown in Fig. 4.1. We have also employed the Halstead Reitan Neuropsychological Battery most recently, and our data with that set of tests is quite preliminary. We have tested only college students to date. Most of the literature, particularly with respect to handedness, has been conducted on college students. This fact limits the generality of findings, but, on the other hand, one might assume that college students supply information about a group functioning at a rather optimal neuropsychological level.

A number of samples of right- and left-handed college students were administered the SIBT over a period of years in our laboratory at Bowling Green State University. These subjects were always tested individually, following the administration of dichotic or tachistoscopic tasks, and prior to securing any FS information on them. Subjects were tested under conditions conducive to high motivation. Except for one sample (McKeever & VanDeventer, 1977), the complete 30 item SIBT was administered with a time limit of 15 minutes. The individual experimenters were always present, although seated at a distance from the subject, and at set intervals gave information to the subject regarding how much time remained (10 minutes, 5 minutes, 2 minutes). The results of the composite of these various samples of right-handed subjects (343 individuals) has been reported (McKeever, Seitz, Hoff, Marino, & Diehl, 1983).

The basic findings for sex-FS groupings are shown in Fig. 4.2. It can be seen that males averaged 3.5 points higher than females on the test. This amounts to approximately .5 standard deviations. It can also be seen that, among females, the FS- (those having no first-degree and no more than one second-degree left-handed relative) scored higher (3.6 points on average) than those having at least

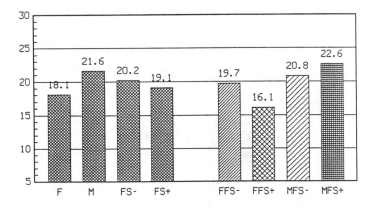

FIGURE 4.2. Mean SIBT scores of females (F), males (M), FS (F-andF+), and sex-FS groups (McKeever, Seltz, Hoff, & Marino, 1983).

one first-degree or more than one second-degree left-handed relative. Among right-handed males, the opposite FS influence on the scores was seen (i.e., the FS+ males scored higher than did the FS-). When a two-factor ANOVA (sex, FS) was applied to the scores of the subjects, a highly significant main effect of sex was seen, with males scoring higher than females ($p < .0001$). In addition, there was a highly significant interaction of the sex and FS factors, with FS females scoring higher than FS+ females, and FS+ males scoring higher than FS- males ($p < .0003$). Post hoc comparisons among the sex-FS groups showed that the FS- females' scores were superior to those of the FS+ females, not different from those of the FS- males, and significantly lower than those of the FS+ males. The FS+ males' scores   were not significantly higher than those of the FS- males ($p < .08$). Thus, the FS+ female scores were significantly lower than those of all other groups.

Subsequently, I reported results on an additional sample of 225 right-handers and 134 left-handers (McKeever, 1986). These results are shown in Fig. 4.3. Results for left-handers are shown in the left half of the figure, and results for the right-handers are shown in the right half of the figure. Males scored significantly higher than females, again, about half a standard deviation higher.

Figure 4.4 presents mean Stafford Identical Blocks Test scores for the handedness-sex-FS subgroups of this study. If we look first at the data for right-handers, it can be seen, that as in the earlier composite sample study, the right-handed FS- women scored substantially higher than the right-handed FS+ women. For males, however, the FS- and FS+ subjects scored similarly, with the FS- actually scoring slightly higher than the FS+. It can also be seen that, except in the FS- left-handed female group, FS- was generally favorable for spatial ability. Analysis of variance showed the scores of males to be higher than those of females across handedness groups, and the scores of right-handers to be higher

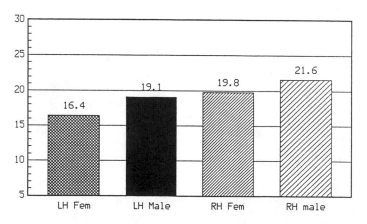

FIGURE 4.3. Mean SIBT scores of handedness-sex groups (McKeever, 1986).

than those of left-handers across sex groups ($p < .003$ and $p < .009$, respectively). Across sex and handedness factors, the FS influence approached, but did not reach, the acceptable level of statistical significance ($p < .07$).

This study also included an additional variable, which I labeled *androgyny*. This was defined in terms of subjects' self-ratings regarding their degree of masculinity and femininity. Each subject rated him or herself on both unipolar scales, and the difference score between scales constituted the androgyny measure. Thus, if a male subject rated himself as extremely masculine (a rating of "7") and extremely low in femininity (a rating of "1"), his androgyny score was 6. For female subjects, the female minus male ratings were used. The factor of androgyny was included because of studies that suggest that androgyny, defined by nonbehavioral measures such as secondary sex characteristics (Broverman et al., 1968; Petersen, 1976) and globally assayed "androgens" (Klaiber et al., 1967; Shute et al, 1983) exerts an influence on spatial ability. Specifically, these findings suggest that highly androgenized males perform less well than less androgenized males, whereas androgenized females perform better than less androgenized females.

Figure 4.5 shows SIBT means for female and male androgynous and non-androgynous subjects. It can be seen that androgynous subjects scored higher in both the female and male samples, across handedness groups. This main effect of androgyny was significant ($p < .004$). There was also a significant ($p < .04$) interaction of handedness, sex, and androgyny, however, and this is shown in Fig. 4.6. It can be seen that androgynous subjects scored higher than nonandrogynous subjects in all handedness-sex groups except among the left-handed females. Thus, among males, regardless of handedness, the subjects rating themselves as highly masculine scored lower than subjects rating themselves as less masculine; among female right-handers, those rating themselves as less feminine scored

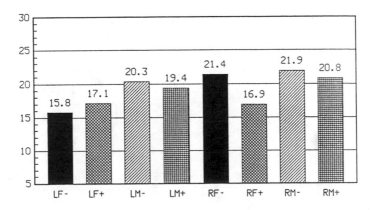

FIGURE 4.4. Mean SIBT scores of left- and right-handed (L and R), FS (-and+) females (F) and males(M) (McKeever, 1986).

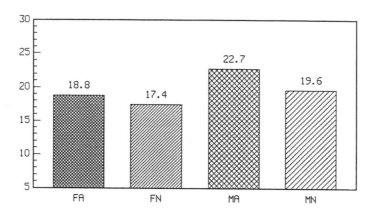

FIGURE 4.5. Mean SIBT scores of female (F) and male (M) androgynous (A) and nonandrogynous (N) subjects (McKeever, 1986).

higher than those rating themselves as more feminine. The results provide some support for the hypothesis that androgyny is related to spatial ability, with the direction of the relationship being anti-intuitive for male subjects. Some data recently obtained by Rich and McKeever (1989) has provided further support for the existence of handedness and sex differences on the SIBT. In a sample of 64 right- handers and 64 left-handers, Rich (1989) found right-handers' scores to be significantly higher than those of left-handers, and males' scores, within both handedness groups, to be significantly higher than those of females. On the MPFB, right-handers again scored significantly higher than did left-handers,

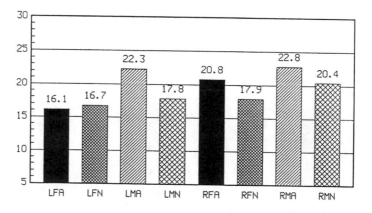

FIGURE 4.6. Mean SIBT score of left-handed (L) and right-handed (R) female (F) and male (M) androgynous (A) and nonandrogynous (N) groups (McKeever, 1986).

within both sexes; no sex difference was obtained on the MPFB, however. Additional evidence for a handedness effect in spatial ability has been obtained by Michael Murray, in his masters thesis research at Northern Arizona University. Murray administered the Halstead-Reitan Neuropsychological Battery to 24 left-handers and 24 right-handers.   Left-handers were found to score significantly lower on the Tactile Performance Test.   This test is clearly a spatial test, performed through tactile-motor channels while blind-folded.   It is possible, nonetheless, that a "visual" transcription of the tactile-motor information is involved in the performance of the task. Most interestingly, Murray found this inferiority of left-handers to be attributable to those left-handers who were FS+. Because of the small sample involved, however, the replicability of this finding must be tested before it is accorded weight in relation to the question of handedness differences in spatial abilities.

Finally, a study of the possible relationship of circulating testosterone levels to performances on the SIBT and the MPFB was undertaken at our Bowling Green State University lab (McKeever, Rich, Deyo, & Conner, 1987). Eighty subjects, approximately equally divided according to sex and handedness variables, were administered both the SIBT and the MPFB. No relationship of testosterone to ability measures was found, but handedness and sex effects were once again obtained on the SIBT, with the directions consistent with those just reported. These effects are shown in Fig. 4.7. No significant effects were found for the MPFB.

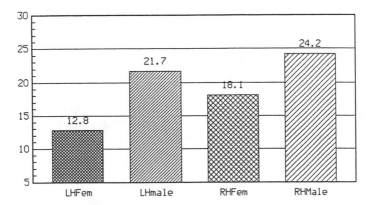

FIGURE 4.7. Mean SIBT scores of left-handed (LH) and right-handed female and male subjects (McKeever, Rich, Deyo, & Connor, 1987).

WHAT IS THE BASIS OF THE APPARENT DIFFERENCE IN SPATIAL ABILITY BETWEEN SEX AND HANDEDNESS GROUPS?

If our experience is valid, and left-handers do show a "deficit" in at least some types of spatial ability, to what can we attribute this lower level of spatial ability? It must be said that the differences we have seen are not dramatic. In the Rich and McKeever (1989) for example, the factor of handedness accounts for only 3.5% of the variance in SIBT scores and 3.1% of the variance in MPFB scores; the factor of sex accounts for 8.6% of the variance in SIBT scores and none of the variance in MPFB scores. These handedness and sex differences are typical of the ones we have obtained with the SIBT. Thus, there is very great overlap between the scores of left- and right-handers, and between males and females, respectively. Furthermore, there may be a variety of specific skills in which left-handers (and women) surpass right-handers (and males). Consistent with this view are the data of Benbow and Stanley (1983) showing that among truly gifted adolescent mathematics students, unexpectedly high percentages of left-handers are represented; and Rich and McKeever (1989) found significantly higher verbal fluency test performances in women as compared to men.

Nonetheless, the question remains as to the basis for the lower scores obtained by left-handers in our studies and many studies by others. As discussed earlier, the hypothesis of Levy (1969) regarding the "crowding" of the right hemisphere by language processing in the left-handed population has adherents. The same hypothesis has served as a putative explanation for the often found lesser spatial ability of females. Evidence for this hypothesis is not compelling, however. McKeever and VanDeventer (1977) found no difference in SIBT performances (or verbal task performances) of subjects who were or were not right-ear dominant on a dichotic digits task. Rich and McKeever (1989) found no association of right-ear advantage scores on the Dichotic Consonant Vowel Task (DCVT) and spatial or verbal task performances of left- and right-handed subjects, despite the existence of handedness differences on the DCVT, SIBT, and MPFB measures. McKeever (1986) did find a very small but significant superiority of left-handers over right-handers on the Shipley Hartford Vocabulary Test, but subsequent studies (e.g., McKeever et al., 1987) failed to replicate this verbal task advantage of left-handers that is posited by the "crowding" hypothesis. Furthermore, with respect to the superiority of males on some spatial tasks, the crowding explanation relies on the view that language lateralization is more bilateral in females than in males. Despite the popularity of this notion, there is considerable evidence against it, at least with respect to tachistoscopic and dichotic language laterality study data (Fairweather, 1976; Hiscock and MacKay, 1985; Krutsch, 1988; McKeever, 1986; McKeever, 1987a; Rich & McKeever, 1989; Seitz and McKeever, 1984; van Eys and McKeever, 1988). Thus, evidence for the crowding explanation of lower spatial task performances of left-handers is not convincing.

A second possible explanation for the superiority of right-handers over left-handers on some spatial tasks might be the existence of pathological left handedness (Bakan, 1971; Satz, 1972) in a proportion of the left-handers tested. Inquiries of subjects, regarding head injuries, or neurological disorders, or possible birth stress should probably be conducted in all studies comparing the performances of left- and right-handers. The fact that many of the studies reporting handedness effects employed subjects who were succeeding in college would seem to mitigate this criticism to some degree. Furthermore, at least some studies (McKeever et al., 1987; Murray, 1988) did assess history of neurological insult, at least as reported by the subjects, and found no differences.

A third possible explanation, suggested by Searleman et al. (1984) as an explanation for SAT score differences within a left-handed sample, might be extended to spatial ability. This is the hypothesis that strongly left-handed FS+ left-handers are less capable than are other types of left-handers. This could be related to the second explanation, in that FS+ could represent pathological left-handedness, with the extent of the "pathology" being reflected in the marked degree of left-hand preference. Although it is traditional to assume that FS+ left-handers are "natural" left-handers, Pipe (1987) has suggested that FS+ status may be a marker for pathological left-handedness. We have not found support for such an extension of this explanation to spatial ability to date. A comparison of the SIBT performances of FS and strength of handedness groups (the latter defined by the Edinburgh Handedness Inventory) was conducted on the left-handed sample studied by McKeever (1986). This comparison was not reported in the 1986 publication, but was presented at a meeting the following year (McKeever, 1987b). The results of the comparison are given in Fig. 4.8. The numbers of cases in the four groups were, respectively, 54, 32, 34, and 15. It can be seen that the groups performed very comparably, and the differences did not approach significance. Furthermore, an analysis of both SIBT and MPFB scores from the Rich & McKeever (1989) study failed to show poorer performances of strongly left-handed FS+ subjects as opposed to other left-handers.

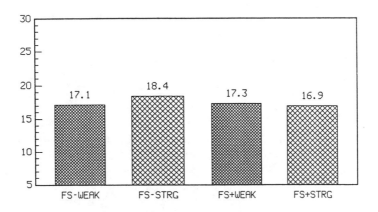

FIGURE 4.8. Mean SIBT scores of weakly (Weak) and strongly (Strg) left-handed FS- and FS+ groups (McKeever, 1987).

CONCLUSIONS AND DIRECTIONS FOR FURTHER RESEARCH

At this point in time, we see no variable that identifies a subgroup of left-handers who can be said to be responsible for the lower performance of unselected groups of left handers on the SIBT, and perhaps on other spatial tasks. Among right-handers, our data has fairly consistently shown that FS+ status is unfavorable for mental rotation ability in females, and possibly slightly favorable in males. The FS- female right-handers are not inferior to males in mental rotation ability, whereas FS+ females are. Unfortunately, we have found no pattern of FS influence on visuo-spatial ability in left-handers. Murray's (1988) finding that the inferiority of left-handers on the Tactile Performance Test was restricted to FS+ left-handers is promising. Murray found poorer performances by FS+ left-handers on a number of other measures of the Halstead-Reitan Neuropsychological Battery as well, but whether these findings will prove replicable remains to be seen.

Finally, I suggest that, despite our failure to find associations of testosterone levels with spatial performances (McKeever et al., 1987), a better understanding of the basis for relationships of handedness to spatial ability may issue from further study of the possible relationship of hormones and spatial ability. In a current study, restricted to an unselected sample of 58 males, we have found some tentative relationships of hormone measures to spatial ability and to FS status. No simple relationships of testosterone or dihydrotestosterone to ability measures were seen, but some relationships were found for two hormone measures. One hormone measure was in terms of deviations from the mean testosterone level of the sample; the other was for deviations of the ratio of dihydrotestosterone to testosterone from the mean value of the sample. Both measures showed significant relationships to the composite score derived from the SIBT and MPFB. In other words, increasing deviations from mean values on these measures were correlated with spatial ability. These findings suggest that curvilinear relationships exist between these variables and spatial ability. Such findings will, of course, require replication because they were not hypothesized and emerged in *post hoc* fashion.

A possibly related variable worthy of investigation concerns immune system disorder history. Rich and McKeever (1989), in her doctoral research, included the variable of history of immune disorder (mostly allergy) as a counterbalanced variable across sex, handedness, and FS groups. As described earlier, she found handedness effects on both the SIBT and MPFB, and a sex effect on the SIBT. In addition, she found an interesting interaction of FS and immune disorder (presence/absence) history. Subjects, regardless of sex or handedness, who were positive or negative for both FS and immune disorder history were significantly superior on the spatial tasks when compared to those who were positive for one factor and negative for the other. A multiple regression equation, incorporating handedness, sex, and the FS/immune disorder variables, with SIBT as the dependent measure, yielded an adjusted R^2 of .172 (p <.0001). Thus, over 17% of the variance was accounted for by the optimal weighting of the predictors. We are currently thinking in terms of the possibility that immune status and FS factors may be differentially related to hormone (specifically, steroid) characteristics. Interactions of the immune system and the hypothalamic-pituitary-gonadal axis are known to occur. If, for example, FS- were related to low steroid levels, and negative immune disorder history were related to high steroid levels, moderate levels might result when both factors were positive or negative. When one factor was positive and the other negative, however, either elevated or depressed levels might be expected. If, as hypothesized by Petersen (1976), intermediate hormone levels are optimal for spatial ability, the optimal combination would occur in those positive or negative for both characteristics. Some other studies suggest possible relationships of laterality, ability, and hormone factors. Benbow and Stanley (1983) found elevated incidences of both allergies and left-handedness in gifted mathematics students. Hampson and Kimura (1988) have shown that tasks that typically yield sex differences also show significant performance fluctuations as a function of the menstrual cycle in females. Such findings, as well as our own, encourage further study of possible hormonal differences in sex and handedness groups that are known to differ in spatial ability.

ENDNOTES

[1] Dr. McKeever is now at the University of Toledo.

REFERENCES

Bakan, P. (1971). Birth order and handedness. *Nature, 229,* 195.

Benbow, C. P., & Stanley, J. C. (1983). Sex differences in mathematical reasoning ability: More facts. *Science, 222,* 1029-1031.

Bradshaw, J. L., Nettleton, N. C., & Taylor, M. J. (1981). Right hemisphere language and cognitive deficit in sinistrals? *Neuropsychologia, 19,* 113-132.

Briggs, G. G., Nebes, R.D., & Kinsbourne, M. (1976). Intellectual differences in relation to personal and family handedness. *Quarterly Journal of Experimental Psychology, 28,* 591-601.

Broverman, D.M., Broverman, I.K., Kobayashi, Y., & Palmer, R.D. (1964). The automatization cognitive style and physical development. *Child Development, 35,* 1343-1359.

Broverman, D.M., Broverman, I.K., Vogel, W., & Palmer, R. D. (1964). the automatization cognitive style and physical development. *Child Development, 13,* 29-38.

Broverman, D.M., Klaiber, E., Kobayashi, Y., & Vogel, W. (1968). Roles of activation and inhibition in sex differences in cognitive abilities. *Psychological Review, 75,* 23-50.

Bryden, M.P., Hécaen, H. & DeAgostini, M. (1983). Patterns of cerebral organization. *Brain and Language, 20,* 249-262.

Cattell, R.B., & Cattell, A. K. S. (1973). *The Culture Fair Intelligence Test*: *Manual*. Champaigne: Charles C. Thomas.

Christiansen, K., and Knussman, R. (1988). sex hormones and cognitive functioning in men. *Neuropsychobiology, 18,* 27-36.

Deutsch, G., Bourbon, W.T., Papanicolaou, A.C., & Eisenberg, H. M. (1988). Visuospatial tasks compared via activation of regional cerebral blood flow. *Neuropsychologia, 26,* 445-452.

Fagan-Dubin, L. (1974). Lateral dominance and the development of cerebral specialization. *Cortex, 10,* 69-74.

Fairweather, H. (1976). Sex differences in cognition. *Cognition, 4,* 231-280.

Flick, G.L. (1966). Sinistrality revisited: a perceptual-motor approach. *Child Development, 37,* 613-622.

Goodglass, H., & Quadfasel, F.A. (1954). Language laterality in left-handed aphasics. *Brain, 77,* 521-548.

Hampson, E., & Kimura, D. (1988). Reciprocal effects of hormonal fluctuations on human motor and perceptual-spatial skills. *Behavioral Neuroscience, 3,* 456-459.

Harris, L.J. (1981). Sex-related variations in spatial skill. In L. Liben, N. Newcombe, & A. Patterson (Eds.) *Spatial representation and behavior across the life span* (pp. 83-125). New York: Academic Press.

Harshman, R. A., Hampson, E., & Berenbaum, S.A. (1983). Individual differences in cognitive abilities and brain organization, Part I: Sex and handedness differences in ability. *Canadian Journal of Psychology, 37,* 144-192.

Hardyck, C., & Petrinovich, L. F. (1977). Left-handedness. *Psychological Bulletin, 84,* 385-404.

Hardyck, C., Petrinovich, L.F., & Goldman, R.D. (1976). Left-handedness and cognitive deficit. *Cortex, 12,* 266-280.

Hicks, R. A., & Beveridge, R. (1978). Handedness and intelligence. *Cortex, 14,* 304-307.

Hiscock, M., & MacKay, M. (1985). The sex difference in dichotic listening: multiple negative findings. *Neuropsychologia, 23,* 441-444.

Klaiber,E. L., Broverman, D. M., & Kobayashi, Y. (1967). The automatization cognitive style, androgens, and monoamine oxidase. *Psychopharmocologia, 11,* 320-336.

Krutsch, A. (1988). *Relationship between auditory and visual tasks of hemispheric language specialization.* Unpublished doctoral dissertation, Bowling Green State University, Bowling Green, OH.

Kutas, M., McCarthy, G., & Donchin, D. (1975). Differences between sinistrals' and dextrals' ability to infer a whole from its parts: A failure to replicate. *Neuropsychologia, 13,* 455-464.

Levy, J. (1969). Possible basis for the evolution of lateral specialization in the human brain. *Nature: London., 224,* 614-615.

Levy, J. (1974). Psychobiological implications of bilateral asymmetry. In S. Diamond & J. G. Beaumont (Eds.) *Hemisphere function in the human brain* (pp. 121-183). London: Paul Elek.

Linn, M. C., & Petersen, A. A. (1985). Emergence and characterization of sex differences in spatial ability: a meta-analysis. *Child Development, 59,* 1479-1498.

Maccoby, E. E., & Jacklin, C. N. (1974). *The psychology of sex differences.* Stanford: Stanford University Press.

McGee, M. G. (1979). Human spatial abilities: Psychometric studies and environmental, genetic, hormonal, and neurological influences. *Psychological Bulletin, 86,* 889-918.

McGlone, J. (1980). Sex differences in functional brain organization: A critical survey. *The Behavioral and Brain Sciences, 3,* 215-227.

McKeever, W. F. (1986). The influences of handedness, sex, familial sinistrality, and androgyny on language laterality, verbal ability, and spatial ability. *Cortex, 22,* 521-537.

McKeever, W. F. (1987a). Cerebral organization and sex: Interesting but complex. In S. U. Philips, S. Steele, C. Tanz (Eds.) *Language, gender, and sex in comparative perspective* (pp. 268-277). Cambridge: Cambridge University Press.

McKeever, W. F. (1987b). *Failure to support hypotheses of cognitive impairment in subgroups of left handers.* Paper presented at The Rocky Mountain Psychological Association meeting, Albuquerque, NM.

McKeever, W. F., Rich, D. A., Deyo, R. A., & Conner, R. L. (1987). Androgens and spatial ability: Failure to find a relationship between testosterone and ability measures. *Bulletin of the Psychonomic Society, 25,* 438-440.

McKeever, W. F., Seitz, K. S., Hoff, A. L., Marino, M. F., & Diehl, J. A. (1983). Interacting sex and familial sinistrality characteristics influence both language lateralization and spatial ability in right handers. *Neuropsychologia, 21,* 661-668.

McKeever, W. F., & VanDeventer, A. D. (1977). Failure to confirm a spatial ability impairment in persons with evidence of right hemisphere speech capability. *Cortex, 13,* 321-326.

Miller, E. (1971). Handedness and the pattern of human ability. *British Journal of Psychology, 62,* 111-112.

Murray, M. G. (1988). *The effects of sex, handedness, familial sinistrality, and handwriting posture on neuropsychological test results.* Unpublished masters thesis, Northern Arizona University, Flagstaff, AZ.

Nebes, R. D. (1971). Handedness and the perception of part-whole relationships. *Cortex, 7,* 350-356.

Oldfield, R. C. (1971). The assessment and analysis of handedness: The Edinburgh Inventory. *Neuropsychologia, 9,* 97-113.

Orme, J. E. (1970). Left-handedness, ability and emotional instability. *British Journal of Social and Clinical Psychology, 9,* 87-88.

Osaka, M. (1984). Peak alpha frequency of EEG during a mental task: task difficulty and hemispheric differences. *Psychophysiology, 21,* 101-105.

Petersen, A. C. (1976). Physical androgyny and cognitive functioning in adolescence. *Developmental Psychology, 12*, 524-533.

Pipe, M. (1987). Pathological left-handedness: Is it familial? *Neuropsychologia, 25*, 571-577.

Rasmussen, T., & Milner, B. (1977). The role of early left-brain injury in determining lateralization of cerebral speech functions. *Annals of the New York Academy of Sciences, 299*, 355-369.

Rich, D. A., & McKeever, W.F. (1990). An investigation of immune system disorder as a "marker" for anomalous dominance. *Brain and Cognition, 12,* 55-72.

Sanders, B., Wilson, J. R., & Vandenberg, S. G. (1982). Handedness and spatial ability. *Cortex, 18*, 79-90.

Satz, P. (1972). Pathological left-handedness: An explanatory model. *Cortex, 8*, 121-135.

Searleman, A., Herrmann, D. J., & Coventry, A. K. (1984). Cognitive abilities and left handedness: An interaction between familial sinistrality and strength of handedness. *Intelligence, 8*, 295-304.

Segalowitz, S. J., & Bryden, M. P. (1983). Individual differences in hemispheric representation of language. In S. J. Segalowitz (Ed.) *Language functions and brain organization* (pp. 341-372). New York: Academic Press.

Seitz, K. S., & McKeever, W. F. (1984). Unilateral versus bilateral presentation methods in the reaction time paradigm. *Brain and Language, 3*, 413-425.

Shute, V. J., Pellegrino, J. W., Hubert, L., & Reynolds, R. W. (1983). The relationship between androgen levels and human spatial abilities. *Bulletin of the Psychonomic Society, 21*, 465-468.

Van Eys, P. L., & McKeever, W. F. (1988). Subject knowledge of the experimenter's interest in handedness and familial sinistrality variables and laterality test outcomes. *Brain and Cognition, 7*, 324-334.

Wittenborn, J. R. (1946). Correlates of handedness among college freshman. *Journal of Educational Psychology, 37*, 161-170.

Yen, W. M. (1975). Sex-linked major-gene influences on selected types of spatial performance. *Behavior Genetics, 5*, 281-298.

5 Dynamic Temporal-Spatial Allocation of Resources in the Human Brain: An Alternative to the Static View of Hemisphere Differences

Dennis L. Molfese
Lisa M. Burger-Judisch
University of Southern Illinois

This chapter speculates that human brain resources are not arranged in a static spatial arrangement within the brain in general and between the two cerebral hemispheres in particular. Instead, the argument is made that the resources of the brain are allocated and reorganized constantly in efforts to deal more efficiently with information processing, decision making, and responding. Although many investigators working within the field would emphatically state that such a model is already widely used, a review of the literature, both past and present, contains numerous reports that argue for a static-based laterality system (see Bryden, 1982, for a review of this position). In this chapter, literature dealing with electrophysiological and behavioral research into one aspect of language processing, speech perception, is used as a database to argue for such a model. In this regard, this chapter provides a review of recent electrophysiological investigations into human speech perception.

This review includes studies that address speech perception in general as well as those that manipulated specific speech cues such as voice onset time (VOT) and place of articulation (PLACE). Such cues have long been recognized as important for the perception of human speech information (Liberman, Cooper, Shankweiler, & Studdert-Kennedy, 1967). Given the complex spatial dimensions noted for even the perception of relatively low levels of language processing, speech perception, and the shifting patterns of this process over developmental periods and across stimulus dimensions, it is argued that the brain's response to environmental and internal factors changes over time in regards to the specific brain regions that work together to process the information. In this regard, the notion of static hemisphere differences only serves to draw our attention away from the more critical issues of brain processing involving the dynamic allocation of resources.

Interestingly, there are numerous parallels in findings across the electrophysiological and behavioral literatures. For example, as Rugg (1983) has noted, inconsistent and variable hemisphere differences have been reported in the electrophysiological evoked potential literature "it would seem clear that there is still a long way to go before it can be stated that EPs give rise to reliable correlates of lateral asymmetries of processing" (Rugg, 1983, p. 382). However, the inconsistencies noted by Rugg in fact occur across other more "traditional" nonelectrophysiological methodologies as well. Blumstein, Goodglass, and Tartter (1975) reported very poor test-retest reliability for adults involved in a dichotic listening task. In her study, ear difference scores noted for specific individuals during the first dichotic test session for speech sounds failed to occur when these same individuals were later retested. Interestingly, although the overall hemisphere differences were found for both test Times 1 and 2, the actual individuals who were characterized by such differences changed! After reviewing the laterality literature, Bryden (1982) also complained about the inconsistency of hemisphere difference findings across different methodologies such as dichotic listening, visual half-field, and handedness studies. Of course, the traditional interpretation, when faced with such inconsistencies, has been to fault the procedure as ineffectual or insensitive to the hemisphere differences we "know" must be present. However, such inconsistencies could also indicate that the phenomenon under study is more complex and dynamic than many in the field have often assumed.

ELECTROPHYSIOLOGICAL PROCEDURES

Before this review proceeds further, an overview of the evoked potential response and its major characteristics is needed. The evoked potential recorded from the scalp is a synchronized portion of the ongoing EEG pattern. It is usually represented as a complex waveform that reflects changes in electrical activity over time. Variations in brain activity are assumed to be reflected by amplitude changes or variations in the height of the waveform at different points in its time course (Callaway, Tueting, & Koslow, 1978). The evoked potential differs from the more traditional EEG measure. The event-related potential (ERP) is a portion of the ongoing EEG activity of the brain that is *time-locked* to the onset of some event in the subject's environment. On the other hand, measures of the ongoing EEG activity are not usually tied to the onset of specific environmental events but instead are evaluated over long periods of time and consequently reflect a wide range of neural activity related to the myriad of neural and body self-regulating systems as well as the various sensory and cognitive functions ongoing in the brain at that time. Because of its time-locked feature, the ERP has been shown more likely to reflect both general and specific aspects of the evoking stimulus and individual's perceptions and decisions immediately following the presentation of that stimulus. Moreover, this time-locking feature enables researchers to pinpoint, with some degree of certainty, portions of the electrical response that occurred while the subject's attention was focused on a discrete event (Molfese, 1983; Nelson & Salapatek 1986; Ruchkin, Sutton, Munson, Silver, & Macar,

1981).

ERPs are generally recorded from electrodes placed over various regions of the scalp that may overlay regions of the brain of interest to the investigators. These scalp electrodes are usually referred to reference electrodes placed on the two ears or the mastoid processes, or even the tip of the nose (Goff, 1974). The electrical activity from these neuroelectrically neutral reference sites is then subtracted from the electrical activity recorded at the scalp. The remaining signal should then reflect, for the most part, changes in electrical activity recorded from each of the scalp positions.

Further inquiry readily indicates that the ERP is not an exact and completely stable pattern reflecting only those discrete neural events directly related to the evoking stimulus, the task, or the subject's state. Rather, it is a by-product of the brain's bioelectrical response to such an event. This process begins at levels well below that of the cortex as the stimulus information is transformed by the sensory systems and progresses through the brainstem, into the midbrain, and on upward into the higher centers of the brain. Such signals must travel through a variety of tissues of different densities, conductivity, and composition (e.g., neurons, glial cells, fiber tracts, cerebral spinal fluid, bone, muscle) before they reach the recording electrodes placed on the scalp. Consequently, the final version of the ERP recorded at the scalp is a composite of a variety of complex factors, some of which relate directly to the testing situation and some of which do not. Moreover, as changes occur moment-by-moment in these factors, changes will occur at the same time in the amplitude of the ERP waveform that reflect both these nontask-related changes as well as changes in a variety of task-related cognitive factors. Because of such variability in the ERP that results in part from continuous changes in the physiology of the subject, many researchers collect a number of ERPs to the same stimulus within a single recording session, sum these responses, and then calculate an averaged evoked response. It is reasoned that this averaged response is more likely to contain the repetitive activity that reflects the processing of the stimulus from one time to the next. The nonstimulus related activity that is not time-locked to the onset of the stimulus would be expected to average out or be minimized in the averaged waveform of the ERP. This procedure, then, helps to improve the signal strength of the ERP while decreasing the noise levels resulting from random voltage changes unrelated to the test situation such as muscle contaminants. Additional analyses are subsequently conducted on the averaged waveforms.

Given that the ERP is characterized by changes in voltage (amplitude) over time, researchers have focused on analyses that evaluate such amplitude changes. The ERP is usually characterized by a series of positive and negative voltage shifts in the waveform. Researchers traditionally identify such shifts by indicating the most positive or negative points reached in the waveform as various latencies following stimulus onset. Thus, in the auditory ERP would be characterized by a series of peaks labeled N100, P200, N240, P300, and so forth. In this case, the N100 component would refer to the large negative deflection that begins approximately 60 msec following stimulus onset, reaches its most negative peak at approximately 100 msec following stimulus onset, and then reaches its prestimulus baseline by approximately 140 msec. The P200 component would reflect the large positive deflection that follows the N100 component, peaking at its most positive point 200 msec following stimulus onset, and then returning to a more negative point to eventually merge with the following N240 peak. Analysis approaches for evaluating the ERP have a range of options that include amplitude and latency measures performed on various peaks of the averaged ERP, area measures, discriminant function procedures, and other multivariate approaches including principal components analysis.

The ERP procedure has a number of strengths. First, it is able to employ identical procedures with all participants, regardless of age or species. Consequently, direct comparisons can be made between various subject groups in terms of discrimination abilities. Although the waveshapes of the ERPs will change from infancy to adulthood and differ across different species, one can assess whether the brain responses recorded from these different populations reliably discriminate between different stimuli, subject groups, and task characteristics. Second, the ERP procedures can be used to obtain response information from subjects who either have difficulty in responding in a normal fashion (as in the case of individuals with brain damage) or who cannot respond because of language or maturity factors (as with young infants and children). Third, the ERPs also provide information concerning both between hemisphere differences as well as within hemisphere differences. Fourth, the procedure provides both spatial (in relation to the brain) and time-related information that may offer insights into not only where but also when certain information is detected and processed. These final two points form the basis for many of the arguments presented in this chapter.

HUMAN SPEECH PERCEPTION: RESPONSES TO GENERAL SPEECH INFORMATION

Studies using evoked potential procedures to study hemisphere differences are a relatively recent phenomenon. As previously noted, the strategies involved in utilizing this procedure have ranged from attempts to test for lateralized differences to studies that evaluate how such lateralized patterns change as a function of changes in stimulus or task factors. The studies outlined in Table 5.1 characterize this first group of studies. As noted, a number of investigators have conducted electrophysiological studies to measure brain responses to speech and nonspeech sounds. Although a number of these studies were conducted to specifically address the issue of hemispheric differences in response to speech sounds (Cohn, 1971; Friedman, Simpson, Ritter, & Rapin, 1975; Galambos, Benson, Smith, Shulman-Galambos, & Osier, 1975; Grabow, Aronson, Rose, & Greene, 1980b; Hillyard & Woods, 1979; Molfese, 1972; Molfese, Freeman, & Palermo, 1975; Morrell & Salamy, 1971; Neville, 1974, 1980; Tanguay, Taub, Doubleday, & Clarkson, 1977), some of the designs were such that additional information could be gleaned concerning the properties of the electrical response to different acoustic dimensions that influenced such hemisphere differences (Molfese, Nunez, Seibert, & Ramaniah, 1976).

The first group of studies, those concerned specifically with attempts to identify evoked potential correlates of hemisphere differences, varied in their degree of success. For the most part, hemisphere differences, when noted, were reported to be variable both between and within subjects. For example, Cohn (1971) recorded AERs to clicks and consonant-vowel-consonant (CVC) words from temporal and central electrodes placed over the left and right hemispheres. The results reflected a great deal of variability across subjects with only 17 adults producing larger left-hemisphere AERs between an early negative peak (N30 - N50) and a later positive peak (P125) in response to the speech stimuli. Responses to the nonspeech clicks, however, appeared more uniform with all 37 adults responding with a larger positive peak over the right hemisphere AERs at 14 ms. Morrell and Salamy (1971), in a related study, recorded AERs from 7 adults to natural speech CVCs at frontal, temporal-parietal, and midline sites. Across their subjects, the region of the AER centered around the negative peak at 100 msec was larger for the temporal-parietal region of the LH than for the RH for all sounds. However, a more recent study by Grabow, Aronson, Rose, & Greene (1980) that looked at the single subject responses of 10 adults instead of group effects failed to replicate the Morrell and Salamy finding.

One example of variability in lateralized patterns within and across populations is typified by the data reported by Molfese (Molfese, 1972; Molfese et al. 1975) in a study of auditory evoked responses to speech and nonspeech sounds by a group of 10 infants, 11 children, and 10 adults. Although the overall analyses indicated larger left-hemisphere effects for speech than for nonspeech sounds (and larger right- than left-hemisphere effects for nonspeech sounds) across all ages studied, inspection of the individual data indicates variability within subjects. Although some subjects indeed generated larger left-hemisphere responses to speech sounds, their response patterns to stimuli of the same general class (speech or nonspeech) were not consistent. That is, some subjects responded to certain speech materials with larger left-hemisphere responses and to other speech materials with larger (or equal) right-hemisphere responses.

This variability in hemispheric responding could be due to a variety of stimulus or task factors that perhaps varied across or even within studies. Indeed, some researchers have speculated that task and stimulus demands may alter the level of differential hemispheric responding (Hillyard & Wood, 1979; Neville, 1974). For example, neither Neville (1974) nor Tanguay et al. (1977) found evidence of hemisphere differences when stimuli were presented *monaurally*. However, in the same study Neville noted a number of hemisphere effects when speech sounds were presented *binaurally*. For example, peak latencies (the time from stimulus onset to the most positive or negative point in a portion of the ERP) were shorter in the left hemisphere than in the right hemisphere for the N1, P2, and N2 components. This finding of hemisphere differences in evoked potential studies using a binaural but not a monaural mode of presentation is consistent with the behavioral literature. As Molfese and Adams (1988) note, ear

TABLE 5.1
GENERAL SPEECH/NONSPEECH DISCRIMINATION

STUDY	AGE	N=	STIMULI	SITES	TASK	RESULTS
Cohn(1971)	adults	37	10 msec square wave Single syllable words ex. cat, bat, rat Binaural presentation	solder disc Pair @ 2cm anterior to external acoustic meatus & in a vertical plane 2 cm from mid-sagittal line	----------	Clicks processed primarily in RH Single syllable words processed bilaterally for 20 Ss, other 17 Ss LH dominence for verbal processing
Morrell & Salamy (1971)	21-39 yrs	7	/pi,pa,epik, epak, a/ Binaural presentation	Central, . Frontal, . Temporo-parietal . over both hemis. Ref = linked ears, eye leads	Report each stimulus heard	N1 (90 msec) in LH > RH LH response 40% > RH corresponding locations

STUDY	AGE	N=	STIMULI	SITES	TASK	RESULTS
Neville (1974)	20-25 yrs	3 females 7 males	Monosyllabic digits . from 1-10 Nonverbal clicks Dichotic & Monaural presentation	C5,C6 Ref=linked mastoids, eye leads	Report all digits heard for both dichotic & monaural conditions & report number of clicks for both conditions	Dichotic Condition: N1(85-130 msec), P2 (185-230 msec), N2 (240-280 msec) for these peaks verbal stimuli latencies earlier in left vs right hemispheres. N1,P2 shorncies in right vs left for nonverbal Greater hemisphere asymmetries for verbal vs. nonverbal P1(20-50 msec) - N1 amplitude greater in left vs right for verbal Monaural Condition: P1, P3(290-350msec) shorter latency in left vs right for verbal P1,N1,N2,P3 shorter latency for verbal vs nonverbal

STUDY	AGE	N=	STIMULI	TASK	SITES	RESULTS
Friedman, Simson, Ritter & Rapin (1975)	19-25 yrs	8	Real speech words ex. kick, cake, pint Human sounds ex. coughing, whistle Binaural presentation	"no task word" & "no task sound" - Ss just listens Vigilence cond. - Ss respond by finger lift to one of 5 stimuli	Pz, left/ right temporo-parietal midway btwn Pz & mastoid, eye leads Ref = nose	LH: N100 latency to words > sounds LH > RH as measured by N100 amplitude to signal words LH > RH as measured by P300 amplitude to nonsignal words P300 to signal stimuli > nonsignal stimuli > " no task" stimuli P300 amplitude produced by sounds > words at all sites
Galambos, Benson, Smith Schulman-Galambos & Osier (1975)	adults	4 male 4 female	Natural speech (pa, ba) Pure tones Binaural presentation	Listen for targets & count them in each of four lists	Gold Cz, Midway bwn T3-P5 & T4-T6 Ref= linked mastoids	P3(350 msec) latency at two hemispheres differed between speech and tones. N1(100 msec) latency difference between speech and tones. P3 at vertex and in part at hemisphere sites had negative peak at 250 msec in target speech response. P3 larger for target tones & shorter in latency than target speech N1 & P2(190 msec) were result of click stimuli

STUDY	AGE	N=	STIMULI	SITES	TASK	RESULTS
Molfese, Freeman & Palermo (1975)	25.9 yrs	5 females 5 males	2 speech syllables /ba/ & /dae/ 2 words /boi/ & /dog/ 2 sounds c-major piano burst of noise Binaural presentation	T3 T4 Ref= linked ears	attend to the sounds	Based P2(160 msec) & N1 (100 msec) 8/10 adults LH > to speech 9/10 adults RH > to piano 10 adults RH > to noise stimuli
Tanguay, Taub, Doubleday & Clarkson (1977)	20.4 yrs	18 males	Voiced stop consonants /b, d, g/ followed by /a/ Monaural presentation	C3, C4, left/right Wernicke's (midway btwn T5 & C3 and T6 &C4), Ref = ipsi-lateral ears,	Attend to stimuli	P2(209-236 msec) latency & AER amplitude > over RH at Wernicke & central sites AER amplidue to contra-lateral ear stimulation > ipsilateral ear stimulation at Wernicke & central sites
Fink, Hillyard & Benson (1978)	twenties	6 male 10 female	/ba, ga, da, ja/ male voice in one channel & female in other channnel control: 10 KHz tone pips & white noise bursts Binaural presentation	gold electrodes Cz and at left/right lateral to C3 & C4 - 10% of inter-aural distance,	Group C: count targets Group P: press button after target (one of four syllables designated as target)	N1 (126 msec) over LH to phonetic stimuli > tonal or noise bursts Sites contralateral to ear of stimulation produced larger N1(126 msec) amplitude

STUDY	AGE	N=	STIMULI	SITES	TASK	RESULTS
Grabow, Aronson, Rose & Greene (1980)	20-37 yrs	9 female 1 male	Phonemic Combinations /epik/ /epak/, /a/, /pi/ /pa/ Nonspeech 2500 Hz 8000 Hz Binaural presentation	F7,F8 C5,C6 P5,P6, Ref = linked mastoids	Ss to remain silent through experiment	N1(90 msec) & P2(160 msec) appeared symmetrical for LH & RH for pure tone & speech sounds
Molfese & Erwin (1981)	20.1 yrs	20 females	3 vowels /i,ae,au/ speech & nonspeech Binaural presentation	T3 T4 T5,P3,P4,T6 Ref = linked ears	Attend to stimulus	T5,T6,P3,P4: normal formant <> sinewave formant (300 & 450 msec) P3,P4: sinewave formant <> all other site x formants P3, P4: /i/ speech <> /ae,c/ speech (160 msec) T3,T4: /ae/ <> /c/, T5,T6: /i/ <> /c/, P3, P4: /i/ <> /ae/ &
Ninomiya & Ikeda (1984)	23-26 yrs	2 female 12 male	2 syllable speech (in Japanese) a. meaningful b. nonsense 2 tone pips a. 300 Hz b. 600 Hz Binaural presentation	frontal, central & parietal, Ref= linked ears	Button press to block of 5 identical sounds vs 4 identical & one mismatch	LH <> RH in meaningful word condition Meaningful words <> tone pips in frontal (160 & 260 msec) Meaningful words <> nonsense words & meaningful words <> tone pips in central region (160 & 350 msec)

differences are commonly reported in dichotic listening tasks where materials are presented binaurally but not in monaural tasks. And yet, the very fact that hemisphere effects appear and disappear as modes of presentation change or as stimulus parameters change underscores the fact that the brain is a dynamic processor whose configuration for processing information does not exhibit a single form. This pattern of complexity becomes more evident when more rigorous controls are established over task and stimulus characteristics as in the case of studies investigating the perception of specific speech cues.

HUMAN SPEECH PERCEPTION:
THE STUDY OF SPECIFIC SPEECH CUES.

Perhaps in the area of speech perception more than any other, systematic electrophysiological investigations have indicated that hemispheric differences in responses to specific acoustic cues such as voice onset time and place of articulation change over developmental periods and display complex patterns of discrimination both within as well as between hemispheres (Molfese, 1978a, 1978b, 1980a, 1980b; Molfese & Hess, 1978; Molfese & Molfese, 1979a; 1988).

The first cue addressed here, VOT, the temporal relationship between laryngeal pulsing and the onset of consonant release, is an important one for the perceived distinction between voiced and voiceless forms of stop consonants such as b and p (Liberman et al. 1967). Adult listeners appear to discriminate a variety of speech sounds by the phonetic labels attached to them. Adults can readily discriminate between consonants from different phonetic categories, such as [ba] and [pa], whereas they perform at only chance levels when attempting to discriminate between two different [ba] sounds that differ acoustically to the same extent as the [ba-pa] difference (Lisker & Abramson, 1970). This pattern of discrimination for *between phonetic category contrasts* while chance levels of discrimination are noted for *within-category contrasts* is referred to as *categorical perception*. Studies with infants (Eilers, Gavin, & Wilson, 1980; Eimas, Siqueland, Jusczyk, & Vigorito, 1971), children (Streeter, 1976), and adult listeners (Lisker & Abramson, 1970) have demonstrated categorical perception and discrimination for a wide range of contrasts such as voicing (*ba, pa*; *ga, ka*) and place of articulation (*ba, da, ga*).

Voice Onset Time

The classic work by Eimas et al. (1971) investigating early categorical perception in young infants, when viewed against a backdrop of reports that language perception skills were lateralized (Kimura, 1961; Shankweiler & Studdert-Kennedy, 1967; Studdert-Kennedy & Shankweiler, 1970), provided one obvious approach to studying early lateralization for specific language-related cues. Clearly, if infants possessed such skills, one would expect that these skills should be lateralized to one hemisphere, generally the left, whereas the other hemisphere (the right) would not show such abilities. Molfese (1978b), in a follow-up to work by Dorman (1974), attempted to determine whether categorical discrimination of VOT could be assessed using ERP procedures and, if present, whether such discriminations were confined to one hemisphere.

Before the work could begin with young infants, Molfese first had to determine whether such effects occurred for adults. To this end, Molfese (1978b) recorded ERPs from the left and right temporal regions of 16 adults during a phoneme identification task. The adults were presented with randomly ordered sequences of synthesized bilabial stop consonants with VOT values of +0 ms, +20 ms, +40 ms, and +60 ms. In the +0 ms case, the onset of consonant release and vocal fold vibration would occur simultaneously, whereas in the +60 ms condition the onset of laryngeal pulsing was delayed for 60 ms after consonant release. The ERPs were recorded in response to each sound; then, after a brief delay, the adults pressed a series of keys to identify the sound they had heard. Two regions of the ERP (one component centered around 135 ms and the second occurring between 300 and 500 ms following stimulus onset) did change systematically as a function of the sound's phonetic category - a categorical discrimination effect. Stop consonant sounds with VOT values of +0 and +20 ms (sounds identified as *ba*) were discriminated from those with VOT values of +40 and +60 ms (sounds identified as *pa*). However, the ERPs did not discriminate between the sounds from the same category. There were no differences in the waveforms between the 0 and +20 ms sounds or between the +40 and +60 ms sounds. Electrophysiological studies employing similar stimuli with a variety of different populations have replicated this finding (Molfese, 1980a; Molfese & Hess, 1978; Molfese & Molfese, 1979b, 1988). Surprisingly, however, in all these studies at least one region of the ERP in which this categorical discrimination effect was noted across the different age groups occurred over the right temporal region.

Similar effects were noted with 4-year-old children in a study involving the velar stop consonants *k*, *g*. Molfese and Hess (1978) recorded AERs from the left and right temporal scalp regions of 12 preschool-age children (mean age = 4 years, 5 months) in response to randomly ordered series of synthesized consonant-vowel syllables in which the initial consonant varied in VOT from +0 ms, to +20 ms, to +40 ms, to +60 ms. Upon analysis of the AERs, they, like Molfese (1978b), also found a categorical discrimination effect whereby one late-occurring portion of the waveform (peak latency = 444 ms) changed systematically in response to consonants from different phonetic categories but did not respond differentially to consonants from within the same phonetic category. As in the case of Molfese (1978b), this effect occurred over the right hemisphere. Unlike the adult study by Molfese, however, they found a second portion of the auditory ERP that occurred earlier in the waveform, before this right-hemisphere effect, and which was detected by electrodes placed over both hemispheres. This earlier auditory ERP component also discriminated the voiced from the voiceless consonants in a categorical manner (peak latencies = 198 and 342 ms). Similar results have recently been reported by Molfese and Molfese (in press) with 3-year-old children.

This work was later extended to include newborn and older infants

(Molfese & Molfese, 1979a). In the work with newborn infants, they presented the four consonant-vowel syllables used by Molfese (1978b) to 16 infants between 2 and 5 months of age (mean = 3 months, 25 days). AERs were again recorded from the left and right temporal locations. Analyses revealed that one portion or component of the auditory ERP, recorded from over the right hemisphere approximately 920 ms following stimulus onset, discriminated between the different speech sounds in a categorical manner. As in the case of Molfese and Hess (1978), they also noted a second portion of the auditory ERP that was present over both hemispheres and that also discriminated between the consonant sounds categorically. The major portion of this component occurred 528 ms following stimulus onset. These results, then, paralleled the findings of Molfese and Hess (1978) in noting two portions of the auditory ERP that discriminated between the speech sounds categorically. These included a bilateral component that occurred first in the waveform, followed by a right-hemisphere lateralized component that occurred later in time and also discriminated between the sounds categorically. A final portion of the ERP waveform was found to differ between the two hemispheres across all of the different stimuli.

A second experiment described by Molfese and Molfese (1979a) failed to note any such bilateral or right-hemisphere lateralized effects with 16 newborn infants under 48 hours of age on the basis of group analyses. However, a recent study by Kurtzberg (personal communication, January, 1985) employing a different evoked potential test procedure suggests that at least some even younger infants may be able to discriminate between voiced and voiceless consonant sounds.

One discrepancy between the adult study of Molfese (1978b) and the studies with children (Molfese & Hess, 1978; Molfese & Molfese, 1988) and infants (Molfese & Molfese, 1979a) concerns the absence of a bilateral effect with the adult population studied by Molfese. At first it was speculated that such a bilateral effect might drop out with further maturation and development. However, recent work with adults involving recording of AERs from more electrode sites (Molfese, 1980a) suggests that the bilateral effect remains in adults but that the area in which this effect can be noted is restricted to a more limited region of the scalp. The difference, then, between the two age groups could be due to the shrinking size of the electrical fields over which the effect can be detected. As individuals age, the scalp potentials become more and more differentiated, with more differences in electrical activity being noted between even closely adjacent electrode sites.

Molfese (1980a) conducted a second study with adults to determine whether the laterality effects noted for the VOT stimuli were elicited by only speech stimuli or whether similar electrophysiological effects could be noted for both speech and nonspeech sounds. Such a comparison would allow conclusions to be reached regarding similarities in mechanisms that might subserve the perception of materials with similar temporal delays (+0-, +20-. +40-, +60-ms). If the right hemisphere and bilateral categorical effects occurred for nonspeech stimuli containing comparable temporal delays, it would be clear that such effects would be due to the temporal nature of the cues rather than to their "speech" quality. Molfese used four tone onset time (TOT) stimuli (from Pisoni, 1977). The overall duration of each TOT stimulus was 230 ms. Each stimulus consisted of two tones in which the higher tone was always 230 msec while the duration of the lower tone was reduced in 20 msec steps across the four stimuli. The four TOT stimuli differed from each other in the onset of the lower frequency tone (500 Hz) relative to the higher frequency tone (1500 Hz). The lower tone began at the same time as the upper tone for the 0-ms TOT stimulus; the lower tone lagged behind the upper tone by 20 ms for the +20-ms TOT stimulus. This delay increased to 40 ms and 60 ms, respectively, for the +40- and +60-ms TOT stimuli. Both tones ended simultaneously. AERs were recorded from 16 adults. Analyses indicated that one region of the auditory ERP centered around 330 ms and common to electrodes placed over the temporal, central, and parietal regions of the right hemisphere categorically discriminated the +0- and +20-ms TOT sounds from the +40- and +60-ms sounds. No comparable changes were noted over the left hemisphere at this latency. However, bilateral responses were noted earlier in time from the parietal regions 145 ms following stimulus onset and over the central areas at 210 ms. Interestingly, these bilateral effects were detected by electrodes placed over regions that were not sampled in the original Molfese (1978b) study. Thus, the lack of bilateral effects in the original study appears to result from the use of a more restricted sampling of electrical activity. Consequently, as in the case of the infant and child studies, processing of the temporal cue appeared to involve both bilateral responses that occurred earlier in time, followed by later right-hemisphere lateralized responses. The work by Molfese and Molfese (1988) with 3-year-old children, employed both the VOT stimuli used by Molfese and Hess (1978) and the TOT stimuli of Molfese (1980a). They found that both stimulus sets produced identical right-hemisphere responses that discriminated the 0-msec and 20-msec TOT sounds from the 40-msec and 60-msec TOT stimuli. It appears, then, that these changes noted in the ERP are indeed the result of responses to temporal delays rather than to some general "speech" quality per se.

Although the right-hemisphere discrimination of the VOT cue seems paradoxical in light of arguments that language processes are carried out primarily by the left hemisphere, two independent developments out of the behavioral literature offer some resolution to this concern. First, clinical studies of VOT suggest that it may be discriminated, if not exclusively, then at least in part, by the right hemisphere (for a review of this literature, see Molfese, Molfese, & Parsons, 1983). For example, Miceli, Caltagirone, Gainotti, and Payer-Rigo (1978), using a nondichotic pair presentation task, noted that the left-brain-damaged aphasic group made fewest errors with stimuli differing in voicing than in place of articulation. Blumstein, Baker, and Goodglass (1977) also noted fewer errors for voicing contrasts than for place contrasts with left-hemisphere damaged Wernicke aphasics. In a related study, Perecman and Kellar (1981), based on their own findings that left-hemisphere-damaged patients continue to match sounds on the basis of voicing but not place, speculated that voicing could be processed by either hemisphere but that the place cue was more likely to be processed by only the left hemisphere. Second, the electrophysiological studies of Molfese and his colleagues point to several regions of the brain that appear responsive to voicing contrasts. A summary of these findings are presented in Table 5.2.

Three general findings have emerged from this series of VOT/TOT studies. First, the discrimination of the temporal delay cue common to voiced and voiceless stop consonants can be detected by electrophysiological measures - specifically, the ERPs recorded from electrodes placed on the scalp over the two hemispheres. Second, from at least 2 months of age, if not before, the infant's brain appears capable of discriminating voiced from voiceless stop consonants in a categorical manner. Third, categorical discrimination across different ages appears to be carried out first by bilaterally represented mechanisms within both hemispheres and then, somewhat later in time, by right-hemisphere lateralized mechanisms.

Place of Articulation

Studies with infants and adults have identified some electrophysiological correlates of the acoustic and phonetic cues important to the perception of consonant place of articulation (Molfese, 1978a, 1980b, 1984; Molfese, Buhrke, & Wang, 1985; Molfese, Linnville, Wetzel, & Leicht, 1985; Molfese & Molfese, 1979b, 1980, 1985; Molfese & Schmidt, 1983). As in the case of the VOT temporal cue, these studies of the place cue identified both lateralized and bilateral hemisphere responses that discriminated between the different consonant sounds. Furthermore, such discriminations were present from birth. However, there were some important differences, both in the development of ERP responses to the place cue and in the character of the lateralized responses to this cue, which distinguished it from VOT. Although both the VOT cue and the place cue are important to speech perception, the brain responses that discriminate between these two types of information appear to emerge at different points in development, are lateralized differently, and are processed at different points in time.

Infants. In a study of place discrimination with newborn and young infants, Molfese and Molfese (1979b) noted a pattern of lateralized and bilateral responses present from birth. In this study, AERs were recorded from the left and right temporal regions (T3 and T4) of 16 full-term newborn human infants within 2 days of birth. During testing the infants were presented series of consonant-vowel syllables that differed in the second formant transition (F2, which signaled the place of articulation information), and formant bandwidth. One auditory ERP component that appeared only over the left-hemisphere recording site discriminated between the two consonant sounds when they contained normal speech formant characteristics (peak latency = 192 ms). A second region of the

TABLE 5.2
VOT STUDIES

STUDY	AGE	N=	STIMULI	SITES	TASK	RESULTS
Dorman (1974)	under-graduates	50	3 CV syllables /ba/ 0 msec VOT (within category) /ba/ 20 msec VOT (standard) /pa/ 40 msec VOT (across category)	single electrode at vertex, ref= right ear	Detect shift stimuli within sequence of standard stimuli	N1 (75-125 msec) P2 (175-225 msec) amplitude for across category stimuli > within category stimuli
Molfese (1978b)	27.0 yrs	8 female 8 male	/ba/, /pa/ w/ VOT of +0, +20, +40, +60 msec	T3 T4 Ref = linked ears	key press to /ba/ vs /pa/	RH: +0,+20 <> +40,+60 (135, 300, 430, 500 msec) LH: +0 <> +60 (300, 430, & 500 msec) LH: +0,+60 <> +20,+40 (135 msec)
Molfese (1980a)	College sophs	16	4 two-tone sequence 500 hz, 1500 hz 1. 0 msec lag 2. 20 msec lag 3. 40 msec lag 4. 60 msec lag	T3,C3,C4,T4 T5,P3,P4,T6 Ref=linked ears	Attend to stimulus	RH: 0 & 20 msec <> 40 & 60 msec (60 msec) LH: 0,20 & 40 msec <> (300 msec) P3 & P4: 0 & 20 msec <> 40 & 60 msec, 0 msec <> 20 msec, 40 msec <> 60 msec (210 msec) P3 & P4: 0 msec <> 20 msec (305 msec) C 3 & C4: 0 & 20 msec <> 40 & 60 msec, P3&P4: 0 & 20 msec <> 40 & 60 msec (145 msec)

STUDY	AGE	N=	STIMULI	SITES	TASK	RESULTS
Molfese, Linnville, Wetzel, Leicht (1985)	23.83 yrs	10 male 6- left 4- right 8 female 3-left 5-right	4 CV syllables 2-/dae/ (P1&P2) 2-/gae/ (P3&P4) Frequency varied for formants 2&3 P1 = 1695 & 3195 Hz P2 = 1845 & 2862 Hz P3 = 1996 & 2525 Hz P4 = 2156 & 2180 Hz	T3,C3,C4,T4 T5,P3,P4,T6 Ref= linked ears, eye leads	key press when hear /dae/ vs /gae/	Parietals: /dae/ (P1 &P2) <> /gae/ (P3 & P4) and /dae/ (P2) <> /gae/ (P3) (475 msec)

auditory ERP varied systematically over both hemispheres and also discriminated between the two speechlike consonant sounds (peak latency = 630 ms).

In a replication and extension of this work, Molfese and Molfese (1985) presented a series of consonant-vowel syllables that varied in place and formant structure. Two different consonant sounds [b, g] combined with three different vowel sounds were presented with speech or nonspeech formant structures. AERs were again recorded from the left and right temporal regions (T3, T4). As in the case of Molfese and Molfese (1979b), analyses identified two regions of the auditory ERP that discriminated the place difference. One AER component, with a peak latency of 168 ms, was detected only over the left-hemisphere site as discriminating between the two different consonant sounds; a second region with a peak latency of 664 ms, discriminated this place difference and was detected by electrodes placed over both hemispheres. Interestingly, the lateralized effect noted for these infants for the place cue occurred before that for the bilateral effect, a finding opposite to that noted for adults studied under similar circumstances (Molfese, 1983). However, the reversal of the temporal relationship between the bilateral and lateralized responses appears to be a legitimate one, given that virtually identical results were found by Molfese and Molfese (1985) and Molfese and Molfese (1979b) with different populations of infants and somewhat different stimulus sets that contained the PLACE variable. This temporal pattern of initial lateralized responses followed by bilateral responses is opposite to that noted previously for both VOT and place cues for adults as well as that found for infants exposed to changes in the VOT/TOT cue. Clearly, such differences in the ERP effects suggest that different mechanisms subserve the perception and discrimination of the different speech-related cues. Furthermore, these mechanisms also appear to change as a function of age and maturation.

The relationship between the lateralized and bilateral responses are not clear at this time. It does appear, however, that the bilateral response may develop after the lateralized one, both ontogenetically as well as phylogenetically. For example, Molfese and Molfese (1980) noted only the presence of left-hemisphere lateralized responses in 11 preterm infants born on average 35.9 weeks postconception. The stimuli for this study consisted of a series of consonant-vowel syllables in which the stop consonants varied in place of articulation, formant structure, and phonemic transition quality. Changes in the place cue signaled either the consonant b or g. The formant structure variable referred to a set of nonspeech sounds that contained formants composed of sinewaves 1 Hz in bandwidth whereas a set of speech sounds contained formants with speech like bandwidths of 60, 90, and 120 Hz for Formants 1 through 3. The phonetic transition quality cue referred to two stimulus properties in which one stimulus set contained formant transitions that normally characterize human speech patterns and the second set contained an unusual pattern not found in the initial consonant position in human speech patterns. AERs were recorded from the left- (T3) and right-hemisphere (T4) temporal regions. As found with the full-term infants (Molfese & Molfese, 1979a), a portion of the auditory ERP recorded from over the left hemisphere discriminated between speech stimuli containing different consonant transition cues. An additional left-hemisphere component differentiated only between the nonphonetic consonants, a finding similar to that reported by Molfese (1978a) with adults, with the exception that adults were sensitive to both phonetic and nonphonetic contrasts. Another auditory ERP component responded differently to speech versus nonspeech formant structures.

Adults. In the first of the adult place discrimination study series, Molfese (1978a) attempted to isolate the neuroelectrical correlates of the second formant transition, the cue to which listeners attend in order to discriminate between different consonant sounds. As noted earlier, the adults attended to a series of consonant-vowel syllables identical to those employed by Molfese and Molfese (1980) with preterm infants. The stop consonants varied in place of articulation, formant structure, and phonemic transition quality. Auditory ERP responses were recorded from the left and right temporal regions of 10 adults in response to randomly ordered series of consonant-vowel syllables that varied in consonant place of articulation, bandwidth, and phonetic transition quality. Two regions of the auditory ERP that peaked at 70 and 300 ms following stimulus onset discriminated consonant phonetic transition quality and place of articulation only over the left-hemisphere temporal electrode site. As in the case of Molfese (1978b), who also used only a single left-hemisphere temporal site, no bilateral place discrimination was noted. Similar left hemisphere place discrimination effects have since been noted by Molfese (1980b, 1984) and Molfese & Schmidt (1983) even though they included auditory ERP data collected from more electrode recording sites over each hemisphere. In these latter studies, consistent discrimination of the place cues were also noted for both hemispheres (bilateral effects). However, one experiment in particular provides a somewhat more in depth analysis of the complexity of the brain's response to stimuli at the phonetic level (Molfese, 1984). In this study, a series of auditory ERPs were collected from 14 audiometrically screened right-handed adults in response to three consonant-vowel syllables, [bi, di, gi]. Ten active scalp electrodes were placed at 10-20 locations (Jasper, 1958) over the left and right frontal, temporal, and parietal areas and referenced to linked ear leads. Each adult pressed one of three keys to identify the sound heard. An analysis procedure involving a principal components analysis and analysis of variance sequence as well as a discriminant function procedure were used to analyze the brain responses. A split half comparison was then run to confirm the original analyses. In all, five distinct regions of the auditory ERP were found to change as a function of changes in consonant place of articulation cues. Among the effects were bilateral ERP components that occurred at 100 msec and 155 msec and that discriminated the [b,d] consonants from the [g] consonant. These were followed in time by a left-hemisphere lateralized component at 295 msec that discriminated the [b] from the [d] from the [g]. A replication and extension of this work by Gelfer (1987) also noted bilateral and lateralized changes in the ERP as a function of consonant place changes, with similar latencies noted for each. A summary of these results concerning place discrimination are presented in Table 5.3.

Several general findings from these adult studies are apparent. First, when multiple electrode sites are tested over both hemispheres, bilateral stimulus discrimination effects are noted. Second, these bilateral effects invariably occur early in the waveform and prior to the onset of the lateralized place discrimination responses. This temporal relationship between bilateral and lateralized effects was already noted in the VOT discrimination studies. During the discrimination process, both hemispheres initially discriminate between the place and VOT stimuli at the same time, somewhere approximately 100 ms following stimulus onset. Shortly afterwards, at approximately 300 ms following stimulus onset, the left hemisphere discriminates between differences in the place cue, whereas the right hemisphere at approximately 400 ms will discriminate the VOT or temporal offset cue.

On the basis of these electrophysiological data, it appears that the brain's response to speech cues are multidimensional across individuals of all ages. Different regions of the auditory ERP elicited by the different auditory stimuli produce both similar and different patterns of activity over time. Two distinctly different speech cues generate bilateral changes in the same region of the AER early in the waveform. For adults, these bilateral responses are then followed in time by complex lateralized patterns that reflect various aspects of the evoking stimuli and the ability of the electrophysiological signal to discriminate between such patterns. Following the lateralized response, the temporal cue, VOT, elicits a late occurring right-hemisphere response, whereas the place cue elicits an earlier left-hemisphere response. Clearly, then, even at the level of speech perception and discrimination it appears that the brain does not simply respond in the same manner to all speech cues. In addition, the patterns of electrical activity evoked by such stimuli change over time and within as well as across the two hemispheres.

SUMMARY AND CONCLUSIONS

This review has attempted to argue that the brain's responses to even relatively "simple" types of processing as in the case of speech perception and discrimination are very complex. A review of the accumulated data indicates that a simple lateralized model of speech perception is inadequate to account for the results obtained across these studies. Instead, both complex lateralized and bilateral processing of the speech cues that change over time would appear to be the rule, rather than the exception. Moreover, the pattern of within-hemisphere processing also appears to be quite complex. Given the complexity of electrical responses, both spatially and temporally, during speech sound discrimination, one would anticipate that such patterns of complexity would increase markedly when syntactic, semantic, and pragmatic dimensions are added (see Molfese, 1983, for a review of these dimensions).

In addition, the research described in this chapter has indicated that there are clear indicators of changes in laterality for speech discrimination patterns

TABLE 5.3
PLACE STUDIES

STUDY	AGE	N=	STIMULI	SITES	TASK	RESULTS
Wood, Goff & Day (1971)	18-20 yrs	10	Stop consonants /ba/ vs. /da/ Fundamental Freq. /ba/ low - 104 Hz /ba/ high - 140 Hz	T3,C3,C4,T4 Ref= linked ears	Ss indicate stimulus heard	RH EP's identical for both tasks LH : linguistic <> nonlinguistic (preresponse period)
Wood (1975)	19-24 yrs	6 male 6 female	Experiment 1 - Place x Frequency /bae/ Fo= 104 Hz /bae/ Fo= 140 Hz /gae/ Fo= 104 Hz /gae/ Fo= 140 Hz	T3,C3,C4,T4 Ref=linked ears	Button Press Control Cond.: Button 1: 104 Hz Button 2: 140 Hz Orthogonal Cond.: Button 1: /bae/ Button 2: /gae/	RH: no differences LH: Pitch task <> place task (60-80 msec to 120-140 msec)
			Experiment 2 - Pitch x Intensity /bae/ @ 140 Hz loud 104 Hz loud 140 Hz soft 104 Hz soft		Button Press Control cond. Orthogonal cond.	No significant effects
			Experiment 3 - Same as Exp. 1 except only second formant transition of stop consonants		Same as Exp. 1	No significant effects

STUDY	AGE	N=	STIMULI	SITES	TASK	RESULTS
			was used (rising vs falling transition) Experiment 4 - Frequency vs pitch contour (falling contour- cue for statement, rising contour- cue for question)		Button Press	No significant effects in prerespons interval Significant effects btwn all dimensions at all sites in motor response interval (between 204 and 500 msec)
Molfese (1978a)	19.5 yrs	2 male 8 female	8 cv syllables /bae/, /gae/ normal/sine formants and speech/nonspeech	T3 T4 Ref= linked ears	-----------	LH: front & back consonants differ between stimuli w/ phonetic & nonphonetic transitions (70 & 300 msec) N2 component more marked for normal formant than for sinewave formant (455 & 305 msec) Response to /b/ was different for low and high right-hand
Molfese, Papanicolaou, Hess & Molfese (1979)	adult	10 right handers	4 meaningful /kaeb/ /paek/ /gaep/ /baek/ 4 nonsense /kaek/ /paeb/ /gaek/ /baep/	T3 T4 Ref= linked ears	press one of 2 keys if heard word of nonsense syllable	Large positive in meaning condition (6-60 msec) Large amplitude in meaning condition (320-440 msec, 240-280 msec) Differences in voicing of initial consonants ex. /b/,/g/ <> /k/,/p/ (65-140 msec)

STUDY	AGE	N=	STIMULI	SITES	TASK	RESULTS
Grabow, Aronson, Offord, Rose & Greene (1980)	young adults	9 females 1 male	/ba/ Fo=104 Hz /ba/ Fo=140 Hz /da/ Fo= 104 Hz	T3,C3,C4,T4 C5,C6 Ref= linked mastoids	Stop Consonant task: Button 1= /ba/, Button 2 = /da/ Frequency Task: Button 1 =/ba/ Fo=104 Hz Button 2= /ba/ Fo=140 Hz	Temporal: LH response lower for time points from mid 50's- mid 80's for both tasks Temporal: LH amplitude smaller for both tasks. Differences btwn tasks not specific to hemispheres Differences btwn tasks not specific for any of 3 homologous sites.
Lawson & Gaillard (1981)	20-25 yrs	10	Speech: /pe,te,ke,we,je, me, ne, ve, fe, se/ Nonspeech: 1000 Hz tone	Fz,C T3,Cz, T4 Pz Ref= linked ears, eye leads	Key press immediately after stimulus	P2 latency : /we/ <> remainder stimuli, /we/ longer than /me/,/ne/ & /ve/ /ve/ N1-P2 amplitude significant for tone,/pe/,/te/,/ke/ & /we/ vs /fe/ & /se/ also /ke/ <> /me/ & /ve/ Plosives shorter EP latencies compared to other consonants

STUDY	AGE	N=	STIMULI	SITES	TASK	RESULTS
Molfese & Schmidt (1983)	20.1 yrs	20 females	12 CV syllables /bi,bae,bc, gi,gae,gc/ - 1st set normal speech formant structure - 2nd set sine wave structure	T3 T4 T5,P3,P4,T6 Ref= linked ears	Identify to themselves the stimuli presented	LH: /b/ <> /g/ (215, 290 & 460 msec) Electrodes over both LH & RH discriminate consonants, parietals <> temporals to vowels (170 msec) LH: /b/ <> /g/ when followed by /ae/, parietals <> temporals when normal formant (120 msec) LH: normal <> sinewave T3,T4: /ae/ <>/c/ for /b/ w/ normal formant T5,T6: /i/ <> /ae,c/ for /g/ w/ normal and /ae/ <> /c/ for /g/ sinewave Parietals: /c/ <> /i/ & /ae/ for /b/ normal or sinewave formant and ae/ <> /i/ & /c/ for /g/ normal or sinewave (40 msec) Parietals: /i/ <> /ae,c/ and T3,T4 <> other sites for normal (70 & 340 msec)

STUDY	AGE	N=	STIMULI	SITES	TASK	RESULTS
Molfese (1984)	21.0 yrs	12 male 2 female	3 Cv syllables /bi,di,gi/	F3,F7,F8,F4 T3 T4 T5,P3,P4,T6 Ref=linked ears, eye leads	key press to identify CV syllable heard	LH: /b/ <> /g/, /d/ <> /g/ (295 msec) /b/ <>/d/ RH: /b/<>/g/,/d/<>/g/ F3,F4,F7,F8,T3,T4: /b/& /d/ <>/g/ T5,T6: /b/&/g/ <> (375 msec) /b/ <>/g/ and /d/<>/g/ (100 msec) /b/<>/g/ and /d/<>/g/ (155 msec) /b/<>/g/ and /d/<>/g/ (205 msec) /b/<>/g/ and /d/<>/g/ (475 msec)
Molfese, Buhrke & Wang (1985)	21 yrs	10 students	4-2 formant syllables /ba/, /da/ formant transition 2- initial 80 msec formant transition	F3,F7,F8,F4 T3,T5,T6,T4 Ref=linked ears, eye leads	Press key when hear /ba/ vs /da/	T6,P4: N305-N410 component > for 80 (340 msec) F3,F7,P3: N100-P210 > to /d/ than /b/ (95 msec)

95

STUDY	AGE	N=	STIMULI	SITES	TASK	RESULTS
Gelfer (1987)	28.0 yrs	6 male 6 female	Synthetic & Natural speech /bi, bae, bc,di dae, dc/ Chirps (above stimuli w/ isolated 2nd & 3rd formant transitions)	T3 T4 Ref= contralat. ears, eye leads	Finger raise to perception of /b/ or /d/ Chirps: Speech instruct. - discrim. as /b/ or /d/ Frequency instruction - discrim hi vs lo	Differentiation of stop consonants and chirps in LH (290 msec) /b/ <> /d/ independent of hemispheres (150 msec) Synthetic vs. Natural speech /b/ & /d/ processed bilaterally (160 msec)

across human developmental periods. There are also distinct patterns of both lateralized and bilateral cerebral involvement from the earliest points in infancy tested. Such patterns of both bilateral and lateralized responses so early in development indicate the need to view infant laterality within a broader framework than the traditional "one hemisphere does all" or "left hemisphere - language hemisphere" model usually employed to describe neural organization in infancy and early childhood. One sometimes senses that the field of developmental neuropsychology in particular (or neuropsychology in general) might have progressed faster and further if our brains were composed of a sphere divided into three major cortical surface regions instead of two hemispheres.

One of the long-standing problems facing neuropsychology researchers concerns the limits of the research tools and experimental designs used to assess normal brain function. These limitations apply to all of our commonly used techniques from dichotic listening to visual half field procedures to haptic presentations to the electrophysiological procedures outlined in this chapter. In many cases these methods only allow us to determine whether or not a difference exists between sensory/cognitive systems that are linked to the two hemispheres. They do not allow us to assess changes in processing over short periods of time. They also generally do not allow us to evaluate the differences in processing that may go on within the hemispheres. Finally, such procedures do not often allow us to readily determine whether the hemisphere differences found resulted from differences in sensation, perception, cognitive/linguistic processing, decision-making strategies, or output strategies. For example, in the case of the dichotic listening procedure, researchers can determine whether or not left-ear performance differs from right-ear performance. If left-ear performance is greater than right-ear performance, we usually assume that the right hemisphere (which receives a majority of its input from the left ear) is more involved in processing the information. Greater right-ear accuracy in identifying strings of letters or words is usually interpreted to mean that the activity is controlled by the left hemisphere. However, such ear differences usually make up only a small percentage of the actual responses made by the subject. In a task involving 100 trials, perhaps 45 correct identifications are made of sounds presented to the left ear while 55 correct identifications are made of sounds presented to the right ear. On only 10% of the trials was there an ear difference. On the other, for 90% of the trials, no differences were noted. Consequently, a great deal of our experimental energies have focused on a relatively small proportion of the subject's behavior. But what about the 90% of the trials on which correct responses were made by both hemispheres? Were they actually the same? The answer may well be "no." In most instances where the first response following stimulus presentation is the one that is scored and recorded, such correct responses change from ear to ear across trials. On one trial the sound presented to the left ear is correctly identified while on the next it may be identified better if presented to the right ear. Consequently, the correct ear response does indeed change across those 90 other trials as well, suggesting that the mechanisms subserving the discrimination or identification task are in fact not static but dynamic as well.   Here may well be a case where a different theoretical framework, one in which the brain's resources and processing modes change over time even within the same task, could lead to a reinterpretation of the data used for so long to support a static view of hemisphere differences.

Perhaps for future research, the question we address should not be so much how do the two hemispheres differ from each other but instead how do they manage their similar and different resources to work so efficiently together over time.

ENDNOTES

[1] While we might respond that such variability is due to some type of random noise in the data, we might wonder about the data where 90% of the signal is noise. However, this "noise" (if it is noise) does seem remarkably consistent from study to the next, both within and across laboratories.

ACKNOWLEDGMENT

Support for this work was provided by the National Science Foundation (BNS 8004429, BNS 8210846), the National Institutes of Health (R01 HD17860) and the Office of Research Development and Administration (2-10947), Southern Illinois University at Carbondale.

REFERENCES

Blumstein, S., Baker, E., & Goodglass, H. (1977). Phonological factors in auditory comprehension in aphasia. *Neuropsychologia, 15*, 19-30.

Blumstein, S., Goodglass, H., Tartter, V., (1975). The reliability of ear advantage in dichotic listening. *Brain and Language, 2*(2), 226-236.

Bryden, M.P. (1982). *Laterality : Functional asymmetry in the intact brain.* New York: Academic Press.

Callaway, E., Tueting, P., & Koslow, S.H. (1978). *Event-related brain potentials and behavior.* New York: Academic Press.

Cohn, R. (1971). Differential cerebral processing of noise and verbal stimuli. *Science, 172*, 599-601.

Dorman, M. (1974). Auditory evoked potential correlates of speech sound discrimination. *Perception & Psychophysics, 15*, 215-220.

Eilers, R., Gavin, W., & Wilson, W. (1980). Linguistic experience and phonemic perception in infancy: A cross-linguistic study. *Child Development, 50*, 14-18.

Eimas, P.D., Siqueland, E., Jusczyk, P., & Vigorito, J. (1971). Speech perception in infants. *Science, 171*, 303-306.

Fink, R., Hillyard, S., & Benson, P. (1978). Event-related brain potentials and selective attention to acoustic and phonetic cues. *Biological Psychology, 6*, 1-16.

Friedman, D., Simpson, R., Ritter, W., & Rapin, I. (1975). Cortical evoked potentials elicited by real speech words and human sounds. *EEG*, *38*, 13-19.

Galambos, R., Benson, P., Smith, T., Shulman-Galambos, C., & Osier, H. (1975). On hemispheric differences in evoked potentials to speech stimuli. *EEG*, *39*, 279-283.

Gelfer, M. (1987). An AER study of stop-consonant discrimination. *Perception & Psychophysics*, *42*(4), 318-327.

Goff, W. (1974). Human average evoked potentials: Procedures for stimulating and recording. In R.F. Thompson & M.M. Patterson (Eds.), *Bioelectric recording techniques, part B: electroencephalography and human brain potentials* (pp. 102-141). New York: Academic Press.

Grabow, J., Aronson, A., Offord, K., Rose, D., & Greene, K. (1980). Hemispheric potentials evoked by speech sounds during discrimination tasks. *Journal of Electroencephalography and Clinical Neurophysiology*, *49*, 48-58.

Grabow, J., Aronson, A., Rose, D., & Greene, K. (1980). Summated potentials evoked by speech sounds for determining cerebral dominance for language. *Journal of Electroencephalography and Clinical Neurophysiology*, *49*, 36-47.

Hillyard, S.A., & Woods, D.L. (1979). Electrophysiological analysis of human brain function. In M. S. Gazzaniga (Eds.), *Handbook of behavioral neurobiology*, (Vol. 2, pp. 345-378). New York: Plenum Press.

Kimura, D. (1961). Cerebral dominance and the perception of verbal stimuli. *Canadian Journal of Psychology*, *15*, 166-171.

Lawson E. A. & Gaillard, A.W.K. (1981). Evoked potentials to consonant-vowel syllables. *Acta Psychogica*, *49*, 17-25.

Liberman, A.M., Cooper, F.S., Shankweiler, D., & Studdert-Kennedy, M. (1967). Perception of the speech code. *Psychological Review*, *74*, 431-461.

Lisker, L., & Abramson, A.S. (1970). The voicing dimension: Some experiments in comparative phonetics. In *Proceedings of the 6th International Congress of Phonetic Sciences* (pp. 563-567). Prague: Academia.

Miceli, G., Caltagirone, C., Gainotti, G., & Payer-Rigo, P. (1978). Discrimination of voice versus place contrasts in aphasia. *Brain and Language*, *6*, 47-51.

Molfese, D.L. (1972). *Cerebral asymmetry in infants, children and adults: Auditory evoked responses to speech and music stimuli.* Unpublished doctoral dissertation, The Pennsylvania State University, University Park, PA.

Molfese, D.L. (1978a). Left and right hemisphere involvement in speech perception: Electrophysiological correlates. *Perceptual Psychophysiology* *23*, 237-243.

Molfese, D.L. (1978b). Neuroelectrical correlates of categorical speech perception in adults. *Brain and Language*, *5*, 25-35.

Molfese, D.L. (1980a). Hemispheric specialization for temporal information: Implications for the perception of voicing cues during speech perception.

Brain and Language, 11, 285-299.

Molfese, D.L. (1980b). The phoneme and the engram: Electrophysiological evidence for the acoustic invariant in stop consonants. *Brain and Language, 9,* 372-376.

Molfese, D.L. (1983). Event related potentials and language processes. In A.W.K. Gaillard & W. Ritter (Eds.), *Tutorials in ERP research: Endogenous components* (pp. 345-368). The Netherlands: North Holland Publishing.

Molfese, D.L. (1984). Left hemisphere sensitivity to consonant sounds not displayed by the right hemisphere: Electrophysiological correlates. *Brain and Language, 22,* 109-127.

Molfese, D.L., & Adams, C. (1988). Auditory evoked responses as an index of laterality: Findings from studies of speech perception. In K. Hugdahl (Ed.), *Handbook of dichotic listening: Theory, methods and research* (pp. 375-396). New York: Wiley.

Molfese, D.L., Buhrke, R.A., & Wang, S. (1985). The right hemisphere and temporal processing of consonant transition durations: Electrophysiological correlates. *Brain and Language, 26,* 49-62.

Molfese, D.L., & Erwin, R. J. (1981). Intrahemispheric differentiation of vowels: Principal component analysis of auditory evoked responses to computer synthesized vowel sounds. *Brain and Language, 13,* 333-344.

Molfese, D.L., Freeman, R.B., & Palermo, D.S. (1975). The ontogeny of brain lateralization for speech & nonspeech stimuli. *Brain & Language, 2,* 356-368.

Molfese, D.L., & Hess, T.M. (1978). Speech perception in nursery school age children: Sex and hemisphere differences. *Journal of Experimental Child Psychology, 26,* 71-84.

Molfese, D.L., Linnville, S., Wetzel, F & Leicht, D. (1985). Electrophysiological correlates of handedness and speech perception contrasts. *Neuropsychologia, 23(1),* 77-86.

Molfese, D.L. & Molfese, V.J. (1979a). Hemisphere and stimulus differences as reflected in the cortical responses of newborn infants to speech stimuli. *Developmental Psychology, 15(5),* 505-511.

Molfese, D.L., & Molfese, V.J. (1979b). Infant speech perception: Learned or innate. In H.A. Whitaker and H. Whitaker (Eds.), *Advances in neurolinguistics.* (Vol. 4, 225-238). New York: Academic Press.

Molfese, D.L., & Molfese, V.J. (1980). Cortical response of preterm infants to phonetic and nonphonetic speech stimuli. *Developmental Psychology, 16(6),* 574-581.

Molfese, D. L., & Molfese, V. J. (1985). Electrophysiological indices of auditory discrimination in newborn infants: The bases for predicting later language development? *Infant Behavior and Development, 8,* 197-211.

Molfese, D.L., & Molfese, V.J. (1988). Right hemisphere responses from preschool children to temporal cues contained in speech and nonspeech materials: Electrophysiological correlates. *Brain and Language, 33,* 245-

259.

Molfese, D.L., & Molfese, V.J. (in press). The use of auditory evoked responses recorded from newborn infants to predict later language skills. In L. Siegel (Ed.) *Research in infant assessment*. White Plains, NY: March of Dimes.

Molfese, D. L., Nunez, V., Seibert, S. M., & Ramaniah, N. V. (1976). Cerebral asymmetry: Changes in factors affecting its development. *Annals of the New York Academy of Sciences*, 280, 821-833.

Molfese, D.L., Papanicolaou, A., Hess, T.M., & Molfese, V.J. (1979). Neuroelectrical correlates of semantic processes. In H. Begleiter (Ed.), *Evoked brain potentials and behavior* (pp. 88-106). New York: Plenum.

Molfese, D.L., & Schmidt, A. (1983). An auditory evoked potential study of consonant perception in different vowel environments. *Brain and Language*, 18, 57-70.

Molfese, V.J., Molfese, D.L., & Parsons, C. (1983). Hemisphere involvement in phonological perception. In S. Segalowitz (Ed.), *Language functions and brain organization* (pp. 29-49). New York: Academic Press.

Morrell, L.K. & Salamy, J.G. (1971). Hemispheric asymmetry of electrocortical responses to speech stimuli. *Science*, 174, 164-166.

Nelson, C. A., & Salapatek, P. (1986). Electrophysiological correlates of infant recognition memory. *Child Development*, 57, 1483-1497.

Neville, H. (1974). Electrographic correlates of lateral asymmetry in the processing of verbal and nonverbal auditory stimuli. *Journal of Psycholinguistic Research*, 3, 151-163.

Neville, H. (1980). Event-related potentials in neuropsychological studies of language. *Brain and Language*, 11, 300-318.

Ninomiya, H., & Ikeda, T. (1984). A waveform dissimilarity of auditory evoked potentials induce by the stimulation of meaningful nouns. *Biological Psychology*, 18(2), 133-147.

Perecman, E., & Kellar, L. (1981). The effect of voice and place among aphasic, nonaphasic right-damaged and normal subjects on a metalinguistic task. *Brain and Language*, 12, 213-223.

Pisoni, D.B. (1977). Identification and discrimination of the relative onset time of two component tones: Implications for voicing perception in stops. *Journal of the Acoustical Society of America*, 61, 1352-1361.

Ruchkin, D., Sutton, S., Munson, R., Silver, K., & Macar, P. (1981). P300 and feedback provided by absence of the stimulus. *Psychophysiology*, 18, 271-282.

Rugg, M.D. (1983). The relationship between evoked potentials and lateral asymmetries of processing. In A.W.K. Gaillard & W. Ritter (Eds.), *Tutorials in ERP research: Endogenous components* (pp. 369-383). The Netherlands: North Holland Publishing.

Shankweiler, M., & Studdert-Kennedy, D. (1967). Identification of consonants and vowels presented to left and right ears. *Quarterly Journal of Experimental Psychology*, 14, 69-63.

Studdert-Kennedy, M., & Shankweiler, D. (1970). Hemisphere specialization for speech perception. *Journal of the Acoustical Society of America, 48,* 579-594.

Streeter, L.A. (1976). Language perception of two-month-old infants shows effects of both innate mechanisms and experience. *Nature, 259,* 39 - 41.

Tanguay, P., Taub, J., Doubleday, C., & Clarkson, D. (1977). An interhemispheric comparison of auditory evoked responses to consonant-vowel stimuli. *Neuropsychologia, 15,* 123-131.

Wood, C. C. (1975). Auditory and phonetic levels of processing in speech perception: Neurophysiological information-processing analyses. *Journal of Experimental Psychology: Human Perception and Performance, 104,* 3-20.

Wood, C., Goff, W., & Day, R. (1971). Auditory evoked potentials during speech perception. *Science, 173,* 1248-1251.

6 Cerebral Laterality in Functional Neuroimaging

Frank B. Wood
D. Lynn Flowers
Cecile E. Naylor
Bowman Gray School of Medicine

Lateral asymmetry of cortical function has been studied for at least a century, but until recently most studies have involved clinical-pathological correlations in lesioned humans. Indeed, the post mortem examination, has become the "gold standard" criterion by which claims of brain behavior relationships have been tested. Although it has always been recognized that the lesioned brain is abnormal, so that inferences about normal function are only indirect, the objective proof provided by an autopsy has prevailed as the empirical touchstone.

Recently, however, for the first time in the history of neuroscience, it has become feasible to investigate the localized functioning of the brain by measures of local metabolism or blood flow during a particular behavioral or cognitive task. This method allows the use of normal humans, and the correlation between task demands themselves and amplitude or intensity of metabolic activity in given regions of the brain. This chapter considers certain details and complications that arise when this method is used to study cerebral lateral asymmetry of function.

Naturally, there are technical and statistical issues, but these have been well reviewed elsewhere. See Stump and Williams (1980) for a review of the older xenon-133 inhalation method of measuring cerebral blood flow (see Frackowiak, Lenzi, Jones, & Heather, 1980 and Raichle, Herscovitch, Minun, & Markham, 1983, for some details of the use of positron emission tomography).

Attention has also been directed to statistical problems and to certain methodological issues (see Wood, 1983 for a general review of these issues as they apply to cerebral laterality research). Wood's review covers certain fundamental issues including variance differences between groups or between activation conditions, correlations between means and variances, non-normal distributions of metabolic activity measurements, and inhomogeneous correlations within the matrix of intercorrelations between regions of metabolic measurements. Traditional statistical approaches, especially ANOVA and MANOVA, have been found inadequate for many purposes, so newer and more comprehensive statistical approaches have been offered. The scaled subprofile model of Moeller, Strother, Sidtis, and Rottenberg, 1987 is perhaps the most thorough and comprehensive (see also the work of Clark, Kessler, Buchsbaum, Margolin, & Holcombe, 1984 and Clark & Stoessl, 1986).

A considerable stream of laterality research, using functional neuroimaging methods, is already flowing. Of these, the studies using completely normal subjects, with behavioral activation paradigms, are naturally the most instructive. Such studies have confirmed expected brain-behavior mappings, particularly in the sensory and motor systems (Knopman, Rubans, Klassen, Meyer, & Niccum, 1980; Roland, Kkinhoj, Larsen, & Lassen, 1977). Cognitive laterality studies have also been done, with the expected verbal versus visual spatial asymmetries of left and right hemisphere functioning (see, for example, Risberg, Halsey, Wills, & Wilson, 1975; Gur & Reivich, 1980).

There have been some complexities, however: Knopman et. al. (1982), showed both right and left activation to a word-meaning task. Moreover, they showed unilateral left- hemisphere activation to both a phonetic and a tonal task. Similarly, Wood, Taylor, Penny & Stump (1980) showed increased left hemisphere activation for a semantic-processing task, but decreased left hemisphere activation for an episodic memory-processing task, even though the stimuli were the same verbal materials in both cases (i.e., lists of words, to be either semantically categorized or episodically recognized).

Overall hemispheric differences have tended to be small in these cognitive activation tasks. This could be because, in the healthy brain, cognitive correlates tend to be manifested by a redistribution of activation within the hemisphere; or, alternatively, that lateral asymmetry is more pronounced in subregions of the hemisphere rather than in the hemisphere as a whole.

A considerable limitation has been posed by all of the studies to date: small sample sizes have restricted the statistical procedures available for evaluating patterns of activation. Larger N studies are essential, not only so that subject variance resulting from factors such as age, sex, intelligence, and anxiety can be considered, but also so that patterns of intercorrelation can be sorted out. Until sample sizes reach perhaps 50 or more, there can be little confidence that the resulting patterns of intercorrelation, among sites of activation, can be reliably estimated.

The study of such intercorrelations is particularly important, if cerebral laterality studies are to proceed beyond the "left brain versus right brain" approach. No one seriously believes that a single hemisphere acts as a monolithic unity, in contrast to the opposite single hemisphere; everyone assumes that there are functional systems within and between hemispheres. The extant studies in functional neuroimaging, however, have seldom approached those questions in a systematic way, for lack of adequate sample sizes.

COMPARISON OF COACTIVATION TASKS

As an illustration of the use of patterns of intercorrelation, to study cerebral laterality phenomena, we offer the following sample of N=60, undergoing two cognitive activation tasks, using the same stimuli and responses.

The tasks involved either identifying words previously heard and repeated aloud (a recognition memory task) or identifying words of a specified length (an orthographic analysis, or spelling task). Each word list was composed of concrete nouns. Lists were the same length, required the same bi-manual response, and contained the same number of task-relevant targets. Thus, the two tasks differed only in what subjects were asked to do with the word lists. The two tasks did differ substantially in difficulty: the spelling task had a significantly higher accuracy of performance than the memory task.

Regional cerebral blood flow was measured directly during the performance of each task, and the direct results are shown in Figure 6.1.

There were eight probes per hemisphere. The index of flow is the Initial Slope Index or ISI of Risberg that reflects mainly gray matter flow and is corrected for noncortical Xenon saturation. In this figure, the ISI is plotted along the ordinate and the numbers along the bottom correspond to the probe sites 1 through 8 in the left and right hemisphere as shown in the brain schematic above.

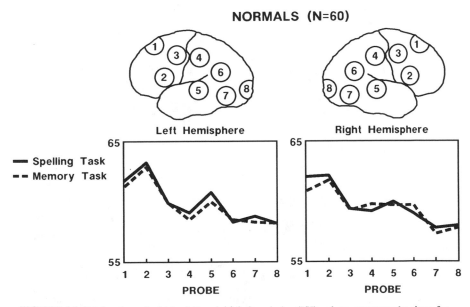

FIGURE 6.1. Regional cerebral blood flow initial slope index (ISI) values, across probe sites, for the spelling task and the memory task.

Note the typically seen hyperfrontality and bilateral activation over auditory areas. It is notable that the two tasks, although not identical, produce quite similar profiles -- suggesting perhaps that many of the same functional areas are involved in both tasks (because they are both auditory language tasks).

To examine lateral asymmetry in localized areas of the hemispheres, we calculated the difference between left and right flow at homologous sites, giving eight dependent measures, where each measure represents the degree of lateral asymmetry of activation at a given site. (Positive scores represented a left-hemisphere advantage.)

We then submitted these eight laterality scores to a formal principal components analysis, to discover the major patterns of communality among them -- that is, to specify any prevailing tendencies for the laterality scores at different sites to vary together. Naturally, the analyses were done separately on the memory task scores and the spelling task scores.

By this method we could discover if lateral asymmetry at one site tended to be accompanied by lateral asymmetry at another site, that is if there were principal factors or components of lateral asymmetry. We could also discover if these factors differed as a result of the task demands.

We were especially interested in the question of whether lateral asymmetry is general to the whole hemisphere, or perhaps confined to smaller

MEMORY TASK

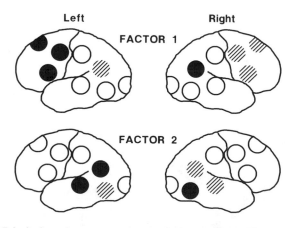

FIGURE 6.2. Principal component structure of homologous probe differences for the memory task. Note: Eight homologous probe difference values are entered in the analysis; therefore, the left and right hemisphere plots for a given component (labeled *factor*) are redundant mirror images. Directionality is indicated by totally dark vs. partially striped shading. Thus, homologous probe pairs with the same shading are positively correlated with the given component (factor). See text for fuller discussion.

subregions. In addition, we naturally wondered if the one task might elicit a more generalized asymmetry than on the other. (Previous work has suggested that the memory task might be expected to engender a more diffuse, less lateralized activation pattern, in which the only asymmetry might be elicited by the stimuli involved--hence in the auditory association cortex or Wernicke's area. By this reasoning, the spelling task, because it is more specifically linguistic, might be expected to recruit more asymmetric left hemisphere activation than the memory task.)

Recognition Memory Results

Considering first the recognition memory task, the first principal component (shown at the top of Figure 6.2)
demonstrates that, rather than a uniform hemispheric response, there is a more restricted pattern of asymmetry involving only the regions that have been shaded. This component alone accounts for 31% of the variance, and it is interesting that it is largely frontal and does not include Wernicke's area. A frontal role in memory tasks has indeed often been proposed (see Wood, 1987 for a review).

There is a novel twist, as well: The angular gyrus asymmetry is inversely correlated with the frontal asymmetries. Thus, there is a reciprocal pattern of asymmetric activation between frontal and posterior regions. Not only does the whole hemisphere not operate unanimously (with respect to lateral asymmetry) but local asymmetry in the frontal region is accompanied by the opposite asymmetry in the angular gyrus.

The second principal component, orthogonal to the first and accounting for 19% of the variance, is also a reciprocal factor: the asymmetry of the temporal-parietal activation is inversely related to the asymmetry of inferior temporo-occipital activation.

Spelling Task Results

In the spelling task, the different instruction has yielded different patterns of activation (bottom of Figure 6.3). This time only the first component is one of reciprocity. The asymmetry of posterior peri-Sylvian activation is inversely correlated with occipital activation asymmetry. Note that the second component is significantly loaded by only a single asymmetry, that of Broca's area. (It may be of interest that the first two components from the spelling task account for somewhat less variance than those from the memory task, 43% and 50%, respectively.)

Figure 6.4 compares the first component of each task-the memory task above and spelling task below. Insofar as the first component can be assumed to represent the most salient brain response to task demands, these two activation patterns demonstrate differential effects of task demands to highly similar stimuli. For our purposes, however, the most important point is that in both cases, the lateral asymmetries are focal, not hemisphere-wide, and they are reciprocal --

involving inverse asymmetries in different regions.

Lateral asymmetry is partial within a hemisphere, and differentially so between task. Because these two tasks differ within the verbal memory domain, one interpretation of the difference in these task-dependent patterns, is that the observed cortical activation patterns reflect the different demands of two different types of memory. The recognition memory task is an episodic memory task (in the terms of the episodic-semantic memory distinction of Tulving). The cortical response to such a task has been suggested (Wood, 1987) to include frontal activation, perhaps because of a greater need to focus attention on immediate and more novel aspects of the stimuli in order to separate the relevant from the irrelevant. Certainly the memory task was the more difficult of the two as judged by task accuracy scores.

The spelling task is a semantic memory task, in the sense of being context-free and not dependent on a particular episode of the subject's past experience. As Wood (1983, 1987) suggested in reviewing the Ojemann brain stimulation mapping studies, such semantic memory processing is expected to engage peri-Sylvian areas, because of the focal language activation required (whereas an episodic memory task would do so only to the extent of stimulus processing and would additionally stimulate areas more distal to the peri Sylvian region).

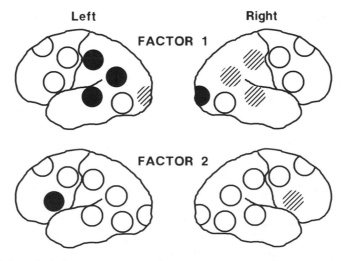

FIGURE 6.3. Principal component of homologous probe differences for the spelling task. (See note for Figure 2).

Sex Differences

Let us now consider another methodological issue, one that has also been frequently related to the question of cerebral lateral asymmetry--sex differences. Because these are considered particularly relevant on verbal and linguistic tasks, we limit our attention to the spelling task in the current paradigm.

Figure 6.5 shows the general pattern of cortical activation plotted by sex. Note that females show generally higher flows, but both groups show the typical pattern of hyperfrontality, that is, an anterior-posterior flow gradient, and both groups show a peak of activation over left temporal regions (Wernicke's area). This peak is singularly important because it is significantly correlated with task accuracy. More specifically, it is the slope or the relative activation at Wernicke's area (Site 5) compared to angular gyrus (Site 6) that is the best predictor of task accuracy. This is true for both males and females. This peak of activation is not predicted by vocabulary or other measures of verbal ability. Furthermore, this relationship between peak activation at Wernicke's area and task accuracy is not found with the recognition memory task. We have found that this peak is flattened in those with a history of reading disability, which we have attributed to a deficit in functioning of left temporal regions. We conclude, therefore, that this task is a linguistic task that selectively activates Wernicke's area in normal individuals.

Given the relevance of the focal Wernicke's area activation, we were

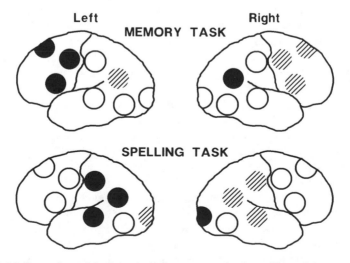

FACTOR 1

FIGURE 6.4. Comparison of the first principal components for the spelling and the memory task.

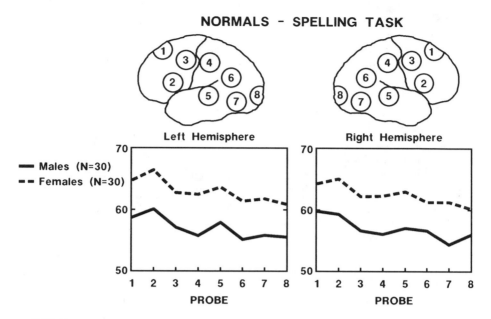

FIGURE 6.5. Regional cerebral blood flow initial slope index (ISI) values, across probe sites, during the spelling task, for males and females.

interested in examining what other brain regions might be linked with this focal activation. In other words, we asked the question: which of the remaining 15 sites correlates with Wernicke's area activation in a multivariate analysis that looked at the unique relationship between Probe 5 and each probe holding all remaining probes constant? There is a strong tendency for all sites to vary together, that is, for there to be a global heightening of activity in any cognitively challenging task; the partial correlation analysis excludes that variance, however.

In males, there is a unique bidirectional relationship between Wernicke's and Broca's area, and no other significant partial correlations with Wernicke's area were found (Figure 6.6). That is, when Wernicke's area is activated, there is a corresponding, tightly coupled activation of Broca's area as well. This comports well with a functional systems model as proposed by Luria, so that these core language areas covary even on a largely receptive task; Broca's and Wernicke's areas are not receptive and expressive "boxes" so to speak. This tight coupling, similar to that reported by Ojemann, might be taken to imply an analysis by synthesis approach, that is, that one listens by making speech or that perception requires production; at least, it appears that Broca's region is intimately involved in language reception in males.

The story is quite different and much more complicated for females, however (Figure 6.7). First, we see no unique coupling between Wernicke's and Broca's areas as for males. Instead, there is a bitemporal coupling, that is, as left

MALES - SPELLING TASK

Left   Right

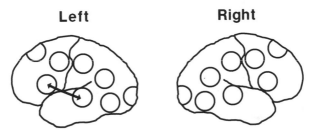

FIGURE 6.6. Pattern of statistically significant (p < .05) partial correlations of ISI flow values between probe sites involving either left Broca's or left Wernicke's area, in males during the spelling task. The partial correlation is independent of all other correlations between either of the two indicated sites and any other sites in either hemisphere.

temporal regions are activated so are right temporal regions. This could be interpreted as providing some support for greater bilateral representation of verbal skills in females. There is also a unique coupling between the left temporal region and a more posterior and inferior region of the left hemisphere. Thus, in females, it is as if this task recruits more cross-hemispheric activation and also more posterior (possibly more purely perceptual) activation than with males.

The stark fact is that the activation at left Wernicke's area is without reference to Broca's area activation. If we are to take seriously the findings in males that support a familiar functional system model must we not also take just as seriously these unambiguously discrepant findings in females? Perhaps one of the reasons that this more complicated picture is only beginning to surface has been our heavy bias toward studying predominantly males in the past.

The correlation between Wernicke's area and task accuracy indicates that both sexes recruit this area to perform this linguistic task. But, the means to the end is very different for females, perhaps even more elaborate--with two independent functional units as compared to one in males. On the recognition memory task, not only was Wernicke's area not related to task accuracy, but there were virtually no unique couplings found between Wernicke's or Broca's area and any other region of the brain and this was true for both males and females. Therefore, this represents a specific pattern of activation in response to a purely linguistic task.

A further question that we could not resist asking was whether, if Broca's area is not coupled with Wernicke's area in females, it is functionally linked with any other regions. The answer is yes, but the picture is even more complicated (Figure 6.8). In females, Broca's region is uniquely coupled with most other cortical regions except Wernicke's area. There are both positive and negative significant relationships. This reveals an extremely rich, complicated, and highly differentiated pattern of unique functional relations between cortical regions in

FEMALES - SPELLING TASK

Left   Right

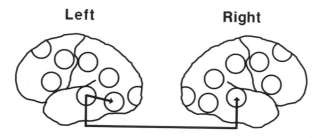

FIGURE 6.7. Pattern of statistically significant (p < .05) correlations of ISI flow values.

FEMALES - SPELLING TASK

Left   Right

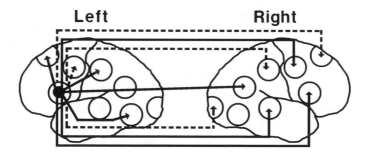

FIGURE 6.8. Pattern of statistically significant (p < .05) correlations of ISI flow values between left Broca's area and any other probe sites, in females during the spelling task. Each partial correlation is independent of all other correlations involving left Broca's area. Postitive correlations are indicated by solid arrows; negative correlations by broken arrows.

the female brain. The meaning of this remains undeveloped but at minimum, it makes a strong statement emphasizing the role of subject variables. Different kinds of subjects (across many dimensions, not just sex) may accomplish the same task in dramatically different ways.

CONCLUSIONS

The data just presented are offered, of course, only in an illustrative manner; if they open up some new avenues of inquiry, they certainly do not close or even conclude those inquiries. Let us consider, nonetheless, the broader implications of the points that are illustrated in these data.

The broadest point of all is the need to incorporate a classically functionalist approach to what has always been perceived as an inherently structuralist issue, namely the question of cerebral laterality. We would do well to take guidance from the structuralist versus functionalist debates of 100 years ago, so as to avoid the perils of an unduly narrow structuralism.

Perhaps the most familiar concept, from those historic debates, is that of "Einstellung" or "set." Broadly, the difference between the memory and spelling tasks is one of task instruction, or set. Even in the last century, it was clear that such set differences could have a profound impact on all aspects of task performance, particularly when any selectivity (specific response to specific subsets of the stimulus field) was involved. No one is surprised, in the late 20th century, that a verbal memory task would differ from a spelling task in the specific set and, therefore, in the specific attentional biases that are involved in the performance of the task. On the other hand, it is somewhat surprising that the "raw" functional landscapes engendered by these two tasks are highly similar, while the patterns of intercorrelation among sites are substantially different. In brief, differential "set" has reorganized the brain without changing its externally apparent posture.

More specific to the issue of cerebral laterality is the fact that this set difference involves reciprocal interactions between different subregions of the two hemispheres. In general, this tends toward a "diagonal laterality" mechanism, whereby asymmetry to the left in one part of the brain is accompanied by asymmetry to the right in another part of the brain. The best example is the first principal component in the memory task; it is a left frontal and right parietal factor, whereby lateral advantage to the left frontal region is correlated with lateral advantage to the right parietal region.

This "diagonal laterality" can be easily analogized to the skeletal muscle system, as that system is organized by a variety of tasks. Consider baseball. The right-handed pitcher makes disproportionate use of the left leg: At the moment of maximum energy use by the right arm (in the actual delivery of the pitch) there is also maximal use of the left leg (on which the pitcher has the entire weight of the body during the pitch). There is thus a diagonal axis of maximum activation, from the left leg to the right arm. This reciprocal asymmetry is required for simple balance: If required to stand on the right foot only, the right-handed pitcher gets seriously off balance and loses considerable "reach" or "purchase" with the right arm. Although only an analogy, the case naturally raises the question whether a similar balance principle operates in cerebral mechanics.

Individual differences are not so purely a functionalist concept as set is, but functionalist approaches are still indispensable to any sophisticated understanding of the above described sex differences. That is because the dramatically different brain organizations in males and females, on the spelling task, are not present on the memory task. In familiar terms, the highly distinctive and unusual female brain organizational pattern on the spelling task is the result of a sex by task interaction. A prevailing structural difference between male and female brains, present on all tasks involving language stimuli, is specifically not demonstrated. We are, therefore, led to inquire about the particular aspects of spelling task activation that are responsible for the dramatically different brain organization patterns that are evoked in males and females on that task. No answer is readily in sight, but it is clear that no answer can be found if the search is confined within the intercranial space: serious attention to the external environment and its task demands is obviously required.

ACKNOWLEDGMENTS

Research reported in this chapter was supported by grants from the National Institute of Child Health and Human Development (P01-HD21887) and the National Institutes of Mental Health (R01-MH39599) to the Bowman Grey School of Medicine.

REFERENCES

Clark, C.M., Kessler, R., Buchsbaum, M.S., Margolin, R.A. and Holcomb, H.H. (1984). Correlational methods for determining regional coupling cerebral glucose metabolism: Pilot study. *Biological Psychiatry 19*, 663-678.

Clark, C.M., & Stoessl, A.J. (1986). Glucose use correlations: A matter of inference. *Journal of Cerebral Blood Flow Metabolism, 6*,(letter)., 511-513.

Frackowiak, R.S.J., Lenzi, G.L., Jones, T., & Heather, J.D. (1980). Quantitative measurement of regional cerebral blood flow and oxygen metabolism in man using 150 and positron emission tomography: Theory, procedure and normal values. *J. Computer Assisted Tomography, 4*,727-736.

Gur, R.C. & Reivich, M. (1980). Cognitive task effects on hemispheric blood flow in humans: Evidence for individual differences in hemispheric activation. *Brain and Language, 9*, 78-92.

Knopman D.S., Rubens, A.B., Klassen, A.C., Meyer, M. W., & Niccum, N. (1980). Regional cerebral blood flow patterns during verbal and nonverbal auditory activation. *Brain and Language, 9*, 93-112.

Moeller, J.R., Strother, S.C., Sidtis, J.J., & Rottenberg D.A. (1987). Scaled subprofile model: A statistical approach to the analysis of functional patterns in positron emission tomographic data. *Journal of Cerebral Blood Flow and Metabolism, 7*,649-658.

Raichle, M.E., Martin, W.R.W., Herscovitch, P., Mintun, M.A., & Markham, J. (1983). Brainblood flow measured with intravenous H2150. II. Implementation and validation. *Journal of Nuclear Medicine, 24*,790-798.

Risberg, J.L., Halsey, J.H., Wills, E.L., & Wilson, E.M. (1975). Hemispheric specialization in normal man studied by bilateral measurements of the regional cerebral blood flow: A study with the 133-Xe technique. *Brain, 98*, 511-524.

Roland, P.E., Kkinhoj, E., Larsen, B., Lassen, N.A. (1977). The role of different cortical areas in the organization of voluntary movements in man: A region cerebral blood flow study. *Acta Neurol Scand*, *56*, 542-543; 277-279.

Stump, D.A. & Williams, R. (1980). The noninvasive measurement of regional cerebral circulation. *Brain and Language*, *9*, 35-46.

Wood, F., Taylor, B., Penny, R., & Stump, D. (1980). Regional cerebral blood flow responses to recognition memory versus semantic classification tasks. *Brain and Language*, *9*, 113-122.

Wood, F. (1983). Cortical and thalamic representation of the episodic and semantic memory systems converging evidence from brain stimulation, local metabolic indicators and human neuropsychology. *Behavior and Brain Science*, *6*, 189-230.

Wood, F. (1987). Focal and diffuse memory activation assessed by localized indicators of CNS metabolism: The semantic-episodic memory distinction. *Human Neurobiology*, *6*, 141-151.

7   Cerebral Laterality and Metacontrol

Joseph B. Hellige
University of Southern California

In 1976, Jerre Levy and Colin Trevarthen distinguished between hemispheric ability and hemispheric dominance and introduced a concept they referred to as *metacontrol*. *Hemispheric ability* refers to how well each cerebral hemisphere can handle a particular information-processing task and has been the subject of a great deal of research over the last two decades. Levy and Trevarthen used the term *hemispheric dominance* to refer to the degree to which each cerebral hemisphere in commissurotomy patients tends to assume control of information processing and behavior. In experiments with four commissurotomy patients, they discovered that the ability differences between the two cerebral hemispheres are not the sole determinant of hemispheric dominance. That is, in commissurotomy patients the hemisphere that assumed control was not always the hemisphere with the greater ability to perform the task. Levy and Trevarthen refer to the neural mechanisms that determine which hemisphere will attempt to control cognitive operations as metacontrol.

The concept of metacontrol is especially important in considering information processing in the neurologically normal brain. An abundance of research indicates that each cerebral hemisphere has its own processing abilities and propensities that can be brought to bear on a variety of tasks. These discoveries have been made by studying patients with appropriate injuries to the cerebral hemispheres and by studying neurologically intact individuals in experimental situations that restrict stimulus input to only one hemisphere at a time or that monitor the output of only one hemisphere at a time (for discussion of these techniques see Hellige, 1983). Except for these unusual laboratory situations, stimuli tend to be presented to both hemispheres and some unified response is required from the individual. An important question concerns the manner in which the two hemispheres (with their different abilities and propensities) work together in these situations where each has access to the same stimulus information. The concept of metacontrol suggests that in at least some cases one hemisphere's preferred mode of processing will dominate and that the dominant hemisphere will not necessarily be the one with superior ability for the task to be performed.

Despite the obvious importance of metacontrol, there have been very few attempts to determine whether metacontrol is a unique feature of commissurotomy patients or whether it extends to the neurologically normal brain. Perhaps the biggest problem in extending the investigation of metacontrol to normal individuals is the difficulty in determining which hemisphere in some sense dominates processing when both have access to the same stimulus information. The purpose of this chapter is to outline a set of procedures for making such a determination and to illustrate the promise of those procedures by reviewing a variety of recent experiments that suggest metacontrol in the neurologically intact human brain.

DETERMINATION OF METACONTROL
AND THE BILATERAL PARADIGM

For many information-processing tasks, it is the case that each cerebral hemisphere has some competence but the processing differs *qualitatively* as a function of which hemisphere is stimulated. The operational definition of a qualitative difference in processing is that the effect of some manipulated task variable produces a different pattern of effects depending on which hemisphere initiates processing. Thus, qualitative differences can be discovered by studying patients with unilateral brain injury (where it is assumed that the intact hemisphere is more involved in information processing) and by studying how the effects of task variables differ as a function of the hemisphere stimulated in neurologically normal individuals. For example, in a tachistoscopic presentation task a qualitative hemispheric difference would be indicated by an interaction of visual field (i.e., hemisphere) and some manipulated task variable.

In order to determine whether the concept of metacontrol extends to the neurologically intact brain, it is useful to use tasks that meet the definition of being performed in qualitatively different ways by the two cerebral hemispheres. Consider a visual half-field task using tachistoscopic presentation of information to the right visual field-left hemisphere (RVF-LH) or the left visual field-right hemisphere (LVF-RH). By including bilateral presentation of the same stimulus simultaneously to both visual fields (hemispheres) it is possible to determine whether the qualitative pattern of results when both hemispheres are stimulated matches the qualitative pattern of results obtained from one visual field (hemisphere) but not the other. When this is the case, it suggests that one hemisphere's mode of processing dominates when a choice can be made and, in this sense, one hemisphere exerts metacontrol (for more detailed discussion of this paradigm see Hellige, 1987).

This tachistoscopic paradigm incorporating bilateral presentation has recently been used with a variety of tasks known to lead to qualitative processing differences between the left and right cerebral hemispheres. In all cases, the qualitative nature of the results on bilateral trials was identical to the qualitative nature of the results from one single visual field but not the other. The next two sections review these studies.

TASKS WITH NO OVERALL HEMISPHERIC SUPERIORITY

The experiments described in this section utilized a variety of different tasks with the common property that neither the left nor the right hemisphere was uniformly superior across all of the experimental conditions within the experiment. Such tasks were chosen so that any effects of metacontrol would be unlikely to be attributed to uniform superiority of one hemisphere or the other. All of these experiments were conducted with right-handed university students as subjects.

Comparison of Cartoon Faces

Hellige, Jonsson and Michimata (1988) had subjects perform a comparison task using cartoon faces that had been shown previously by Sergent (1982, 1984) to produce qualitatively different patterns of results as a function of the cerebral hemisphere stimulated. On each trial of this experiment a single target cartoon face was presented for one sec at the subject's fixation point. When this face disappeared, a probe face was presented for 250 msec to the LVF-RH or to the RVF-LH or the same probe face was presented for 250 msec to both visual fields simultaneously (bilateral trials). The subject was asked to indicate as quickly as possible whether the target and probe faces were identical or not. When the two faces differed, they were identical except for one of four variable features (hair, eyes, mouth, or jaw).

When the two faces were not identical, the reaction time (RT) to make a correct response depended on which single feature was different in the two faces. In general agreement with Sergent's (1982, 1984) earlier findings, the pattern of feature location effects was significantly different for LVF-RH and RVF-LH trials, consistent with her conclusion that the two hemispheres perform this task in qualitatively different ways (see Sergent, 1982, 1984 for discussion of the nature of this qualitative difference). Note that the interaction of feature location and visual field meets our operational definition of a qualitative processing difference between the two cerebral hemispheres.

Of particular interest was the finding that the pattern of feature location effects on bilateral trials was identical to the pattern of feature location effects on RVF-LH trials and, therefore, different from the pattern of feature location effects on LVF-RH trials. This was true even though neither of the two unilateral visual field conditions was uniformly superior for this face comparison task. That is, the similarity of the results on bilateral trials and RVF-LH trials cannot be attributed to an overall superiority of the left hemisphere in performing the face comparison task. In fact, as Hellige et al. (1988) discuss, the pattern of results on bilateral trials follows the pattern of results on RVF-LH trials even for those feature location differences that were processed faster on LVF-RH trials. This dissociation of metacontrol and hemispheric superiority is similar to the findings reported by Levy and Trevarthen (1976) in their study of commissurotomy patients.

Same/Different Judgments About Letters

When subjects are asked to indicate as quickly as possible whether two simultaneously presented letters are same or different it is frequently the case that RT is faster for same than for different pairs. This effect has been referred to as the fast same effect and its interpretation has been a matter of considerable debate (see Farell, 1985).

When the letters to be compared are presented briefly to either the LVF-RH or RVF-LH on each trial it is often the case that the "fast same" effect is restricted to RVF-LH trials (e.g., Bagnara, Boles, Simion & Umilta, 1983; Egeth & Epstein, 1972), producing a significant same/different by visual field interaction. As Bagnara et al. argue, such an interaction indicates that the two hemispheres perform the letter comparison task in qualitatively different ways (see Bagnara et al. for consideration of several alternative interpretations of this qualitative difference).

The existence of such a qualitative difference and the fact that the "fast same" effect is generally found in studies that present the letter pairs in central vision (i.e., when the information is accessible to both hemispheres) suggests that the mode of processing employed by the left hemisphere may dominate this task when both hemispheres have access to the same stimulus information. In order to test this, Hellige and Michimata (1989a) included bilateral stimulus presentation in a same/different letter comparison experiment.

Hellige and Michimata (1989a) required subjects to indicate as quickly as possible whether or not two letters presented one above the other were physically identical. The stimuli consisted of all possible pairs of the symmetrical uppercase letters T, H and X. In addition, for reasons that are not germane for the present chapter, on half of the trials the stimuli were presented clearly in focus and on half of the trials the stimuli were moderately out of focus. On different trials the letter pair was projected to only the LVF-RH, only the RVF-LH or the same letter pair was projected simultaneously to both visual field locations (bilateral trials). Subjects were told that on bilateral trials the letter pair projected to one visual field would always be identical to the letter pair projected to the other visual field.

The relevant results are summarized in Figure 1, which shows the RT of correct responses for same and different letter pairs presented in each of the three visual field conditions. The results with Clear and Blurred stimuli are shown in the upper and lower panels, respectively.

For both clear and blurred stimuli, RT was faster to same letter pairs than to different letter pairs (i.e., the fast same effect was obtained). Of more importance is the fact that, consistent with the findings of Bagnara et al. (1983), there was an LVF-RH versus RVF-LH by same/different interaction for both clear and blurred stimuli. As Fig. 7.1 illustrates this interaction occurs because the fast same effect is present on RVF-LH trials but not on LVF-RH trials. It is also interesting to note that neither visual field (hemisphere) was uniformly superior to the other for performing this letter comparison task. That is, the two hemispheres have approximately equal competence to perform the task but are predisposed to

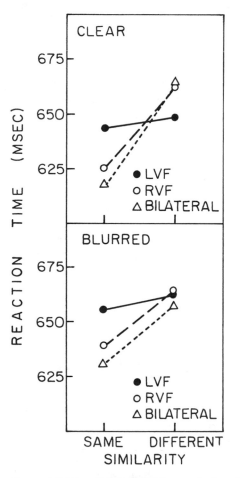

FIGURE 7.1. Reaction time to SAME and DIFFERENT letter pairs for stimuli presented to left visual field (LVF), right visual field (RVF) and both visual fields (BILATERAL). Results with Clear and Blurred stimuli are shown in the upper and lower panels, respectively. From Hellige and Michimata (1989a).

go about it in qualitatively different ways.

Figure 7.1 also illustrates the fact that the qualitative pattern of results on bilateral trials (i.e., the presence of the fast same effect) was identical to the pattern obtained on RVF-LH trials. This finding suggests that once again the mode of processing preferred by the left cerebral hemisphere is utilized when both hemispheres have access to the same stimulus information.

HEMISPHERIC DIFFERENCES IN SPATIAL PROCESSING

It has been known for some time that the right cerebral hemisphere is superior to the left for processing a variety of nonverbal visuospatial information (e.g., Bradshaw & Nettleton, 1983). More recently, evidence has accumulated for the hypothesis that the brain computes two different kinds of spatial-relation representations: one used to assign a spatial relation to a category such as "outside of" or "above" and the other used to specify metric distance with precision (e.g., Kosslyn, 1987, this volume). Furthermore, Kosslyn (1987) has suggested that although the right cerebral hemisphere makes more effective use of the "metric distance" processing subsystem (consistent with the body of accumulated evidence) it is the left cerebral hemisphere that makes more effective use of the "categorization" processing subsystem. Hellige and Michimata (1989b) have provided a test of this hypothesis and have also investigated the pattern of results with bilateral presentation of stimulus information.

On each trial of the experiment reported by Hellige and Michimata (1988b) subjects were shown a stimulus consisting of a horizontal line and a small dot in one of 12 possible locations (6 at different distances above the line and 6 at different distances below the line). Each subject used these stimuli to perform both a categorization task and a metric distance judgment task, during different experimental sessions.

The categorization task required subjects to indicate as quickly as possible whether or not the dot on each trial was above or below the line, ignoring its distance from the line. The distance judgment task required subjects to indicate whether the dot on each trial was near the line or far from the line, ignoring whether the dot was above or below the line. In order to be able to make this judgment, subjects were trained to refer to the six dot locations nearest the line on either side as "near" and to refer to the six dot locations farthest from the line on either side as "far."

On each trial, the stimulus information was presented briefly to only the RVF-LH, only the LVF-RH or the same stimulus information was presented to both visual field locations simultaneously (bilateral trials). The relevant results from this experiment are summarized in Fig. 7.2, which shows the RT of correct responses for both the Above/Below task and the Near/Far task. The parameter is visual field condition.

Consistent with Kosslyn's (1987) hypothesis, RTs were faster on RVF-LH trials than on LVF-RH trials for the above/below task and faster on LVF-RH trials than on RVF-LH trials for the near/far task. This pattern of results produced a significant LVF-RH versus RVF-LH by task interaction, with no significant main effect of hemisphere. That is, as in the experiments reviewed earlier, there was no overall superiority of one hemisphere or the other for processing these stimuli. Instead, both hemispheres have some competence to process them but are predisposed toward efficient use of different subsystems for representing spatial relations.

Before examining the results on bilateral trials it is instructive to reconceptualize the Visual Field by Task interaction found on unilateral trials. Note that the RT difference between the above/below and near/far tasks is greater on RVF-LH trials than on LVF-RH trials. If the left hemisphere is biased toward the use of a categorization processing subsystem then this might be expected to lead to faster processing during the Above/Below task (for which a categorical subsystem is well-adapted) than during the Near/Far task (for which a categorical system is not well-adapted). By way of contrast, a right hemisphere bias toward use of a metric distance processing subsystem would serve to reduce the RT advantage for the above/below task.

Averaged across both tasks, the RTs on bilateral trials were faster than on unilateral trials. That is, there is a beneficial effect of having two redundant stimuli on bilateral trials. Of more importance is the fact that on bilateral trials the RT advantage for the above/below task was equal to the magnitude of that advantage on RVF-LH trials and significantly greater than the magnitude of that advantage on LVF-RH trials. That is, the qualitative pattern of RT effects was identical for RVF-LH and bilateral trials and both were different from LVF-RH trials. This suggests that on bilateral trials subjects were biased toward the use of the same spatial processing subsystem that was characteristic of left-hemisphere trials.

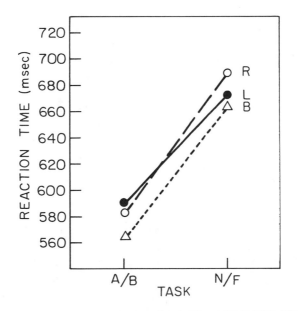

FIGURE 7.2. Reaction time for the ABOVE/BELOW (A/B) and NEAR/FAR (N/F) tasks for stimuli presented to the left visual field (L), right visual field (R) and both visual fields (B). From Hellige and Michimata (1989b).

COMMON CHARACTERISTICS AND POSSIBLE INTERPRETATIONS

The experiments reviewed in this section make different information processing demands and yet certain aspects of their results are very similar. For example, in each of these experiments the qualitative pattern of results on bilateral trials was identical to the qualitative pattern obtained on RVF-LH trials and both were different from the qualitative pattern obtained on LVF-RH trials. From this it would be tempting to conclude that when both hemispheres of right-handed adults are presented with the same stimulus information, the mode of processing favored by the left hemisphere is utilized regardless of specific task demands. Although such a conclusion is consistent with the studies reviewed so far, it is not consistent with other recent studies summarized in the next section. Therefore, it is instructive to consider other similarities among those experiments that have already been described.

Despite there being different preferred modes of processing on LVF-RH and RVF-LH trials, in the tasks used by Hellige, Jonnson, & Michimata (1988) and by Hellige and Michimata (1989a, 1989b) neither mode of processing was uniformly superior to the other. That is, there was no overall superiority of one hemisphere in these experiments. Furthermore, it is unlikely that in any of these experiments it was the case that either of the two modes of processing was completely unavailable to the hemisphere that was not biased in its favor. As a result of this, it seems unlikely that the overall level of performance on bilateral trials would depend on which mode of processing was used. Perhaps under these conditions right-handed adults do have a very general bias toward left hemisphere metacontrol; that is, toward the mode of processing favored by the left hemisphere. However, the experiments reviewed in the next section make it clear that when these conditions change things can be quite different.

A TASK WITH LEFT HEMISPHERE SUPERIORITY

In order to extend the investigation of metacontrol to a task that produces an overall advantage in favor of one hemisphere, Hellige, Taylor, and Eng (1989) required subjects to identify consonant-vowel-consonant (CVC) nonsense syllables presented briefly and followed by a mask. On each trial during their experiments a CVC was presented to only the LVF-RH, only the RVF-LH or the same CVC was presented to both fields simultaneously (bilateral trials). The stimuli and task were patterned after an experiment reported by Levy, Heller, Banich and Burton (1983) in which it was found that qualitatively different modes of CVC processing were used on LVF-RH and RVF-LH trials.

As expected for a verbal task, Levy et al. (1983) reported a RVF-LH advantage for identifying CVCs correctly. In addition, on trials where the response was incorrect, the pattern of errors was qualitatively different on LVF-RH and RVF-LH trials. This qualitative difference was determined in the following way.

Errors were classified into one of three types and the normalized frequency of the types compared. A first-letter error (FE) occurred when the first letter of the CVC was not reported correctly but the last letter was reported correctly. A last-letter error (LE) occurred when the last letter of the CVC was not reported correctly but the first letter was reported correctly. Correctness of the vowel was irrelevant in scoring for FEs and LEs. All remaining types of errors were classified as other errors (OEs). Levy et al. computed a qualitative error score (QE) for each visual field as [(LE - FE) / (Total Errors)] for that visual field. Dividing by the total number of errors for the appropriate visual field normalizes the LE - FE difference, which is important for separating *qualitative* processing differences from the overall RVF-LH advantage.

Levy et al. (1983) found that the QE score was greater on LVF-RH trials than on RVF-LH trials. They suggest that the relatively large QE score on LVF-RH trials occurs because the right hemisphere lacks a phonetic processing mechanism and, consequently, processes the CVC in a letter-by-letter fashion beginning with the first letter. When this mode of processing is utilized, the first letter is more likely to be identified than the final letter. Of course, the left hemisphere is also capable of using a letter-by-letter mode of processing. However, Levy et al. suggest that the left hemisphere supplements or replaces a letter-by-letter mode of processing with phonetic processing mechanisms that treat the CVC as a single linguistic unit. They propose that it is the application of this phonetic processing mode that reduces the QE score on RVF-LH trials.

By including bilateral presentation of the same CVC to both hemispheres, Hellige, Jonnson, & Michimata (1988) wanted to determine which hemisphere's preferred mode of processing would emerge when both hemispheres had equal access to the stimulus information. In view of the fact that the mode of processing characteristic of RVF-LH trials leads to better performance, it might be expected that the mode of processing on bilateral trials would be identical that used on RVF-LH trials. In this case, the normalized error pattern on bilateral trials should be identical to the normalized error pattern on RVF-LH trials.

Despite its intuitive appeal, the possibility just outlined has a potential drawback. If Levy et al. (1983) are correct in their claim that the right hemisphere lacks a phonetic processing mechanism, then it is unlikely that the phonetic mode of processing could be applied to both stimuli on bilateral trials. Instead, processing might be restricted to the RVF-LH stimulus (of course, the two stimuli are identical on bilateral trials, but we have seen how redundant information can improve performance under some circumstances). In view of this, there might be an advantage in using the nonlinguistic mode of processing (characteristic of the right hemisphere on unilateral trials) on bilateral trials because it can be used by both hemispheres and, therefore, applied to each of the two redundant stimuli.

Hellige et al. (1989) adjusted stimulus duration after each experimental trial so that the overall error rate would be approximately 50% averaged across all three visual field conditions. This procedure ensures that there will be a sufficient number of errors in each visual field condition to make a qualitative analysis of error types reasonable. They report the results from two experiments that differed only in that Experiment 1 required subjects to identify a small digit presented at the subject's fixation point simultaneously with the presentation of a lateralized CVC whereas in Experiment 2 the fixation digits were eliminated. Despite this difference in procedure, the results of the two experiments were very similar.

In both experiments, the total number of errors was significantly lower on RVF-LH trials than on LVF-RH trials. This is consistent with the well-established superiority of the left hemisphere for aspects of linguistic processing. The total number of errors on bilateral trials was either equal to (Experiment 1) or lower than (Experiment 2) the number of errors on RVF-LH trials. At first glance, this *quantitative* similarity on RVF-LH and bilateral trials might be taken as an indication that the *qualitative* mode of processing on bilateral trials was identical to the mode characteristic of RVF-LH trials. However, examination of the qualitative pattern of errors indicates that this was not at all the case.

Figure 7.3 shows the normalized percentage of the three types of errors (FE, LE, OE) for each of the three visual field conditions. The results from Experiments 1 and 2 are shown in the upper and lower panels, respectively. It is important to note that each normalized score was obtained by taking the number of errors of a particular type for a single visual field and dividing by the total number of errors for that visual field. Consequently, these scores represent the qualitative error pattern for each visual field uncontaminated by any quantitative difference in terms of the overall number of errors.

With respect to the two unilateral visual fields, the results obtained by Hellige et al. (1989) replicated the qualitative hemispheric difference reported by Levy et al. (1983). Specifically, the proportion of LEs was much higher than the proportion of FEs on LVF-RH trials and this difference was significantly smaller on RVF-LH trials. Of particular interest is the fact that the qualitative error pattern on bilateral trials was identical to the qualitative error pattern on LVF-RH trials and significantly different from the qualitative error pattern on RVF-LH trials. This finding indicates that for this task the mode of processing characteristic of the right hemisphere on unilateral trials was employed on bilateral trials which provided the same stimulus information to both hemispheres.

In view of the fact that the task used by Hellige et al. (1989) involved verbal stimuli and that it produced an RVF-LH advantage, the use of the "inferior" letter-by-letter mode of processing on bilateral trials is counterintuitive. However, as noted earlier one potential advantage of this mode of processing is that it is available to both cerebral hemispheres whereas a more phonetic mode is not. By applying this "inferior" mode of processing to each of two redundant stimuli it may be possible to achieve an overall error rate even lower than that obtained on RVF-LH trials.

In fact, the overall error rate on bilateral trials was equal to or lower than the overall error rate on RVF-LH trials. Of course, in both experiments the overall error rate on bilateral trials was much lower than the overall error rate on LVF-RH trials--this despite the identity of qualitative error patterns for these two visual field conditions. In an attempt to account for these findings, Hellige et al.

(1989) assumed that on bilateral trials the mode of processing characteristic of the right hemisphere was used to process each of the two stimulus items, with the processing of the two stimuli contributing independently to response accuracy. A mathematical version of this model was used to predict the percentage of trials on which the different error types should occur on bilateral trials (i.e., to predict the quantitative as well as qualitative error performance). As Fig. 7.4 shows, the agreement between this model and the data obtained on bilateral trials was excellent. At the same time, the bilateral results are clearly inconsistent with the

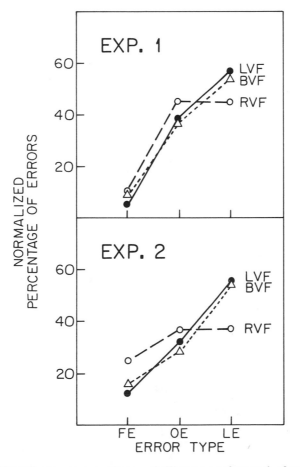

FIGURE 7.3. Normalized percentage of errors of different types from each of two experiments (FE = first letter errors; LE = last letter errors; OE = other errors). The parameter in each panel is visual field of stimulus presentation (LVF = left visual field; RVF = right visual field; BVF = BILATERAL presentation). After Hellige et al. (1989).

notion that the mode of processing characteristic of the left hemisphere is applied to either of the two redundant stimuli.

The results reported by Hellige et al. (1989) are important because they indicate that the left-hemisphere metacontrol suggested by the studies reviewed in previous sections of this chapter does not generalize to all tasks. Instead, in right-handed adults --- the emergence of one hemisphere's preferred mode of processing likely depends on a variety of task demands that have yet to be discovered. In addition, the results reported by Hellige et al. provide the clearest evidence yet that in the neurologically intact brain the mode of processing that

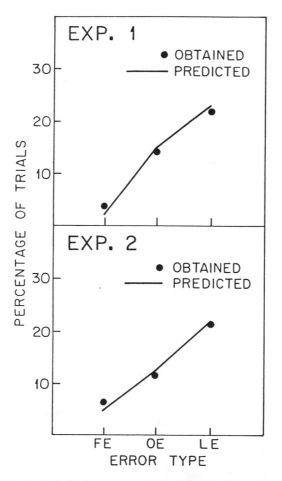

FIGURE 7.4. Predicted and obtained percentage of trials on which different types of errors occur for BILATERAL stimulus presentation. The upper and lower panels present the results from two different experiments. FE = first letter errors, LE = last letter errors and OE = other errors. After Hellige et al. (1989).

emerges both hemispheres have access to the same relevant stimulus information is not when determined completely by which single hemisphere has superior ability to perform the task. This finding is clearly reminiscent of the work of Levy and Trevarthen (1976) with commissurotomy patients.

It is interesting to speculate why, on the bilateral trials of the CVC experiments, each cerebral hemisphere did not process the stimulus with which it was presented by using the best mode of processing available to it. As Hellige et al. (1989) argued, this would have produced a qualitative error pattern different from either of the two unilateral patterns and would have further reduced the overall error rate on bilateral trials. One plausible reason is that with bilateral presentation it is inefficient (perhaps impossible) for an intact organism to engage in mutually inconsistent modes of processing at the same time. With respect to the processing of CVCs, it has been argued that when phonetic processing is used there is a very rapid or global distribution of attention across the letters whereas nonlinguistic processing results in a slower, item-by-item sequential distribution of attention (Levy & Kueck, 1986). It may be the difficulty of simultaneously distributing attention in these two different ways that makes it inefficient for both modes of processing to be used at the same time. More generally, the difficulty created by the simultaneous use of mutually inconsistent modes of processing may necessitate a metacontrol mechanism.

CONCLUDING COMMENTS AND DIRECTIONS FOR THE FUTURE

This chapter outlines a technique using bilateral stimulus presentation that shows promise for extending the study of metacontrol to the intact brain. The studies conducted to date all suggest that when both hemispheres receive identical input, the mode of processing characteristic of one hemisphere governs performance. This pattern of results is not a necessary outcome of the bilateral paradigm. In fact, I have outlined elsewhere (Hellige, 1987) other plausible patterns of effects that might be expected and when my colleagues and I began this series of studies we fully expected to encounter some of these patterns. The fact that we have not does not, of course, mean that one or the other hemisphere's preferred mode of processing must always dominate for all tasks. However, given the variety of tasks that have been used it is clear that such patterns are pervasive. It is equally clear that which mode of processing dominates depends on a variety of specific task demands that are only beginning to be investigated. This section considers briefly two of the ways in which investigations of metacontrol might be fruitfully extended.

One way in which it is important to extend the present results is to consider individual differences in the relationship of bilateral performance to performance on RVF-LH and LVF-RH trials. Subjects in all of the experiments reviewed here were right-handed university students. Although the relationship between cerebral laterality (in terms of the relative abilities of the two hemispheres) and handedness is far from perfect, it is the case that left-handers are more heterogeneous with respect to cerebral laterality than are right-handers.

Consequently, the mean results from a group of left handers typically show smaller, less reliable laterality effects than do the corresponding results from a group of right handers. It is possible that handedness is more strongly related to an individual's tendency to rely more on the processes of one hemisphere compared to the other when given a choice. The development of the bilateral paradigm makes it possible to separate such biases from the pattern of hemispheric abilities per se.

Even among right-handed university students there is individual variation both in terms of hemispheric abilities and in terms of whether the qualitative pattern of results on bilateral trials is more similar to the LVF-RH or RVF-LH pattern. In the studies reviewed in this chapter, 75%-85% of the right-handed subjects produced data consistent with the patterns shown in the group means. However, for the remaining subjects the bilateral pattern was more similar to the pattern shown by the visual field (hemisphere) opposite the majority trend. At the present time we do not know whether this individual variation represents random error or whether it reflects meaningful individual differences in patterns of metacontrol and whether such individual differences are related to what others have termed "hemisphericity" (e.g., Kinsbourne, 1982) Given that at least some of the variation among right-handers in hemispheric *superiorities* is reliable across tasks (e.g., Hellige, Bloch, & Taylor, 1988), there is reason to investigate the variability in metacontrol.

Although the logic of the bilateral paradigm has been developed for visual half-field studies, it can be extended in a reasonably straightforward way to other modalities such as dichotic listening and the presentation of tactile information. Such extensions would provide important converging investigation of issues related to metacontrol just as the extension to a variety of modalities has provided converging tests of hypotheses about hemispheric abilities.   In fact, the presentation of tactile information may prove particularly interesting because stimuli are not apprehended all at once. Therefore, measuring the nature and time of tactile exploration with each hand may lead to important insights about hemispheric dominance, hemispheric interaction, and metacontrol.

An important challenge facing cognitive neuropsychologists is to account for the emergence of unified information processing from a brain consisting of a variety of processing subsystems. The left and right cerebral hemispheres may be characterized as two very general subsystems with different processing propensities and biases.   Understanding interhemispheric interaction and the conditions for metacontrol can provide important clues about the emergence of unified information processing. The procedures outlined in this chapter provide a promising behavioral technique for increasing that understanding.

ACKNOWLEDGMENT

The research reported in this chapter was supported in part by Grant BNS - 8908305 from the National Science Foundation and by an Academic Challenge Award from the State of Ohio to the University of Toledo Department of

Psychology which provided a visiting professorship for Dr. Hellige.

REFERENCES

Bagnara, S., Boles, D. B., Simion, F., & Umilta, C. (1983). Symmetry and similarity effects in the comparison of visual patterns. *Perception & Psychophysics, 34*, 578-584.

Bradshaw, J. L., & Nettleton, N. C. (1983). *Human cerebral Asymmetry.* Englewood Cliffs, N J: Prentice-Hall

Egeth, H. E., & Epstein, J. (1972). Differential specialization of the cerebral hemispheres for the perception of sameness and difference. *Perception & Psychophysics, 12*, 218-220.

Farell, B. (1985). Same-different judgments: A review of current controversies in perceptual comparisons. *Psychological Bulletin, 98*, 419-456.

Hellige, J. B. (Editor). (1983). *Cerebral hemisphere asymmetry: Method, theory and application.* New York: Praeger.

Hellige, J. B. (1987). Interhemispheric interaction: Models paradigms and recent findings. In D. Ottoson (Ed.), *Duality and unity of the brain* (pp. 454-456). Hampshire, England: McMillan.

Hellige, J. B., Bloch, M. I., & Taylor, A. K. (1988). Multi-task investigation of individual differences in hemispheric asymmetry. *Journal of Experimental Psychology: Human Perception and Performance, 14*, 176-187.

Hellige, J. B., Jonsson, J. E., & Michimata, C. (1988). Processing from LVF, RVF and BILATERAL Presentations: Metacontrol and interhemispheric interaction. *Brain and Cognition, 7*, 39-53.

Hellige, J. B., & Michimata, C. (1989a). Visual laterality for letter comparison: Effects of stimulus factors, response factors and metacontrol. *Bulletin of the Psychonomic Society, 27*, 441-444.

Hellige, J. B., & Michimata, C. (1989b). Categorization versus distance: Hemispheric differences for processing spatial information. *Memory & Cognition.*

Hellige, J. B., Taylor, A. K., & Eng, T. L. (1989). Interhemispheric interaction when both hemispheres have access to the same stimulus information. *Journal of Experimental Psychology: Human Perception and Performance*, in press.

Kinsbourne, M. (1982). Hemispheric specialization and the growth of human understanding. *American Psychologist, 37*, 411-420.

Kosslyn, S. (1987). Seeing and hearing in the cerebral hemispheres. *Psychological Review, 94*, 148-175.

Levy, J., Heller, W., Banich, M. T., & Burton, L. A. (1983). Are variations among right-handed individuals in perceptual asymmetries caused by characteristic arousal differences between hemispheres? *Journal of Experimental Psychology: Human Perception and Performance, 9*, 329-359.

Levy, J., & Kueck, L. (1986). A right hemispatial advantage on a verbal free-vision task. *Brain and Language, 27*, 24-37.

Levy, J., & Trevarthen, C. (1976). Metacontrol of hemispheric function in human split-brain patients. *Journal of Experimental Psychology: Human Perception and Performance, 2*, 299-312.

Sergent, J. (1982). About face: Left-hemisphere involvement in processing of physiognomies. *Journal of Experimental Psychology: Human Perception and Performance, 8*, 253-272.

Sergent, J. (1984). Configural processing of faces in the left and right cerebral hemispheres. *Journal of Experimental Psychology: Human Perception and Performance, 10*, 554-572.

8 Shadow and Substance: Attentional Irrelevancies and Perceptual Constraints in the Hemispheric Processing of Language Stimuli

Curtis Hardyck
University of California, Berkeley

After a lot of work by a great many researchers over a good many years, we still seem to have no good theoretical model of how interhemispheric transfer is effected and what is transferred. Particularly vexatious is the area of language. The closest approximation extant to a rock-solid finding in the study of human cerebral lateralization is the common finding that language tasks are done more accurately and with greater speed in the right visual field-left hemisphere (RVF-LH) than in the left visual field-right hemisphere (LVF-RH).

In a field noted for the instability of many of its findings, this constancy of language studies is all the more striking. When the results of research on a language task done within visual half-fields is reported, we are quite safe in assuming that an RVF-LH advantage will be found, regardless of the particular parameters of the investigation. Despite the development of interesting models of transfer such as that proposed by Moscovitch (1986), we still lack a linkage between theory and data for language transfer processes.

Our own investigations (for a detailed account of this work, see Hardyck, Chiarello, Dronkers, & Simpson, 1985) have focused on the influence of attentional allocation on language processing within visual fields, work initially stimulated by a hypothesis put forth by Bryden. Bryden (1978) argued quite convincingly that lateralization researchers tended to place too much reliance on interpretations of observed cerebral lateralization differences as indicative of structural differences in the brain. Before concluding that structural differences account for our observations, we should be certain that other equally plausible explanations have been eliminated. Bryden suggested that attentional bias, perhaps related to handedness, could account for many of the observed asymmetries, and went on to justify his position by reporting data on dichotic listening offering strong support for the idea that attentional bias could account for much of the variance in hemisphere differences. Our goal was to determine whether similar biases could explain many of the differences found in visual field phenomena.

In our examination of this problem, we were influenced considerably by the work of Posner (Posner, 1978, 1980; Posner, Snyder, & Davidson, 1980) and his colleagues on the fundamental parameters of attention. However, Posner's work centered around the study of attentional allocation to relatively simple sensory detection tasks--tasks that we did not expect to show hemisphere differences.

For our work , we selected the lexical decision task--deciding whether or not a letter string is an English word. It is well established as a measure of access to the internal lexicon and is easily scaled for degrees of difficulty. Our words were taken from the norms of Toglia and Battig (1978) and had high ratings on imagery, concreteness, and familiarity. Our nonwords were all pronounceable and consonant with the rules of English orthography. Figures 8.1a and 8.1b illustrate the type of word and nonword stimuli used in our studies. Stimuli are set 2.0 deg of visual angle from the fixation point and span a horizontal distance of 2.0 deg.

In our first experiment, we began by establishing a baseline of performance to letter strings presented randomly for 100 msec. to the right or left of a fixation point. We found stable differences in accuracy of judgement with a 20% advantage in the RVF-LH. Following the establishment of this baseline, we then asked subjects to try and improve performance to stimuli presented to the left (or right) of the fixation point.

Manipulations of attention without concern for possible subject bias in eye movements are made possible by use of an eye movement monitor interfaced to the computer that controls the stimulus display. We sample eye position every 16 msec and if the subject is not fixated on the defined point, the stimulus item is not

(a)   **HUMOT**

(b)   **MONEY**

FIGURES 8.1A. and 8.1B. (A) Sample non word letter string positioned in the left visual field-right hemisphere. (B) Sample word letter string positioned in the right visual field-left hemisphere.

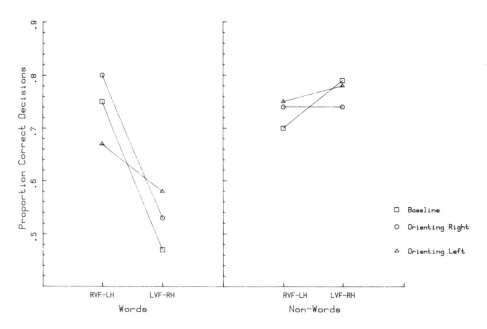

FIGURE 8.2. Experiment 1. Response accuracy within visual fields for baseline, orienting right instruction, and orienting left instruction conditions (RVF-LH = right visual field-left hemisphere. LVF-RH = left visual field-right hemisphere)

shown until a stable fixation is achieved. This allows us to manipulate attentional bias conditions without fear of introducing involuntary eye shifts. The results of attempting to induce an attentional bias through instruction are shown in Figure 8.2.

Our first interpretation of these results was that attention seemed shiftable to the left but not to the right. However, this finding turned out to be more apparent than real, because our analysis of variance indicated a complete lack of any interaction of condition with visual field. Instructing subjects to bias their attention in a given direction has no discernible effect on accuracy. Interestingly, there is an effect attributable to attentional bias instruction present in reaction time. The mean reaction times for RVF-LH and LVF-RH for baseline performance are .955 and .1,125 ms. Under instructions to improve performance in the RVF-LH, the mean reaction times are .715 and .816, essentially unchanged in relative level from the baseline performance. However, when subjects are given instructions to improve performance to stimuli appearing to the left of the fixation point, RVF-LH mean time is .825 and LVF-RH is .823. We interpret this as evidence that our instructions did have an attentional effect, but only on speed of response. Basically, subjects took less time to produce the same error rate found in the baseline condition.

It will have been noted that nonwords do not display the same response patterns as do words. For nonwords, accuracy of identification is about the same in both visual fields. Discussion of this result will be delayed until other experimental results are presented.

A logical next step was to consider the possibility that attention shifting might be facilitated by the use of some cue location information. To test this we replaced our central fixation point with an indicator of location of the next trial item.

In this experiment, after the establishment of a baseline performance of 200 trials randomly to the right or the left of a central fixation point, subjects saw either a right-pointing or a left-pointing indicator. They were told that the direction indicated was the location of the next letter string and that the indicators were always correct. This had no more real effect than instructing subjects to do better on the right or left. Results are shown in Figure 8.3.

Having a perfectly valid cue as to the location of the next stimulus item is no help at all in making accurate judgments about the nature of that stimulus.

The possibility then had to be considered that timing was critical--that the interval between when our cue was presented and the stimulus appeared was somehow not optimal for the allocating of attention. One possible experimental manipulation would be to remove the need to allocate attention other than as a fixed choice for a longer period of time. To test this, we carried out another

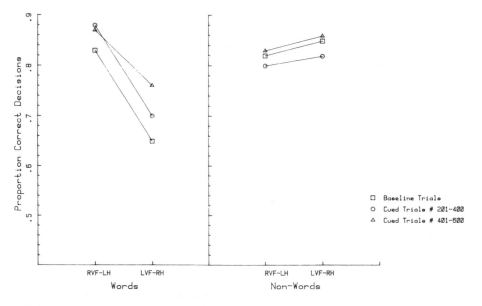

FIGURE 8.3. Experiment 2. Response accuracy within visual fields for baseline and position cued conditions. (RVF-LH = right visual field-left hemisphere. LVF-RH = left visual field-right hemisphere)

experiment where, following the establishment of the customary baseline, trials were run in blocks of 200 trials either to the right or the left of the fixation point This was not at all effective, as can be seen in Figure 8.4.

As an aid to accuracy of judgments, knowing exactly where an item will appear is of almost no help at all over random right-left presentations. Right and left visual field differences in accuracy in the lexical decision task are not affected at a level sufficiently beyond chance expectations by instructions, changing cues, or fixed locations. As a final confirmation of this, we ran two more experiments. In our fourth experiment, we simply ran 600 trials with no instructions other than how to do the task. The results are shown in Figure 8.5.

Information gained from this experiment is (a) that our earlier fears about the ineffectiveness of our experimental manipulations were entirely justified, and (b) subjects doing the same thing for 600 trials show the effects of boredom around the 400th+ trial.

Our last experiment in this series was an examination of the effects of nonspecific exhortation. Subjects in this experiment, after finishing the baseline trials, were urged to try and do better, but with no specifics as to where or how to do better. This produced the result shown in Figure 8.6.

As a criterion experiment for demonstrating lack of interactive effects,

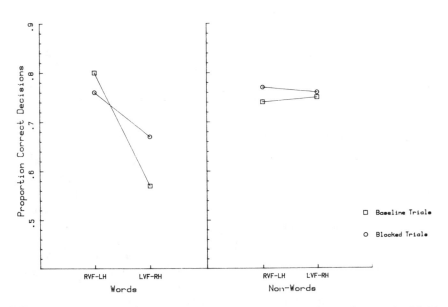

FIGURE 8.4. Experiment 3. Response accuracy in each visual field for baseline and visual field blocked conditions. (RVF-LH = right visual field-left hemisphere. LVF-RH = left visual field-right hemisphere).

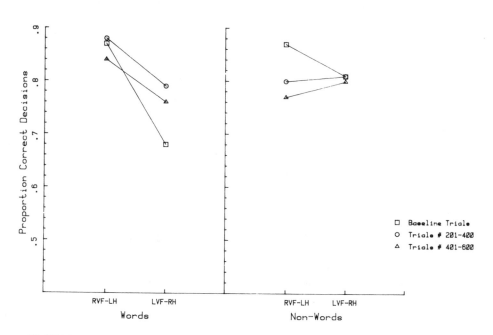

FIGURE 8.5. Experiment 4. Response accuracy within visual fields across trial blocks in the absence of attentional instructions. (RVF-LH = right visual field-left hemisphere. LVF-RH = left visual field-right hemisphere).

this last experiment is hard to surpass. In Figure 8.7, the baseline and experimental performance for all five experiments are shown, scaled to a common metric. It is evident that all attempted manipulations of accuracy are ineffective and that differences present are limited to simple practice effects.

Given these above results, it seems fairly clear that attempts to manipulate attention in language tasks do not produce improvements in accuracy of identification.

Does this mean that attention in tasks of this sort is not allocatable? Posner took an interesting position on this question. He argued that if a complex cognitive task is to be performed, attention will be focused on the task and not on the spatial location where the task is to be found (Posner, 1980). Perhaps so. However, our reaction- time analysis, especially for the first experiment, suggests to us that attention was successfully manipulated. Under the baseline conditions in the first experiment, reaction times were considerably faster to the RVF-LH. When we asked subjects to do better to items on the right, there was no essential change in reaction time from the baseline condition. When subjects were asked to try and improve their performance to items on the left, the reaction times for right and left visual fields were virtually identical. This suggests to us that attentional manipulations were effective, but had no effect on accuracy.

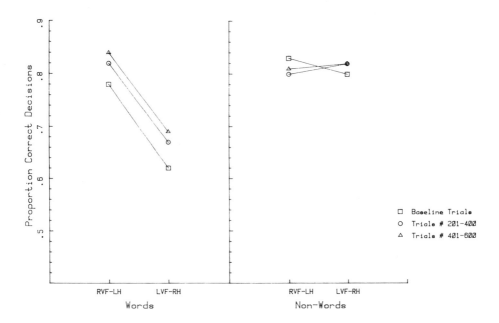

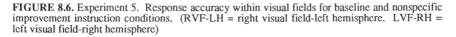

FIGURE 8.6. Experiment 5. Response accuracy within visual fields for baseline and nonspecific improvement instruction conditions. (RVF-LH = right visual field-left hemisphere. LVF-RH = left visual field-right hemisphere)

Left unexplained are the nonword data. How do we construct an explanation that allows substantial hemisphere differences in ability to recognize a letter string as an English word and simultaneously allows nonword discrimination to be equally good and extremely accurate in both hemispheres ?

If we carry out signal-detection analyses on the data of these five experiments, we find that the difference between right- and left-hemisphere performance is due almost entirely to failures in the LVF-RH to recognize words as words. The converse does not happen-non words are not categorized more frequently as words. In both visual fields, the percentage of nonwords categorized as words is around .12%, averaged over all experiments. In contrast, the percentage of words labeled as nonwords is 20% higher in the LVF.

It was at this point that we began to consider more seriously a theoretical position that we had earlier thought highly improbable--the viewpoint advanced by Friedman and Polson (1981; Friedman, Polson, Dafoe, and Gaskill, 1982) that the human cerebral hemispheres can be conceptualized as two independent resource systems operating in parallel, with each system totally dependent on its own resources and unable to call on the resources of the other hemisphere. In this framework, each hemisphere can do any task , but differences in hemisphere performance reflect differences in resources available within the hemispheres. If we apply the Friedman-Polson formulation to the data of the five experiments just

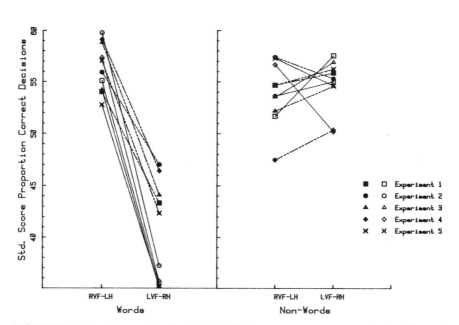

FIGURE 8.7. Experiments 1-5. Standardized (Std) response accuracy scores for baseline and experimental conditions. (Open symbols represent baseline conditions; filled symbols represent experimental conditions).

reported, we can develop a model in which language information entering a given visual-field hemisphere is processed within that hemisphere using only the resources present in that hemisphere. Interhemispheric transfer seems to be limited to information about the end decision.

This application of the Friedman-Polson model requires two lexicons that use the same decision rules (if a word cannot be found in the lexicon, decide that it is not a word), but that differ considerably in size.

Improbable or not, this particular model can be tested. If the assumption is made, consistent with the Friedman-Polson model, that each hemisphere processes the language initially received in the appropriate visual field, doubling the workload should produce a decrement in overall performance, but no change in relative hemispheric performance. If all language processing is carried out in the left hemisphere, then RVF-LH performance should drop drastically under conditions of a double workload

As a test of this model, we carried out two experiments in which two stimuli were shown simultaneously, with one stimulus item in each visual field. Following the stimulus display, an indicator appeared signifying which item of the two was to be answered. The subject had to view both items, and remember them, but had to make only one response. Under these conditions, if processing is done in the visual- field hemisphere where the stimuli are initially received, the performance should be at a lower level than the baseline performance but should

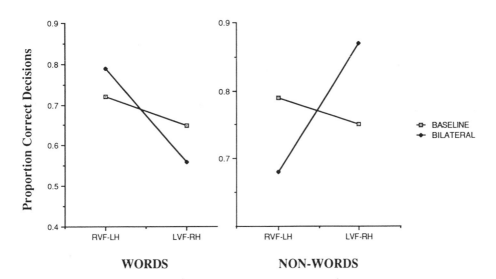

FIGURE 8.8. Response accuracy within visual fields (baseline condition) and between visual fields (bilateral presentation condition). (RVF-LH = right visual field-left hemisphere. LVF-RH = left visual field-right hemisphere)

maintain the same relative level of accuracy within visual fields.

The effects of displaying two stimuli simultaneously, one in each visual field, are shown in Figure 8.8.

These results are exactly in accord with what we expect in a system where resources cannot be shared. However, an entirely appropriate criticism of this study was made by Bertelson (1986), who pointed out that a really adequate test of this hypothesis would test pairs of stimuli within each visual field as well as between. We repeated this study including conditions where two stimuli are presented in each visual field as well as one in each visual field. The conditions were the same as before. Two stimuli were presented simultaneously followed by an indicator specifying the stimulus requiring the lexical decision.

We can see in Figure 8.9 that doubling the workload intrahemispherically substantially lowers the level of performance accuracy for both right and left hemispheres. However, the relative performance difference--right and left-- remains quite similar to that found in the baseline condition.

Given the cumulative negative results of our efforts to explain hemisphere differences as the effect of attentional bias, we thought it appropriate to begin examination of another aspect of our data. Because our findings are in general supportive of the concept of two separate and unequal lexicons, we have

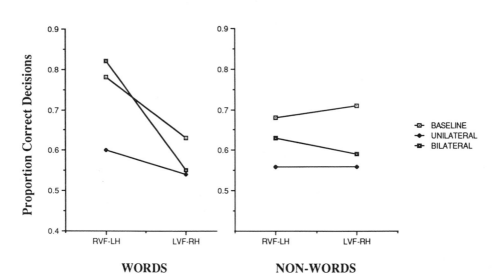

FIGURE 8.9. Response accuracy within visual fields for single presentation (baseline), dual presentation (unilateral) and between visual fields (bilateral).(RVF-LH = right visual field-left hemisphere. LVF-RH = left visual field-right hemisphere).

turned our efforts in this direction.

One of our first efforts was suggested by a linguist colleague--Catherine O'Connor--who suggested to us that if our idea of two lexicons with no sharing of information was correct, subjects exposed to a repeated series of lexical decision tasks should on a repeated series, judge the same items to be correct and mistake the same items as in the first showing. An illustration of the logic is provided by the expectations for a standard vocabulary test. A subject missing some words and having no opportunity to learn new vocabulary should make the same errors on a repeat of the vocabulary test. To test this, we had eight of our subjects who participated in the dual- stimulus experiment return a month later and repeat the baseline condition, consisting of 200 trials with single stimuli appearing to the right or left. In repeating this condition we used the identical order given these subjects at the time they participated in the dual stimulus experiment.

Given the fact that accuracy for both words and nonwords is quite high in the RVF for both the initial and the repeated sessions, the degree of agreement will naturally be quite high. Of greatest interest here is the agreement between the initial and repeated sessions for the LVF for words only, because the level of performance for words is sufficiently low (.62) to allow substantial change to appear. Two assumptions are made here. The first, relevant to the separate lexicons hypothesis, is that there will not have been any great change in the right-hemisphere lexicon in the 1-month interval between the experiments.

The second, more problematical assumption, refers to an alternate hypothesis that can be put forth--the callosal transfer with some loss of information hypothesis that is still a viable alternative explanation. It seems reasonable to argue that an information loss hypothesis must be a random one--that there is nothing systematic about information loss during transmission across the corpus callosum. On the basis of this hypothesis we assume that if callosal transfer of language information complete with errors in transmission is taking place, there should be relatively little agreement for errors--words not recognized at one time might be recognized on a second trial and some words correctly identified the first time might be missed on the second trial. What we find over these eight subjects is an average agreement of .77, this being the combined agreements of correctly identified and wrongly identified over both experiments. When compared to the kinds of reliabilities found for test-retest in vocabulary tests., reliabilities in the range of .78-.84 are found, offering reasonable support for our results. Subjects perform on a repetition of a lexical task with remarkable consistency in repeating correct and incorrect judgments.

A different approach has been used by Zoe Kersteen-Tucker (1988). She is examining the question of information redundancy in making visual field decisions.   Her approach has been to provide more information within the left visual field in an effort to produce similar levels of performance on the lexical decision tasks. The assumptions made are quite similar to those made in the repeated series just described. If a word is not present within a lexicon and there is no communication to another larger lexicon, then repeated exposures to a letter string will not produce much improvement in accuracy. However, if failure to identify a letter string correctly on one exposure is due to transmission errors, then a repeated exposure should produce a correct decision.

Her first experimental condition allowed subjects to signal that they would like a repeated showing of a letter string. Conditions were the same as for the initial exposure, requiring fixation before the stimulus display was shown.

Our expectations were that the number of requests for repeat exposures would be much higher for the LVF. We expected that this would reduce the difference in relative performance between the hemispheres, although we had no specific prediction about the extent. Early in our series, we found that subjects were asking for RVF repeats more often than for LVF and that the relative performance level was increasing rather than decreasing.   When we asked subjects why they did not ask for LVF repeats, the most common comment was "It's no help!".

We then went to a condition where each RVF trial is shown once and each LVF trial twice (again requiring that fixation be maintained before receiving the second exposure). Although this experiment is still in progress, it is evident that LVF performance is improved, but is still not equivalent to RVF performance. We are currently debating whether to go to a condition where we do three, four or even more exposures of an item in the LVF. Under these sorts of conditions, if we can never achieve equivalent performance between the hemispheres, I think we can then argue that whatever is transferred across the corpus callosum, it is not language--at least not in much detail.

Another way to examine the problem of interhemispheric transfer is to use conditions where transfer of information must take place in order for the subject to make a judgment. In this experiment, we again used the lexical decision stimuli presented as in the experiments discussed earlier, but two letter strings are shown either within a visual field or with one item in each visual field. The basic procedure is identical to the dual item experiment presented earlier. However, the judgment the subject has to make is a same-different judgment about the pair of stimuli. If both stimuli are words, or both are nonwords, the judgment is "same." If one item is a word and the other a nonword, the judgment is "different."

The condition of most interest here is of course, the interhemispheric condition, with one item in each visual field. If information is transferred and judgments made in the left hemisphere, then performance in the interhemispheric condition should equal performance in the RVF. If there is no communication between hemispheres other than the decision reached, then the circumstances are equivalent to conditions where two judges must agree on a decision--a condition where accuracy can be no better than that achieved by the worst judge.

Let me review the model used. We are arguing that both hemispheres use the same rules in reaching a decision about the status of a letter string--if you cannot find it in your lexicon, decide that it is not a word-- and that differences in hemisphere performance reflect differences in the sizes of these lexicons. The difference in performance accuracy between the hemispheres consists almost entirely of LVF decisions that a stimulus is not a word. Decisions that a nonword is a word are made with equal frequency by both hemispheres and average 12% in our earlier work.

This means that accuracy on interhemispheric trials must be analyzed into two parts. Those trials where both items are words and those trials where the item in the LVF is a word should have more errors than those trials where both items are nonwords or where the item in the LVF is a nonword. In this condition--both words or a word in the LVF--the accuracy rate should approximate the LVF accuracy rate for words. In the second condition both nonwords or a nonword in the LVF--the accuracy rate should approximate the accuracy rate found in both RVF and LVF for nonwords.

As we can see in Figure 8.10a and 8.10b, this is almost exactly what happens. In Figure 8.10a, we can see the proportions of correct decisions made in the RVF, the LVF and the bilateral condition. The average accuracy rate for the bilateral condition is virtually identical to the accuracy rate for the LVF--a result exactly to be expected if agreement between two judges has as an upper limit, the performance of the least accurate judge. When we break the bilateral data into the conditions described earlier, we obtain the result. shown in Figure 8.10b. To a remarkable degree, the results for the bilateral condition when separated into two components, parallel the results for the RVF and LVF.

The material presented to this point offers a fair amount of supportive evidence for the hypothesis of two lexicons, one to each hemisphere, with what appears to be little useful interchange of information. Given the data accumulated to date, can we eliminate the hypothesis that all verbal processing is done in the left hemisphere and that poor performance on material first input to the LVF-RH is due to errors in transmission from the RH to the LH? Other than citing Cohen's (1982) position that it is difficult to conceive of a system that allows sensory end-organ transmissions of remarkable fidelity, but does not permit accurate internal transmission, this explanation cannot be eliminated.

However, another way to place the interhemispheric transfer hypothesis at risk is to eliminate as far as possible, data-limited experiments. In the experiments reported so far, stimuli subtended approximately 2.0 deg of visual angle, were located 2.5 deg from a fixation point and were exposed for 100 msec. They can hardly be described as other than data limited. It seems necessary to examine data limitations as closely as possible as a first step in trying to differentiate between the two hypotheses .

One obvious sensory limitation is size and clarity of display. I have mentioned before, in other contexts (Hardyck, 1983) that in some ways, we all do the same experiment. When the perceptual laterality literature is reviewed and the parameters of different experiments compared, the extent to which we use the same parameters is quite striking. We all tend to use the same size displays with similar kinds of typefaces and similar placements of eccentricity from the point of

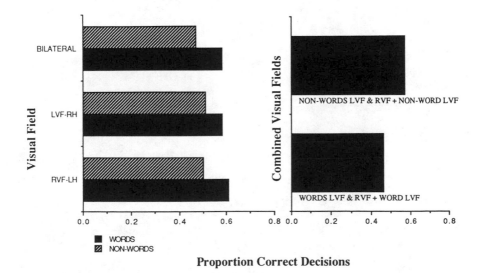

Proportion Correct Decisions

FIGURE 8.10A and B. (A). (left) Response accuracy within and between visual fields for judgements of pairs of letter strings as "same (both words or non words) or "different" (one word and one non word) (RVF-LH = right visual field-left hemisphere. LVF-RH = left visual field-right hemisphere). (B). (right) Response accuracy when visual fields are combined to represent within visual field accuracy rates for bilateral presentations.

fixation.

As a first step in examining the effects of sensory limitations, we repeated one of our earlier lexical decision experiments varying size and spatial frequency. Our original attention work was done with stimuli prepared as slides and projected to a back screen. When we went to video based displays, we did try some work with stimuli as shown in Figure 8.11.

Use of this type of fuzzy display produces a marked effect on visual field differences, diminishing the differences usually found with language stimuli. The data collected using this display have not been reported and there are no plans to do so, given the high attenuation of visual field differences found with use of this kind of display.

Using a high-resolution video display--in our case a Digital VR260 with pixel density of 824 x 1024, we can do sharp edge displays that are directly comparable to earlier work, as shown in Figure 8.12 using both a 40 point size covering 3 deg of visual angle (shown in Figure 12) and a 66 point size which covers 5 degrees of visual angle..

Does size make any difference in visual field performance? Yes, but not in a way that helps right hemisphere performance. Results of another lexical

FIGURE 8.11. Display quality of standard video with pixel density of 12 (vertical) x 16 (horizontal) per centimeter.

decision experiment in which we varied both stimulus size and high-pass spatial frequencies revealed the following effects for size, as shown in Figure 8.13.

The net effect of boosting size and thus providing some amplification of lower spatial frequencies, is to improve RVF-LH performance relative to LVF-RH performance. Clearly, large high-quality displays help, but they help the visual field in which performance is already superior.

Relatively little work has been done on the effects of spatial frequency manipulation on language. As we know from the excellent work done by Sergent (1983,1985), spatial frequency filtering has been shown to have hemisphere-specific effects when applied to the problems of face recognition. Attempts to find similar correlations for language stimuli have not been very successful, although the majority of studies using language stimuli have been low pass filtered or perhaps low-pass emphasis studies, where lower spatial frequencies are emphasized by increasing the stimulus size or by blurring the stimuli so as to attenuate the higher spatial frequencies. Usually, what happens in these experiments is that LVF-RH performance is not improved, but RVF-LH performance deteriorates. It is some support for the spatial frequency hypothesis but not very good support.

FIGURE 8.12. Display quality of computer video display with pixel density of 30 (vertical) x 45 (horizontal) per centimeter. Display shown in figure is 66 point type spanning 5 degrees of visual angle at a viewing distance of 123 cm.

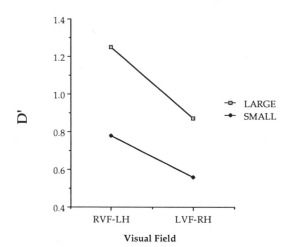

Figure 8.13. Signal detection accuracy within visual fields as a function of size of stimulus display (Large = 66 point type spanning 5 degrees of visual angle at a viewing distance of 123 cm. Small = 40 point type spanning 3 degrees of visual angle at a viewing distance of 123 cm. RVF-LH = right visual field-left hemisphere. LVF-RH = left visual field-right hemisphere).

To date, at least to my knowledge, there are no published studies of high-pass filtering on language stimuli We were fortunate to recently acquire both appropriate computing hardware and the necessary software to allow digital filtering of our language stimuli. For example the fonts used in the present experiment, when low-pass filtered to remove all cycles per picture width (cppw) above 13, appear as shown in Figure 8.14. and as in Figure 8.15 when filtered to remove all cppw below 40. What effect do these filtered stimuli have on lexical decision performance? We would expect that LVF-RH performance would be most affected because the computational filtering process removes those frequencies that are apparently most efficiently processed in the right hemisphere. Results are shown in Figure 8.16.

Neither the size or the frequency effects are effective in enhancing performance of the RVF-LH relative to the LVF-RH. High-pass filtering has just as damaging an effect on performance in the RVF-LH as does low-pass filtering. Left-hemisphere language-processing mechanisms resemble a high-performance engine extremely sensitive to the quality of fuel provided. Use low octane fuel and you have extremely poor performance. Provide super grade high octane fuel and you get superb performance. Right-hemisphere mechanisms by contrast, resemble low-speed diesel engines that deliver a limited level of performance, but can maintain that performance on almost any kind of low grade combustible fuel.

Can some reasonable fraction of visual-field differences in language tasks be attributed to exposure time? One hundred and eighty msec is as long as we normally allow in visual field experiments, but it is scarcely conducive to

FIGURE 8.14. Digitally filtered letter string in 40 point type with all frequencies removed above 13 cycles per picture width of 5.08 cm.

FIGURE 8.15. Digitally filtered letter string in 40 point type with all frequencies removed below 40 cycles per picture width of 5.08 cm.

leisurely viewing. We have completed two lexical decision experiments with differing exposure times; one with an exposure time of 700 msec, the other with an exposure time of 150 msec. The long exposure-time experiment was done by sampling eye position every 16 msec and discarding those trials where the subject was not able to maintain fixation for the trial duration. Did a long exposure time help? Results are shown in Figure 8.17.

The answer is yes, but the help is present where it is least needed. There seems to be nothing that can be done to bring right hemisphere performance up to left hemisphere performance. In an experiment currently underway in which we are trying 600 msec in both visual fields, 150 msec in both visual fields and two differential conditions--one being 600 in the LVF and 150 in the RVF, the other being the reverse of the one just described, results midway through data collection still indicate an RVF-LH superiority, despite the drastically longer exposure times for the LVF-RH.

I have two messages with end this chapter. The first is that we have paid too much attention to the message and not enough to the medium in which it is transmitted Variations in stimulus quality make a great deal of difference and this difference does not seem to be hemisphere independent, nor is it easily predictable. Who would have expected that high-pass and low-pass filtering would produce the same effects for language, when we have seen so clearly what the effects of low-pass filtering are on face recognition?

What explanation will suffice for the observed differences in performance in face recognition and language recognition? The first possibility that occurs to me is that the same phenomenon may actually be present in face recognition

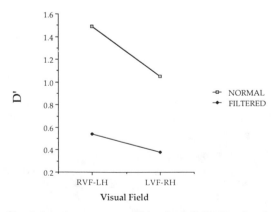

FIGURE 8.16. Signal detection accuracy within visual fields as a function of digital spatial frequency filtering. (Normal = average of 40 point and 66 point unfiltered displays. Filtered = average of 66 point and 40 point type with all frequencies below 40 cycles per picture width removed. RVF-LH = right visual field-left hemisphere. LVF-RH = left visual field-right hemisphere).

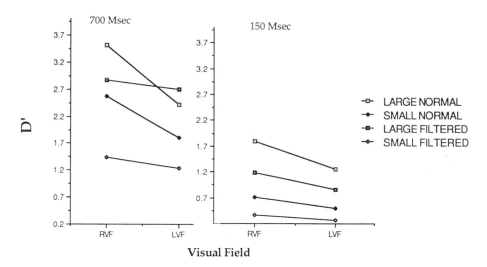

FIGURE 8.17. Signal detection accuracy within visual fields as a function of size of display, spatial frequency filtering and exposure time. (Large Normal = 66 point type, unfiltered. Small Normal = 40 point type, unfiltered. Large Filtered = 66 point type with all frequencies below 40 cycles per picture width removed. Small Filtered = 40 point type with all frequencies below 40 cycles per picture width removed (RVF-LH = right visual field-left hemisphere. LVF-RH = left visual field-right hemisphere).

because we do not yet, to my knowledge, have a face-recognition experiment with high-pass filtering. If we find no RVF-LH advantages for recognition of faces under high-pass filtering conditions, we will have to raise questions about the generality of the spatial frequency-hemisphere hypothesis.

Another possibility is that frequency effects are present, but are detectable only in those phenomena where near-equivalent hemispheric performance is possible. As evidence for this point, it can be noted that the commissurotomy patients who participated in the Levy, Trevarthen, and Sperry (1972) chimeric faces experiment were equally good at recognizing faces with either hemisphere, differing in mode of response, but not in accuracy of performance. In this context, I might mention that prosopagnosia does not exist without bilateral damage , but language can be relatively unaffected with severe right- hemisphere damage.

The second message harks back to the point I began with concerning the nature of language processing. We have the argument I put forth that both hemispheres contain lexicons of differing sizes that do not interact. The venerable alternative is that all language is processed in the left hemisphere, right hemisphere input suffering from the long, arduous and difficult journey across the corpus callosum. The critical experiment has yet to be done, or perhaps even invented. However, I would like to raise an explanatory issue that evolves from the data I have presented here. If the argument that right hemisphere language processing appears poorer because of degradation during transfer, then this explanation should take into account the paradoxical circumstances that when we degrade the stimulus input ourselves before subjecting it to the collosal journey, the effect is somehow less than when we input directly to the left hemisphere. In every condition, stimulus degradation has less impact on right-hemisphere input than on left- hemisphere input. It seems to me that to explain this, we would have to postulate a self-cancelling error process that works very systematically under some conditions but not in others or argue that right-hemisphere processing has deleterious effects on good quality stimuli, but not on poor quality stimuli.

If I am to argue for a position of two separate unequal and noninteracting lexicons, I should be prepared to answer the objection that two lexicons of the type I describe is neither a sensible or efficient design. Granted, if any of us had been retained as a consultant on the design of people, we would probably not have come up with a design of the type I am advocating here. However, we are accumulating increasing amounts of evidence that evolution may not always produce a grand design but may often settle for an ad hoc solution that gets the job done under most circumstances.   Several researchers have advanced such arguments. Dawkins (1986) has provided one of the more detailed expositions in his recent book *The Blind Watchmaker*. Within the field of psychology, the best known advocate of this position is Ramachandran (1985) with his "utility theory." I have no direct evidence I can offer for this point of view. However, I end by arguing that the idea of two lexicons has a lot going for it as an explanation that accounts for the data in a reasonably straightforward manner.

ACKNOWLEDGMENTS

I would like to express my appreciation to Zoe Kersteen-Tucker, Paul Lebby, and Xiao Lan for their help in carrying out several of the experiments described here and for their thoughtful criticisms.

REFERENCES

Bertelson, P. (1986, June). What is transferred? And under what circumstances? Discussion presented in The Symposium on Theoretical Models of Interhemispheric Transfer, *International Neuropsychology Society*, Aachen, Germany, June 25-28.
Bryden, M.P. (1978). Attentional factors in the detection of hemispheric asymmetries. In G. Underwood (Ed.) *Strategies of information processing* (pp. 571-582). New York: Academic Press.
Cohen, G. (1982). Theoretical interpretations of lateral asymmetries. In J. G. Beaumont (Ed.) *Divided visual field studies of cerebral organization* (87-111). London: Academic Press.
Dawkins, R. (1986). *The blind watchmaker*. New York: Norton.
Friedman, A., & Polson, M. C. (1981). Hemispheres as independent resource

systems: Limited-capacity processing and cerebral specialization. *Journal of Experimental Psychology, Human Perception and Performance*, *7*, 1031-1058.

Friedman, A., Polson, M.C., Dafoe, C., & Gaskill, S. (1982). Dividing attention within and between hemispheres: Evidence for two modes of stimulus analysis. *Journal of Experimental Psychology: Human Perception and Performance*, *8*, 625-650.

Hardyck, C. (1983). Seeing each other's points of view: Visual perceptual lateralization. In J. B. Hellige   (Ed.) *Cerebral hemisphere asymmetry: Method, theory and research*. New York: Praeger.

Hardyck, C., Chiarello, C., Dronkers, N.F., & Simpson, G.V. (1985). Orienting attention within visual fields: How effective is interhemispheric transfer? *Journal of Experimental Psychology: Human Perception and Performance*, *11*, 650-666.

Kersteen-Tucker, Z. (1988). *Effects of repeated stimulus exposure on lateralized lexical decisions*. Unpublished manuscript.

Levy, J., Trevarthen, C., & Sperry, R.W. (1972). Perception of bilateral chimeric figures following hemisphere deconnection. *Brain*, *95*, 61-78.

Moscovitch, M.   (1986). Afferent and efferent models of visual perceptual asymmetries. *Neuropsychologica*, *24*(1), 91-114.

Posner, M. I. (1978). *Chronometric explorations of mind*. Hillsdale, NJ: Lawrence Erlbaum Associates.

Posner, M. I. (1980). Orienting of attention. *Quarterly Journal of Experimental Psychology*, *32*, 3-25.

Posner, M. I., Snyder, C. R. R., & Davidson, B. J. (1980). Attention and the detection of signals. *Journal of Experimental Psychology: General, 109*, 160-174.

Ramachandran, V.S. (1985). The neurobiology of perception. (guest editorial). *Perception*, *14*(2), 97-103

Sergent, J. (1983). Role of the input in visual hemisphere asymmetries. *Psychological Bulletin. 93*, 481-512.

Sergent, J. (1985). Influence of task and input factors on hemispheric involvement in face processing. *Journal of Experimental Psychology: Human Perception and Performance*, *11*, 846-861.

Toglia, M. P., & Battig, W. (1978). *Handbook of Semantic Word Norms*. Hillsdale, NJ: Lawrence Erlbaum Associates.

9 The Use of Computer Models in the Study of Cerebral Lateralization

Michael H. Van Kleeck
Massachusetts Institute of Technology

Stephen M. Kosslyn
Harvard University

Since its 19th-century beginnings in the work of neuropsychologists such as Paul Broca and John Hughlings Jackson, the study of human cerebral asymmetry has grown into a large and flourishing field of investigation that draws on a wide variety of modern experimental and biomedical procedures. Many of these procedures rely on the digital computer, which has proven invaluable in neuropsychological applications ranging from computer-controlled stimulus presentation to computerized imaging of brain structure and function. There is one application of computers, however, that has been conspicuous by its absence from studies of cerebral asymmetry: computer modeling. Despite its wide use and proven value in cognitive psychology (not to mention numerous other scientific fields), computer modeling has rarely been used in cognitive neuropsychological studies of laterality (for an exception, see Kosslyn, Sokolov, & Chen, 1989). This chapter is to illustrate the ways in which computer models can make contributions to investigations of hemispheric functional asymmetry.

The chapter is divided into two parts. In the first, we discuss general issues involved in computer modeling: the benefits of computer models, constraints on theories and models, and the appropriateness of different kinds of models for different levels of analysis. This section includes a brief, non-technical introduction to types of models, including the parallel distributed processing (PDP) models that have recently received so much attention in cognitive psychology, computer science, and cognitive neuroscience (Anderson & Rosenfeld, 1988; Feldman, 1985; Grossberg, 1988; McClelland & Rumelhart, 1986b; Rumelhart & McClelland, 1986b). In the second part, we illustrate the concepts and techniques reviewed in the first part by discussing existing and prospective applications of computer modeling to such topics as the development of lateralization, functional asymmetry in the normal adult brain, individual differences in cerebral asymmetry, the relationship of functional asymmetries to the consequences of brain damage, the structural substrate of lateral differences, and the computational consequences of hemispheric specialization.

155

GENERAL ISSUES IN COMPUTER MODELING

Several general issues are relevant to the use of computer models in the study of laterality. These issues include the practical benefits of computer modeling, the necessity of motivating and constraining computer models, and the relationship between levels of analysis and types of models.

Practical Benefits

Computer modeling provides a number of benefits to theoreticians and experimentalists. First, the use of a computer model encourages a careful, precise analysis of the phenomena that are to be modeled, including an explicit formulation of theoretical assumptions. Computers cannot be programmed by handwaving, nor will they gloss over inconsistencies. Furthermore, just as computer models force the theorist to formulate assumptions explicitly, they also generate explicit predictions in the form of simulation output. Second, computer models can be used to simulate experiments that would be technically difficult or ethically problematic. Third, computer models are easily scrutinized, measured, and manipulated. The internal workings of the model are open to inspection, analysis, and modification, and the output of the model is explicit and quantifiable. Thus the modeler can easily collect detailed information on all aspects of the model, by performing a series of controlled, replicable simulations that systematically vary theoretically critical assumptions and parameters.The benefits of computer modeling, however, are not without parallel dangers. Once a computer program has been written that successfully accomplishes some task, it is tempting to view the program as tantamount to a proof of the implicit theory of the cognitive structures and processes actually used to accomplish the task. But there may have been many alternative models that could have accomplished the task equally well; computers are extremely flexible devices that can be programmed in a variety of ways to achieve the same outcome. It is therefore dangerous to view a program as a cognitively and biologically valid theory of processing simply because the program works. Additional constraints are essential.

Constraints on Theories and Models

Three types of considerations are particularly important as constraints on theories of cognitive processing and on the computer models that embody those theories: behavioral, neurobiological, and computational.

Behavioral Constraints. Behavioral constraints are primary in the sense that they describe the phenomena that must be accounted for by the theory embodied in a computer model. Although there may be numerous models that can produce the requisite behavior, at least as many typically cannot. Thus, the behavioral abilities to be explained serve as constraints: They narrow down the class of acceptable models. These constraints simply consist of the abilities that the brain has and hence that the working model must display. In a complete model of visual cognition, for example, the behavioral abilities that must be accounted for include object recognition, visual imagery, navigation, and tracking of moving objects.

Neurobiological Constraints. Neurobiological (neuroanatomical and neurophysiological) evidence also serves as an important constraint on the theories embodied in computer models. Neuroanatomical evidence includes facts about structure at macrolevels (e.g., corresponding to lobes and major pathways) and microlevels (e.g., differences in cell types and synaptic structures). Neurophysiological evidence includes facts about the chemical and electrical properties of cells, obtained by such methods as single-cell recording. Neurobiological evidence helps us to formulate neurologically plausible theories and to develop computer models that mimic actual neural subsystems.

Computational Constraints. A third type of constraint on theories and computer models derives from a computational analysis of what kinds of information processing would be necessary to build a device that behaves as does the brain (cf. Marr, 1982). A computational analysis produces a set of candidate "computations," which in principle can take the available input and produce the requisite output. A computation is a systematic, informationally interpretable transformation of input to output. Theorists often posit that a computation or set of related computations are carried out by a *processing subsystem*, which is simply a group of neurons that work together to carry out one or more related computations. A computational theory of such a subsystem specifies four things: the purpose of the computation carried out by the subsystem, the input, the output, and the boundary conditions that must be satisfied for successful operation of the computation (which are often thought of as "assumptions" that must be satisfied for the computation to succeed; see Marr, 1982).

A computational theory of a processing subsystem treats the subsystem as a "black box" with specified input/output properties. A complete analysis of the subsystem, however, must include not only a theory of the computation but also a theory of the algorithm used by the subsystem. The theory of the algorithm opens up the black box and describes the processes that perform the computation, including the data structures that are used. The distinction between computation and algorithm can be illustrated by considering the mathematical operation of multiplying two numbers. This computation can be carried out by several different algorithms: For example, one could add one of the numbers to itself repeatedly, or one could convert the numbers to logarithms and add them.

Levels of Analysis and Types of Computer Models

The distinction between computation and algorithm is not an absolute one but rather depends on the level of analysis that is taken as a reference point. When viewed from the perspective of a higher level computation, a particular operation may be viewed as part of an algorithm for that computation, but when viewed from a lower level perspective, the same operation may be treated as a computation in its own right. For example, addition can be considered part of an algorithm for the higher level operation of multiplication, as described earlier, but on a lower level, addition can also be viewed as a computation in itself. Similarly, in the analysis of complex systems, the notions of computation and algorithm recur on every level as one proceeds from coarse, high level analyses to more detailed, lower level analyses. For any behavioral ability exhibited by a system, we can begin by specifying a coarse theory of the computation. Next we can specify an algorithm for carrying out the computation. The steps that compose the algorithm can in turn be treated as computations in their own right, with corresponding algorithms. By starting with a relatively coarse level of analysis and proceeding to more and more fine-grained analyses, we avoid being overwhelmed at the outset by low-level details of strategy and implementation.

High-Level, Multi-subsystem Analyses. Standard symbol-processing models. We have argued that computer models and the theories that they embody should be motivated by three kinds of considerations -- behavioral, neurobiological, and computational -- that are applied first at a relatively coarse level of analysis and then at successively more fine-grained levels. The types of computer models that are most appropriate depend on the level of analysis. For the initial high-level approach to a problem, when the behavior to be modeled is a complex one involving many subcomponents, standard symbol-processing models often may be most convenient. Such models represent processes as a series of subroutines (corresponding to processing subsystems); these subroutines communicate via symbolic representations, which are organized into data structures, such as lists and arrays. In order for such models to be plausibly applicable to problems in neuropsychology, the communication paths between subsystems in the model should reflect what is known about information flow in the brain, and the input/output transformations performed by the subsystems should be the kind that can easily be performed by actual neural networks. The methods by which these transformations are actually performed in the model need not have a high degree of neural realism, as long as each input/output relation is consistent with what a real neural network could accomplish; in other words, each subsystem should function as a "virtual" neural network.

Fine-Grained Analyses of Particular Subsystems. PDP models. As a computer model continues to be refined to incorporate more fine-grained analyses and to move closer to modeling the details of neural implementation, PDP models (also called *connectionist models* and *neural network models*) become more appropriate, especially as models of particular subsystems within a larger overall model. Before devising one of these models, it is important to ensure that the model is solving a "well-formed" problem, one that the brain is faced with. Thus, it often makes sense to devise PDP models only after prior computational analyses have been done to delineate the computations that need to be performed. PDP models have recently been the subject of intensive investigation in cognitive psychology and computer science because of their computational power and (relative) biological plausibility. Several useful collections of papers are now available (e.g., Anderson & Rosenfeld, 1988; Feldman, 1985; Grossberg, 1988; McClelland & Rumelhart, 1986b; Rumelhart & McClelland, 1986b), so we do not attempt an extended discussion here but rather simply summarize a few of the important characteristics of PDP models.

PDP models generally consist of a set of processing units, each with its own state of activation, and a set of weighted connections by which activation is transferred among units. The units are often organized into groups; in a frequently used arrangement, one group of units serves as input units, another serves as output units, and a third internal (or "hidden") group serves as an intermediate layer between the input and output units. In this arrangement, there are no connections within groups, and the only intergroup connections are between the input units and the hidden units and between the hidden units and the output units. When a pattern of activation is imposed on the input units, activation is passed along the weighted connections to the units of the hidden layer and thence to the output units, producing a new pattern of activation that is the "response" to the input.

One reason for the recent upsurge of interest in PDP models has been the discovery of powerful rules for learning input/output mappings in networks of the type just described. Learning in these networks consists of adjusting the weights on connections, which determine the output that will be produced for a particular input. One particularly powerful rule for this sort of learning is known as the generalized delta rule, or back-propagation (Rumelhart, Hinton, & Williams, 1986). During a series of learning trials, back-propagation changes the weight on each connection in a network by an amount proportional to the product of (a) an error signal associated with the unit receiving input from the connection and (b) the output of the unit sending activation along that connection. For a unit in the output layer, the error signal is based on the difference between the desired output and the actual output for that unit. For a unit in the hidden layer, the error signal is based on the error signals of the output units to which the hidden unit has connections, as well as on the strengths of those connections. Thus, the error signals are propagated backwards through the network and drive changes to the weights on the connections, in such a way as to decrease the amount of error on subsequent trials. Over the course of many trials, the back-propagation learning rule attempts to minimize the squares of the differences between the actual and desired output values, summed over all output units and all input/output pairs. Back-propagation is in essence an extremely powerful and flexible technique for nonlinear least squares regression, with the particular advantage that unlike traditional regression procedures, back-propagation does not require the user to know in advance the appropriate functional form for modeling a particular input/output mapping (Hecht-Nielsen, 1988).

PDP models are often claimed to be well suited for modeling neural processing subsystems because of their biological and psychological plausibility. The biological plausibility of PDP models rests on several structural and functional correspondences between PDP models and real neural networks (see Rumelhart & McClelland, 1986c). Like the brain, a PDP model computes by using a large number of relatively simple processing units (which may be thought of as corresponding to groups of neurons or highly simplified individual neurons). Each unit receives input from and sends output to a large number of other units via excitatory and inhibitory connections (analogous to synapses). Moreover, just as learning in neural systems depends on synaptic plasticity (for a review, see Squire, 1987), learning in PDP models is accomplished by modifying connections. The performance of PDP models, like that of the brain, usually does not depend critically on any particular unit or connection; knowledge is represented in a distributed fashion, and as a result, damage to a small part of the system generally results in graceful degradation rather than catastrophic failure. Finally, perhaps the most important biologically plausible characteristic of PDP models is their ability to carry out the nonlinear input/output mappings (involving interactions among various aspects of the input) that characterize biological systems at levels ranging from single-cell response properties to high-level behavioral abilities.

The psychological plausibility of PDP models rests on the ease with which they exhibit phenomena such as generalization, priming, constructive inference from partial descriptions, and the formation of prototypes (McClelland & Rumelhart, 1986b; Rumelhart & McClelland, 1986b). Many psychological operations that are easy for humans are also easy to accomplish in these networks. Indeed, it often is easy to mimic a psychological phenomenon such as generalization without even trying to do so (it is a natural property of some network models), whereas most standard symbol-processing models can be brought to behave appropriately only with difficulty. To be sure, not all psychological phenomena yield so readily to the PDP approach; indeed, some aspects of human cognitive processing pose substantial problems for current PDP models. For example, PDP models have difficulty with type/token distinctions and with the use of variables (Norman, 1986), and as a result, the models often fail to capture the rich structure of domains such as language (Pinker & Prince, 1988; cf. Fodor & Pylyshyn, 1988; Lachter & Bever, 1988; Rumelhart & McClelland, 1986a). Nonetheless, PDP models do succeed in modeling a wide range of psychological phenomena with relative ease.

An additional virtue of PDP models is their ability to help elucidate what kinds of internal representations are useful for extracting information from input in order to solve a particular problem. These representations can be studied by examining the response properties of units in the hidden layer and the output layer of a PDP network. For example, Lehky and Sejnowski (1988) configured a network to solve a "shape-from-shading" problem: Given shaded images as input, the network learned to compute the orientation and principal curvatures of the surfaces depicted by the images. To solve this problem, many of the units in the hidden layer developed response properties resembling those of simple cells in visual cortex, and some output units developed response properties resembling those of end-stopped complex cells.   In addition to clarifying the types of representations that are useful for extracting shape information from shading, the network also suggests hypotheses about the functions of the actual cortical cells whose response properties resemble those observed in the network.

USING COMPUTER MODELS TO STUDY CEREBRAL ASYMMETRY

We now proceed to some examples of how the general modeling strategies and types of models discussed here can be employed in the study of hemispheric functional asymmetry. First we discuss the use of high-level models in the study of complex interactions among several processing subsystems, and then we consider lower level models of individual subsystems.   Our focus is on asymmetry in the subsystems involved in the later stages of visual recognition -- those stages that draw on stored knowledge, as opposed to earlier stages of processing (e.g., the detection of edges on the basis of intensity differences), which are driven entirely by the information contained in the stimulus.

High-Level Models: Interactions Among Several Subsystems

Computer models are well suited for examining how lateral differences can arise from complex interactions among processing subsystems. As our main example we will use a computer model of the development of visual cerebral lateralization called BRIAN (Bilateral Recognition and Imagery Adaptive Networks; Kosslyn, 1987; Kosslyn, Flynn, Amsterdam, & Wang, in press; Kosslyn, Sokolov, & Chen, 1989).   This development is assumed to occur during early childhood and involves lateralization of specific processing subsystems.   Because the basic mechanisms of lateralization that we discuss in relation to BRIAN are largely independent of the particular subsystems in the model, we do not present a summary of all the subsystems here but instead describe individual ones as necessary (for details on the subsystems, see Kosslyn, Flynn, Amsterdam, & Wang, in press).

  Lateralization in BRIAN is explained in terms of three key ideas: adaptive subsystems that are "tuned" by feedback; interhemispheric processing degradation; and central bilateral control.

Adaptive Subsystems. Each processing subsystem "adapts" with practice so that it is able to perform frequently encountered tasks more reliably and quickly.   One mechanism that may underlie this "tuning" with practice is suggested by neuroanatomical studies.   In all cases examined to date, afferent pathways between visual areas are accompanied by corresponding efferent pathways (Maunsell & Newsome, 1987; Van Essen, 1985; Van Essen & Maunsell, 1983).   Furthermore, the two types of pathways are typically of comparable size, which suggests a rich bidirectional exchange of information. This two-way communication channel may allow one subsystem that receives information from a second subsystem to provide feedback that trains the second subsystem to produce the same output more efficiently in the future.

Interhemispheric-processing Degradation. Several sources of evidence suggest that when information originates in one hemisphere, the processing of that information is less effective in the opposite hemisphere. For example, shape-sensitive cells in area IT of the macaque show stronger responses when a stimulus is presented to the contralateral visual field (and thus is presented directly to the responding hemisphere) than when the stimulus is presented to the ipsilateral visual field (and thus must cross the callosum to reach the responding hemisphere; e.g., see Gross, Rocha-Miranda, & Bender, 1972). This asymmetry could result from at least three factors. First, the number of projections to these cells across the callosum is smaller than the number of projections within a hemisphere (e.g., Desimone, Fleming, & Gross, 1980, pp. 45-50). Second, both hemispheres may share a single limited-capacity pool of activation (cf. Holtzman & Gazzaniga, 1982). If so, then the hemispheres would indirectly inhibit each other: The more one hemisphere draws activation (e.g., by initially receiving a stimulus), the less activation will be available for the other hemisphere (cf. Kinsbourne, 1973, 1975; Kinsbourne & Hiscock, 1983). Third, the two hemispheres could inhibit each other directly. Studies of visual attention have yielded evidence of cross-hemisphere inhibition (e.g., Hughes & Zimba, 1985, 1987), although it is not clear whether this inhibition is direct or indirect.

The important point is that information transmitted across the hemispheres is processed less effectively in the target hemisphere than in the originating hemisphere. This effect will occur not only with afferent input but also with efferent information, such as the feedback discussed earlier. As a result, feedback will be less effective when it must cross to the opposite hemisphere, so that subsystems in that hemisphere will not be trained as effectively as the homologous ones on the side of the subsystem that originated the feedback.

In what circumstances will feedback originate on one side? This question is addressed by the third key idea, the notion of "central" bilateral control.

"Central" Bilateral Control. The control of bodily movements is typically shared by the two hemispheres, with each being responsible for the contralateral side of the body. However, rapid sequences of precise, ordered movements that extend over both halves of the body introduce the problem of coordination and synchronization of control subsystems in opposite hemispheres. If rapid, precise, bilateral movements were controlled by two separate motor programs generated independently by homologous subsystems, there would be an increased risk of failures of coordination due to inconsistencies between the programs. A more effective solution would use a single motor program generated in a single subsystem. This subsystem could then control a pair of "slave" subsystems that would carry out the easier, less error-prone task of executing the motor programs (i.e., actually performing the movements) on each side of the body.

Kosslyn (1987) hypothesized that this type of "centralized" control of rapid, precise, bilateral movements is achieved by innate lateralization of certain motor programming subsystems (cf. Gazzaniga & LeDoux, 1978; Geschwind, 1975; Kimura, 1976, 1977; Levy, 1969; Mateer, 1978; Nottebohm, 1970, 1979; Summers & Sharp, 1979; Sussman & Westbury, 1978; Zangwill, 1976.)   In particular, he posited two such innately lateralized subsystems, one for the control of speech output and the other for the control of rapid bilateral visual search patterns.   Evidence for a lateralized speech output control subsystem has been obtained from studies of brain-damaged patients and studies of the suppression of activity during direct electrical stimulation of the cortex (e.g. Benson, 1967; Mazzocchi & Vignolo, 1979; Naeser, Hayward, Laughlin, & Zatz, 1981; Ojemann & Mateer, 1979).   The results from these studies demonstrate that the control of speech output is usually lateralized to one hemisphere, typically the left. Moreover, such unilateral control is not limited to adults but instead appears to be present very early in life (for reviews, see Kinsbourne & Hiscock, 1983; Witelson, 1977).   The evidence for a lateralized subsystem for the control of visual search is not as compelling as the evidence for a left-sided unilateral speech output controller, but the right hemisphere does seem to be more involved than the left in disorders of spatial attention (De Renzi, 1982; Heilman, Watson, & Valenstein, 1985).

The Snowball Effect.   We began with the idea of adaptive subsystems that are tuned by feedback, and then we noted that the strength and effectiveness of feedback will be attenuated when it must cross from a unilateral source to a recipient subsystem in the opposite hemisphere.   We have now argued that there are two control subsystems that are innately lateralized.   The combination of these ideas is sufficient to produce lateralization of the entire system via a "snowball" effect, which can be illustrated by the following simple example.

Suppose that a baby produces an utterance to express a thought (e.g., the thought "dog" when the baby sees a dog).   The production of even a single-word utterance such as "dog" requires instructions to be sent to the speech output control subsystem.   Presumably the concept "dog" is paired with a set of such instructions in associative long-term memory, along with other properties of dogs. The output instructions are accessed by a "categorical property lookup" subsystem, which accesses information stored in discrete categories.   This subsystem operates on both sides and passes the accessed instructions to the speech output control subsystem, which is on the left side.   When that subsystem is used, it has the effect (for any or all of the three reasons noted earlier) of producing degraded feedback to the categorical property lookup subsystem on the right side.   Over the course of many trials, this differentially effective feedback will cause the categorical property lookup subsystem on the left to become stronger than the one on the right.   Once this difference starts to emerge, the snowball effect is underway, for the stronger left-sided subsystem begins to play the same role as did the innately lateralized speech output subsystem: When used, its own feedback to other subsystems is more effective on the left than on the right. Those other subsystems in turn begin to become more efficient on the left than on the right; in this way, lateralization percolates through the system.

Thus, we posit that a basic form of lateralization is innate. What develops is the degree and type of lateralization of other subsystems (see Kosslyn, Sokolov, & Chen, 1989, for more justification of this assumption). To date, no developmental work has been done to test this hypothesis; the available data suggest that infants have at least some language functions lateralized, but the data do not bear on the lateralization of other kinds of processing.

Although the concepts used in BRIAN to explore the possible development of lateralization in early childhood are relatively simple, their interactions in the context of a multi-subsystem theory can become extremely complex. Furthermore, if parameters such as activation imbalance, degree of inhibition, and the degree of innate lateralization of the speech output and search pattern control subsystems are allowed to vary, the range of potential outcomes rapidly grows large. The programming of the theory as a computer model therefore takes on special importance, for the multiplicity of possible variations defies hand simulation. Such otherwise unmanageable complexity and variability lies at the heart of areas such as individual differences in laterality and the effects of lateralized brain damage. Those areas are therefore particularly appropriate for exploration via computer simulations.

Individual Differences. Kosslyn, Sokolov, and Chen (in press) used the BRIAN model to investigate how the development of lateralization (which was presumed to occur largely in very early childhood) would be influenced by variations in four parameters: innate lateralization of speech output control, innate lateralization of search pattern control, degree of interhemispheric processing degradation, and relative frequencies of different tasks performed by the simulated system. The results showed that changes in even a single parameter sufficed to produce substantial differences in an overall measure of the lateralization of the entire system. Furthermore, beneath this relatively coarse measure of system lateralization lay a rich pattern of subsystem differences. This detailed level of structure lies beyond that typically addressed in neuropsychological experiments but constitutes fertile ground for new investigation. In particular, there is a need for neuropsychological tests that evaluate the relative strengths of different subsystems in the two hemispheres. In our laboratory, for example, we are currently developing a battery of tests that will allow evaluation of selected subsystems used in visual mental imagery. Although the design of such tests poses a number of methodological difficulties, if appropriate tests can be developed they will be valuable not only in the theoretical understanding of individual differences in laterality but also in applied areas such as education, in which knowledge of the strengths and weaknesses of a particular person's processing subsystems could be used to design individualized instructional programs.

Brain Damage. The ease of investigating complex interactions that makes computer models so well suited for studying individual differences also renders such models ideal for exploring the relationship between cerebral asymmetries and the consequences of localized brain damage. Indeed, once a precise model of lateralization in normal performance has been developed, it is a relatively simple matter to "lesion" the model and examine the resulting deficits in performance. Furthermore, whereas the lesions found in human patients are often diffuse and cut across several functional subsystems and connecting pathways, the lesions simulated in computer models can be precisely controlled and replicated.

Although we have not yet systematically applied the simulated lesion technique to a lateralized version of BRIAN, Kosslyn, Flynn, Amsterdam, and Wang (in press) have explored the effects of damage on a nonlateralized version. Two kinds of damage were investigated: damage to subsystems and damage to connections between subsystems. Perhaps the most striking result was the wide variety of alternative constellations of damage that can lead to a particular deficit. Visual associative agnosia, for example, was found to result from any one of over 30 distinct types of damage. The knowledge gleaned from computer simulations of brain damage may be used not only to aid diagnosis but also to develop customized rehabilitation programs focusing on alternative task strategies (i.e., combinations of subsystems working in concert) that remain viable following a particular pattern of damage.

Lower-Level Models: Properties of Individual Subsystems

So far we have been focusing on complex interactions among multiple subsystems as a driving force in the development of lateralized processing. Such interactions are especially appropriate for investigation with computer models such as BRIAN, in which processing subsystems are implemented as subroutines that function as virtual networks. Virtual networks perform the kind of input/output transformations that actual neural networks would perform, but for reasons of computational feasibility these transformations are implemented with standard symbol-processing algorithms and data structures rather than with the more biologically plausible but computationally intensive PDP models.

Given the limitations of currently available computers, the use of virtual networks is almost a necessity for higher level models such as BRIAN that attempt to describe complex, multi-component behaviors such as visual object recognition. Once a plausible, working model at this high level has been constructed, however, PDP models have an important role to play. The choice of subsystems in the higher level model embodies a set of hypotheses about the problems solved by the particular neural networks that instantiate the subsystems. After the construction of a working simulation has shown this set of hypotheses to be internally coherent, it becomes appropriate to turn attention to the detailed workings of individual subsystems. Indeed, some aspects of performance will only be understood if the internal workings of individual subsystems are understood. For this purpose, PDP models are ideal, because with the move toward a more fine-grained level of analysis, we approach more closely the neural substrate of behavior, and consequently the biological plausibility of our models takes on added importance.

   Structural Basis of Adaptive Tuning. Several types of questions relevant
to hemispheric functional asymmetry can be usefully addressed with PDP models.
For example, as described previously, in BRIAN the notion of adaptive tuning via
differential feedback plays a critical role in lateralization. PDP models can be
used to investigate the kinds of within-subsystem structural changes that are
involved in adaptive tuning and that result in lateral differences. One paradigm
for examining this issue involves taking two initially identical PDP networks and
giving them different amounts of training on the same input/output mapping. The
network that receives more training will presumably perform the task more
accurately (i.e., with lower mean error over one complete sequence of
input/output pairs), but the interesting question concerns the internal
representations that underlie the more proficient performance.

   Suppose that the task is a visual one, where the input units have a spatial
structure and thus form a visual pattern. We might then expect to find differences
between the two networks in the *receptive* field structures of the hidden (internal)
processing units (i.e., in the pattern of connectivity between the input units and
the hidden units); in addition, we might also find differences in the *projective*
field structures of the hidden units (i.e., in the pattern of connectivity between the
hidden units and the output units; cf. Lehky & Sejnowski, 1988). For example,
the hidden units in one network might have large receptive fields (strong
connections to a large subset of the input units), whereas the hidden units in the
other network might have relatively small receptive fields (strong connections to
only a small subset of the input units). Such an organization would mimic
differential sensitivity to high versus low spatial frequency input, analogous to the
hemispheric differences suggested by Sergent (1982). Or the receptive fields
might differ not in size but in shape, with those in one network being long and
narrow and those in the other being square or circular.

   In addition to differences in receptive fields, we might also find
differences in the projective field structures of the hidden units. For example,
suppose that the networks have been trained to take a visual pattern as input and
to extract two types of information, such as shape and location (Rueckl, Cave, &
Kosslyn, 1989), or curvature orientation and curvature magnitude (Lehky &
Sejnowski, 1988); in addition, suppose that each type of information is
represented on a separate subset of output units. Following the different amounts
of training received by the two networks, we might find that in one network, most
of the hidden units had broad projective fields that included output units from
both subsets; thus most of the hidden units would contribute to the computation of
both types of information. In contrast, the other network might have developed
hidden units with narrow projective fields that rarely included output units from
more than one subset; thus, each hidden unit in this network would participate in
the computation of only one of the two types of information. If differences such
as these are found as the result of differential training regimes, they provide
potentially testable neuropsychological hypotheses about the structural properties

that underlie the development of lateral differences in the brain.

As another example of the use of PDP models in the investigation of structural properties underlying hemispheric asymmetry, consider a possible difference in the representation of visual categories in the left and right hemispheres. Pilot studies from our laboratory on memory for pictures of prototypical versus distorted objects are consistent with the hypothesis that the left hemisphere uses relatively broad categories, which group many examples into a single class, whereas the right hemisphere uses narrower categories and thereby preserves more distinctions between individual examples (Hillger, Kosslyn, & Chabris, 1988). PDP models provide an excellent method for developing predictions based on this hypothesis. The first step is to configure two networks in such a way that one uses broad categories and the other uses narrow categories. This can be accomplished by training the two networks on stimulus sets that have different amounts of within-category variation. (Note that such training is not intended to model the development of lateralization but instead is simply a practical technique for bringing the networks to initial levels of performance that approximately represent the hypothesized functional differences between the two hemispheres.) For example, suppose that the task for both networks is to classify shapes as triangles or rectangles. One network can be trained on a stimulus set in which all triangles are very different from each other (e.g., different in the relative sizes of the internal angles) and all rectangles are also quite different from each other (e.g., different in the ratio of length to width). The large amount of within-category variation in the stimulus set will require the network to develop broad categories in order to classify the training stimuli correctly. In contrast, the other network can be trained on a stimulus set in which all triangles are quite similar to each other and all rectangles are quite similar to each other. The high degree of within-category similarity in this stimulus set will allow the network to use relatively narrow categories for classifying the training stimuli.

Once the two networks have been configured in this way, with categories of different widths, one can introduce new exemplars from each category and observe differences in the number of trials required for each network to learn to classify the new stimuli correctly. If the hypothesis of hemispheric differences in the width of visual categories is correct, then the between-network differences in learning time should have implications for hemispheric differences in the processing of novel exemplars of previously learned categories. Furthermore, the patterns of connectivity among the units in each network would suggest possible structural bases for hemispheric differences in the width of visual categories

Computational Efficiency. Another area in which PDP models can provide valuable insights concerns the computational consequences of the development of lateralized processing. In particular, given a fixed quantity of physical neural tissue and a wide variety of problems to solve, does hemispheric specialization result in more efficient processing? PDP models are particularly appropriate for such questions of resources and capacity, because in contrast to standard symbol-processing models, which typically represent processing capacity only as an abstract quantity, PDP models explicitly include concrete processing resources -- units and connections -- that have potential biological parallels.

One useful paradigm for investigating the computational consequences of the division and specialization of resources involves comparing the performance of "split" and "unsplit" networks that are trained to perform the same tasks (see Rueckl, Cave, & Kosslyn, 1989). For example, suppose that a network must solve two problems simultaneously, with the answer to one problem represented on one subset of the output units and the answer to the other represented on the remaining output units. In an unsplit network, all of the hidden units are connected to all of the output units, so that each hidden unit can contribute to the solution of both problems. In contrast, the units in the split network are divided into two groups, each of which connects to only one subset of the output units. Thus in the split network, each hidden unit can contribute to the solution of only one problem. (Of course, the unsplit network could in principle evolve the same solution as the split net, by learning to set the proper weights to zero; in our experience, however, this does not happen.) The performance of the two networks can be compared by measuring either the mean error over one complete sequence of input/output pairs after a fixed number of learning trials, or by counting the number of learning trials needed to reach a fixed error criterion. If the split net outperforms the unsplit net, this difference in performance suggests that specialization of resources, as in the development of lateral differences, brings increases in computational power and efficiency for performing the target task.

The technique of comparing split and unsplit networks has recently been used to investigate the computational consequences of having separate cortical visual systems for the processing of shape and location information, as is true in primates (Rueckl, Cave, & Kosslyn, 1989; cf. Ungerleider & Mishkin, 1982). Split and unsplit networks containing equal total numbers of hidden units were trained to identify the shapes and locations of simple input patterns laid out on a square grid. The task was learned substantially faster by appropriately split networks, in which one subset of the hidden units identified shapes and the other subset computed locations. Thus, the separation of shape and location processing yielded improvements in overall computational efficiency. In our laboratory we are currently using the same split/unsplit technique to examine the computational consequences of hemispheric specialization for global versus local processing of hierarchical visual stimuli (for a review of relevant empirical studies, see Van Kleeck, in press).

Brain Damage. The same properties that make PDP models so well suited for examining questions of computational resources and efficiency also make them appropriate for investigations of lateralized brain damage at a more fine-grained level of analysis than is possible with high-level symbol-processing models. In particular, the inclusion in PDP models of separate classes of discrete processing resources -- units and weighted connections -- allows the modeler to simulate the effects of different varieties of partial damage to subsystems. For example, suppose that two initially identical networks, representing homologous subsystems in opposite hemispheres, have attained different levels of effectiveness due to differences in the quality of feedback during training. (In a back-propagation network, such differences in feedback can be implemented as differences in the variability of the reference output against which the actual output is compared in order to compute the error signal that will be back-propagated through the network.) The modeler can then examine how the two differentially proficient networks will be affected by various amounts of one or more types of partial damage, such as the removal of units (corresponding in a general way to the destruction of cell bodies), removal of connections (corresponding to synaptic damage), addition of random noise to the unit activations or connection weights (corresponding to biochemical irregularities), or changes in the learning rate (corresponding to generalized psychopharmacological changes). Although these varieties of partial damage have not yet been widely used to compare networks with different training histories, McClelland and Rumelhart (1986a) have shown that reductions in the learning rate of a network can yield patterns of performance that simulate certain aspects of residual learning and spared learning in bitemporal amnesia.

In addition to its potential to illuminate the different types of performance deficits caused by different varieties of damage, the partial-damage technique also allows examination of the relationship between types of internal representations and subsequent resistance to damage (cf. Wood, 1982). For example, suppose that as a result of different types of training on the same task, two networks (A and B) develop different internal structures. Network A might learn the task via specialization of units within the network, so that a relatively small subset of units bears primary responsibility for accomplishing the task. In this case, the consequences of partial damage to the network are likely to be highly variable and to depend on the precise location of the damage. If units in the critical subset are spared, performance will remain high, but if units in the critical subset are damaged, performance will deteriorate dramatically. In contrast, suppose that Network B learned the task by developing more distributed internal representations than Network A, so that in Network B, a large proportion of the hidden units contributes substantially to task performance. In this case, the consequences of partial damage will probably be less extreme and will not depend critically on the location of the damage; regardless of location, damage will be likely to yield only moderate deficits in performance.

A related issue that can also be easily examined with the partial-damage technique is the relationship between types of initial internal representations and subsequent ability to recover from damage when training is re-initiated. In the specialized Network A just described, the task is accomplished via specialization of a small number of hidden units, and the remaining units are left relatively uncommitted. Network B, on the other hand, uses a more distributed representation, and consequently most units participate in performing the input/output mapping. Following damage, the differences in degree of prior commitment of units in Networks A and B may substantially affect the rate at which each network can relearn the original mapping.

Perhaps the most important point of this discussion is the difficulty of precisely anticipating all of the aspects of how a certain model will behave. The models allow one to chart the consequences of specific theoretical assumptions in detail, which is often impossible if one stays with relatively vague, verbal theories. Indeed, it is often unclear exactly what is predicted by such informal theories at all. For example, Marshall (1981) has noted that the frequently invoked left-hemisphere/analytic, right-hemisphere/holistic dichotomy is sufficiently vague to yield two opposing predictions about a task as simple as matching circles to arcs (Nebes, 1978; cf. Cooper, 1981). This situation does not arise with computer models, which for better or for worse make explicit predictions.

CONCLUSIONS

Computer models that are motivated and constrained by behavioral, neurobiological, and computational considerations are a valuable tool for investigators of hemispheric functional asymmetry. From high-level explorations of the interactions of multiple processing subsystems, to fine-grained analyses of the structure and function of individual subsystems, computer models allow a level of precision, explicitness, and predictive power that is otherwise virtually impossible to achieve. With computer models, we can develop theories involving complex interactions among many processes and still derive precise predictions about behavior in specific circumstances.

No one doubts that subtle task and stimulus properties affect performance in studies of laterality, but the complexity of the underlying variables has proven daunting. As a result, the neuropsychological literature to date contains numerous examples of theories that conflict and experiments that fail to replicate. New data alone cannot remedy this state of affairs, nor can new theories if they are vague and ill-specified. Computer models, however, can help find a way out of this impasse, for they encourage precise specification of theories and thereby lead to explicit predictions that can guide the collection of theoretically relevant data. With the addition of computer models to our armamentarium of investigational techniques, we have a powerful method for bringing order to the complex realities of human cerebral asymmetry.

ACKNOWLEDGMENTS

Preparation of this chapter was supported in part by a National Science Foundation Graduate Fellowship and a Fairchild Foundation Postdoctoral Fellowship (M. H. Van Kleeck), and by Air Force Office of Scientific Research Grant 88-0012 (S. M. Kosslyn) supplemented by support from the Office of Naval Research. We thank Kyle Cave, Chris Chabris, Lynn Hillger, and Jay Rueckl for valuable comments on a draft of the chapter.

REFERENCES

Anderson, J. A., & Rosenfeld, E. (Eds.). (1988). *Neurocomputing: Foundations of research*. Cambridge, MA: MIT Press.

Benson, D. F. (1967). Fluency in aphasia: Correlation with radioactive scan localization. *Cortex, 3*, 373-394.

Cooper, W. E. (1981). The analytic/holistic distinction applied to the speech of patients with hemispheric brain damage. *Behavioral and Brain Sciences, 4*, 68-69.

De Renzi, E. (1982). *Disorders of space exploration and cognition*. New York: Wiley.

Desimone, R., Fleming, J., & Gross, C. G. (1980). Prestriate afferents to inferior temporal cortex: An HRP study. *Brain Research, 184*, 41-55.

Feldman, J. A. (Ed.). (1985). Special issue: Connectionist models and their applications. *Cognitive Science, 9*, 1-169.

Fodor, J. A. & Pylyshyn, Z. W. (1988). Connectionism and cognitive architecture: A critical analysis. *Cognition, 28*, 3-71.

Gazzaniga, M. S., & LeDoux, J. E. (1978). *The integrated mind*. New York: Plenum Press.

Geschwind, N. (1975). The apraxias: Neural mechanisms of disorders of learned movement. *American Scientist, 63*, 188-195.

Gross, C. G., Rocha-Miranda, C. E., & Bender, D. B. (1972). Visual properties of neurons in inferotemporal cortex of the macaque. *Journal of Neurophysiology, XXXV*, 96-111.

Grossberg, S. (Ed.). (1988). *Neural networks and natural intelligence*. Cambridge, MA: MIT Press.

Hecht-Nielsen, R. (1988). Theory of the backpropagation neural network. *Neural Networks, 1, Supplement 1 (Abstracts of the First Annual INNS Meeting, Boston, 1988)*, 445.

Heilman, K. M., Watson, R. T., & Valenstein, E. (1985). Neglect and related disorders. In K. M. Heilman & E. Valenstein (Eds.), *Clinical neuropsychology* (2nd ed., pp. 243-293). New York: Oxford University Press.

Hillger, L. A., & Kosslyn, S. M., & Chabris, C. (1988). *Left- versus right-hemisphere memory for prototypical and distorted pictures*. Unpublished Harvard University manuscript, Cambridge, MA.

Holtzman, J. D., & Gazzaniga, M. S. (1982). Dual task interactions due exclusively to limits in processing resources. *Science, 218*, 1325-1327.

Hughes, H. C., & Zimba, L. D. (1985). Spatial maps of directed visual attention. *Journal of Experimental Psychology: Human Perception and Performance, 11*, 409-430.

Hughes, H. C., & Zimba, L. D. (1987). Natural boundaries for the spatial spread of directed visual attention. *Neuropsychologia, 25*, 5-18.

Kimura, D. (1976). The neural basis of language qua gesture. In H. Whitaker &

H. A. Whitaker (Eds.), *Studies in neurolinguistics* (Vol. 2, pp. 145-156). New York: Academic Press.

Kimura, D. (1977). Acquisition of a motor skill after left hemisphere damage. *Brain, 100*, 527-542.

Kinsbourne, M. (1973). The control of attention by interaction between the cerebral hemispheres. In S. Kornblum (Ed.), *Attention and performance* (Vol 4, pp. 239-256). New York: Academic Press.

Kinsbourne, M. (1975). The mechanism of hemispheric control of the lateral gradient of attention. In P. M. A. Rabbitt & S. Dornic (Eds.), *Attention and Performance* (Vol 5, pp. 81-97). New York: Academic Press.

Kinsbourne, M., & Hiscock, M. (1983). The normal and deviant development of functional lateralization of the brain. In P. H. Mussen, M. M. Haith, & J. J. Campos (Eds.), *Handbook of child psychology: Vol. 2. Infancy and developmental psychobiology* (4th. ed, pp. 157-280). New York: Wiley.

Kosslyn, S. M. (1987). Seeing and imagining in the cerebral hemispheres: A computational approach. *Psychological Review, 94*, 148-175.

Kosslyn, S. M., Flynn, R. A., Amsterdam, J. B., & Wang, G. (in press). Components of high-level vision: A cognitive neuroscience analysis and accounts of neurological syndromes. *Cognition*.

Kosslyn, S. M., Sokolov, M. A., & Chen, J. C. (1989). The lateralization of BRIAN: A computational theory and model of visual hemispheric specialization. In D. Klahr & K. Kotovsky (Eds.), *Complex information processing: The impact of Herbert A. Simon* (pp. 3-29). Hillsdale, NJ: Lawrence Erlbaum Associates.

Lachter, J., & Bever, T. G. (1988). The relation between linguistic structure and associative theories of language learning -- A constructive critique of some connectionist learning models. *Cognition, 28*, 195-247.

Lehky, S. R., and Sejnowski, T. J. (1988). Network model of shape-from-shading: Neural function arises from both receptive and projective fields. *Nature, 333*, 452-454.

Levy, J. (1969). Possible basis for the evolution of lateral specialization of the human brain. *Nature, 224*, 614-615.

Marr, D. (1982). *Vision: A computational investigation into the human representation and processing of visual information.* New York: W. H. Freeman.

Marshall, J. (1981). Hemispheric specialization: What, how, and why. *Behavioral and Brain Sciences, 4*, 72-73.

Mateer, C. (1978). Impairments of nonverbal oral movements after left hemisphere damage: A followup analysis of errors. *Brain and Language, 6*, 334-341.

Maunsell, J. H. R., & Newsome, W. T. (1987). Visual processing in monkey extrastriate cortex. *Annual Review of Neuroscience, 10*, 363-401.

Mazzocchi, F., & Vignolo, L. A. (1979). Localisation of lesions in aphasia: Clinical-CT scan correlations in stroke patients. *Cortex, 15*, 627-654.

McClelland, J. L., & Rumelhart, D. E. (1986a). Amnesia and distributed memory. In J. L. McClelland & D. E. Rumelhart (Eds.), *Parallel distributed processing: Explorations in the microstructure of cognition. Vol. 2: Psychological and biological models* (pp. 503-527). Cambridge, MA: MIT Press.

McClelland, J. L., & Rumelhart, D. E. (1986b). *Parallel distributed processing: Explorations in the microstructure of cognition. Vol. 2: Psychological and biological models*. Cambridge, MA: MIT Press.

Naeser, M. A., Hayward, R. W., Laughlin, S. A., & Zatz, L. M. (1981). Quantitative CT scan studies in aphasia. I. Infarct size and CT numbers. *Brain and Language, 12*, 140-164.

Nebes, R.D. (1978). Direct examination of cognitive function in the right and left hemispheres. In M. Kinsbourne (Ed.), *Asymmetrical function of the brain* (pp. 99-137). Cambridge: Cambridge University Press.

Norman, D. A. (1986). Reflections on cognition and parallel distributed processing. In J. L. McClelland & D. E. Rumelhart (Eds.), *Parallel distributed processing: Explorations in the microstructure of cognition. Vol. 2: Psychological and biological models* (pp. 531-546). Cambridge, MA: MIT Press.

Nottebohm, F. (1970). Ontogeny of bird song. *Science, 167*, 950-956.

Nottebohm, F. (1979). Origins and mechanisms in the establishment of cerebral dominance. In M. S. Gazzaniga (Ed.), *Handbook of behavioral neurobiology: Vol. 2. Neuropsychology* (pp. 295-344). New York: Plenum Press.

Ojemann, G. A., & Mateer, C. (1979). Human language cortex: Localization of memory, syntax, and sequential motor-phoneme identification systems. *Science, 205*, 1401-1403.

Pinker, S., & Prince, A. (1988). On language and connectionism: Analysis of a parallel distributed processing model of language acquisition. *Cognition, 28*, 73-193.

Rueckl, J. G., Cave, K. R., & Kosslyn, S. M. (1989). Why are "what" and "where" processed by separate cortical visual systems? A computational investigation. *Journal of Cognitive Neuroscience, 1*, 171-186.

Rumelhart, D. E., Hinton, G. E., & Williams, R. J. (1986). Learning internal representations by error propagation. In D. E. Rumelhart & J. L. McClelland (Eds.), *Parallel distributed processing: Explorations in the microstructure of cognition. Vol. 1: Foundations* (pp. 318-362). Cambridge, MA: MIT Press.

Rumelhart, D. E., & McClelland, J. L. (1986a). On learning the past tenses of English verbs. In J. L. McClelland & D. E. Rumelhart (Eds.), *Parallel distributed processing: Explorations in the microstructure of cognition. Vol. 2: Psychological and biological models* (pp. 216-271). Cambridge, MA: MIT Press.

Rumelhart, D. E., & McClelland, J. L. (1986b). *Parallel distributed processing: Explorations in the microstructure of cognition. Vol. 1: Foundations*. Cambridge, MA: MIT Press.

Rumelhart, D. E., & McClelland, J. L. (1986c). PDP models and general issues in cognitive science. In D. E. Rumelhart & J. L. McClelland (Eds.), *Parallel distributed processing: Explorations in the microstructure of cognition. Vol. 1: Foundations* (pp. 110-146). Cambridge, MA: MIT Press.

Sergent, J. (1982). The cerebral balance of power: Confrontation or cooperation? *Journal of Experimental Psychology: Human Perception and Performance, 8,* 253-272.

Summers, J. J., & Sharp, C. A. (1979). Bilateral effects of concurrent verbal and spatial rehearsal on complex motor sequencing. *Neuropsychologia, 17,* 331-343.

Squire, L. R. (1987). *Memory and brain.* New York: Oxford University Press.

Sussman, H. M., & Westbury, J. R. (1978). A laterality effect in isometric and isotonic labial tracking. *Journal of Speech and Hearing Research, 21,* 563-579.

Ungerleider, L. G., & Mishkin, M. (1982). Two cortical visual systems. In D. J. Ingle, M. A. Goodale, & R. J. W. Mansfield (Eds.), *Analysis of visual behavior* (pp. 549-586). Cambridge, MA: MIT Press.

Van Essen, D. C. (1985). Functional organization of primate visual cortex. In A. Peters & E. G. Jones (Eds.), *Cerebral cortex* (Vol. 3, pp. 259-329). New York: Plenum.

Van Essen, D. C., & Maunsell, J. H. R. (1983, September). Hierarchical organization and functional streams in the visual cortex. *Trends in Neurosciences,* 370-375.

Van Kleeck, M. H. (in press). Hemispheric differences in global versus local processing of hierarchical visual stimuli by normal subjects: New data and a meta-analysis of previous studies. *Neuropsychologia.*

Witelson, S. F. (1977). Early hemisphere specialization and interhemisphere plasticity: An empirical and theoretical review. In S. J. Segalowitz & F. A. Gruber (Eds.), *Language development and neurological theory* (pp. 213-287). New York: Academic Press.

Wood, C. C. (1982). Implications of simulated lesion experiments for the interpretation of lesions in real nervous systems. In M. A. Arbib, D. Caplan, & J. C. Marshall (Eds.), *Neural models of language processes* (pp. 485-509). New York: Academic Press.

Zangwill, O. (1976). Thought and the brain. *British Journal of Psychology, 67,* 301-314.

10 Ups and Downs in Cerebral Lateralization

Justine Sergent
Montreal Neurological Institute

Michael C. Corballis
University of Auckland

The search for principles that could uniquely characterize the processing differences underlying hemispheric functions has, for several decades, been the main focus of investigation in the study of cerebral lateralization. It has led to the identification of dichotomous dimensions distinguishing the respective competences of the hemispheres, and specifically to three broad categories along which the two hemispheres are assumed to divide their particular capacities. One is concerned with the nature of the *information* that each hemisphere would be specialized for dealing with, and it is best illustrated by the verbal/visuospatial dichotomy. Another has considered the nature of the *operations*, or the cognitive style, predominantly mediated by each hemisphere, and it is exemplified by the distinction between analytic and holistic modes of processing. The third broad category is concerned with the nature of the *representations* of information within each hemisphere, and it has led to the suggestion of an unequal ability of the hemispheres to operate on different spatial frequency contents of the information.

Each of these dichotomies focuses on one aspect of the functional properties of the cerebral hemispheres and each has found some form of justification in the findings of various experimental studies conducted on normal and neurological populations. For instance, when dealing with brain-damaged patients in a clinical context, the validity of the verbal/visuospatial dichotomy is almost immediately evident, and it offers a highly reliable basis for telling apart left and right hemisphere damaged patients. Similarly, the analytic/holistic dichotomy can discriminate reasonably well between left and right posterior patients in visual perceptual tasks, as can the spatial-frequency hypothesis when tested with low-pass and high-pass stimuli.

Although each of these dichotomies may provide useful approximations of the functional properties of the cerebral hemispheres at a higher order level, it is now clear that they cannot account for all the diverse manifestations of hemispheric asymmetry, and they offer little insight into the many operations that compose and underlie the realization of a given function. For one thing, these dichotomies consider each hemisphere as a processing unit and tend to attribute a unique functional property to a structure that is composed of many subsystems performing a large variety of operations. Yet there is certainly more functional similarity between homotopic areas of the two hemispheres than between anterior and posterior areas of one hemisphere. For another, it leads to investigations that seek to compare the capacities of the hemispheres in broadly defined functions that are in fact the product of many processing components.

The idea that the brain is organized into distinct areas of relative functional autonomy and specialization is a basic principle of neuropsychology and it is supported and illustrated by the selectivity of behavioral deficits that result from focal cerebral injury. With respect to the cerebral lateralization of functions, Allen (1983) has presented cogent arguments for a reformulation of hemispheric specialization in terms of smaller processing entities assumed to differ in their function and in their distribution within the hemispheres. Allen's suggestion was motivated by recent research in cognitive psychology indicating that mental faculties so far conceived as unitary functions, such as reading, face recognition, or imagery, are better described and understood as being composed of distinct processing units or modules that perform specific operations and whose separate activation is required for the realization of such functions. Thus, according to this view, not only is the brain divided into structures subserving specific functions, but each function is also assumed to be composed of subprocesses considered as basic operational units. This new perspective has led to the elaboration of "computational" models of information processing that specify the various steps necessary to carry out a particular task, based on a formal componential analysis of the problem that the system is trying to solve, that is, of what has to be computed to achieve a given goal.

Although Allen remained at a purely theoretical level, the first attempts at devising computational models of cerebral lateralization were made by Farah (1984) and by Kosslyn (1987) within a theory of visual imagery. They suggested that mental imagery involves a number of separate modules, some of which are shared with perception, and that the realization of a given imagery task involves the activation of relevant processing modules, with different modules being used at certain stages of processing depending on the nature of the task.

This approach offers a very promising theoretical framework for investigations into the respective contribution of the cerebral hemispheres to the realization of specific functions, and it certainly constitutes an advance over the more global evaluations of hemisphere specialization typical of the dichotomies approach. This is not to say that the latter are no longer useful and, as we see later, they bear on aspects of functional properties of the hemispheres that a computational approach is not designed to take into account. However, for the empirical study of cognitive functions, computational approaches provide a rigorous procedure that imposes consideration of the various operations that must be implemented in the realization of a given function and may thus allow a more refined and thorough specification of the role of each hemisphere in this realization. This chapter offers an illustration of this approach to the study of visual imagery and specifically the problem of mental rotation. Discussion of the merits of the various approaches to the study of functional cerebral lateralization is deferred until the end of the chapter.

PROCESSING OF DISORIENTED PATTERNS

The recognition of a visual object typically involves a mapping of the input onto some stored representation that specifies the object's structure, and this requires a computation of the correspondence between the retinal description of the object and the underlying invariant properties that characterize its uniqueness. Because retinally based descriptions are many and diverse as a result of the variety of formats, size, contrast, or orientation in which an object can appear, a series of transformations and normalizations of these descriptions must be implemented to achieve an appropriate fit with the corresponding internal representation. The nature of these transformations varies as a function of factors such as the deviation from the canonical perspective, the visual properties of the object, or the type of information that must be extracted from the seen object, suggesting that the visual system can resort to different solutions to achieve object recognition. Recent evidence from the study of brain damaged patients indicates that this flexibility and adaptivity of the visual system may partly result from different modes of processing of the two cerebral hemispheres. For instance, Humphreys and Riddoch (1984) found that right-hemisphere damaged patients were defective at recognizing objects presented from an unconventional perspective that foreshortened the objects' principal axis but preserved their distinctive features (see also Warrington & Taylor, 1978). In contrast, right-hemisphere damage did not affect the recognition of the same objects presented from an unconventional perspective that concealed the object's salient features but not its principal axis (Humphreys & Riddoch, 1984; but see Warrington & James, 1986). Although pointing to hemispheric asymmetry in object recognition, particularly when presentation of the object departs from its conventional view, these findings also illustrate different ways of accessing the stored representation of an object from its retinal descriptions.

A special case of this general problem is encountered when a two-dimensional pattern appears in an orientation that departs from its normal upright, after rotation in the picture plane. Although such a disorientation leaves undisturbed the spatial arrangement of the component features, it modifies the coordinate system along which they are normally processed, which may require, under certain circumstances, some mental rotation of the image to bring it in alignment with its stored representation. This is typically the case in tasks involving left-right discrimination or the discrimination of mirror-image forms appearing in different angular orientations, as initially demonstrated by Cooper and Shepard (1973, 1975; see Figure 10.1 for examples of stimuli). When subjects were timed as they decided whether a disoriented alphanumeric character (or hand) was in its normal or backward version (or a left or right hand), the function relating the reaction times (RTs) to the angular orientation of the pattern showed a sharp increase with departure from its upright. Cooper and Shepard interpreted this function as evidence of a mental rotation of the pattern to the upright before a decision was made.

Before examining the respective contribution of the cerebral hemispheres to mental rotation, two points need to be made. First, disorientation of a pattern is not necessarily detrimental to its recognition, and, when it is, it is not necessarily corrected by a process of mental rotation. Thus, disoriented letters can be identified as quickly as upright letters (Corballis, 1982), and disoriented patterns can be recognized or named at a speed which seems to rule out the operation of mental rotation (Corballis & Nagourney, 1978; Eley, 1982). So far, the most robust evidence of the involvement of mental rotation in the processing of disoriented patterns has been found in tasks requiring the *discrimination* of left from right or of normal from mirror-reversed version of an object, whereas the *identification* of disoriented patterns has yielded a variety of results that are sensitive to many experimental factors. This issue is still the object of debate and controversy, and it bears important implications for the understanding of properties of mental representations (see Corballis, 1988; Jolicoeur, 1988). A second point concerns the criteria for determining whether or not mental rotation

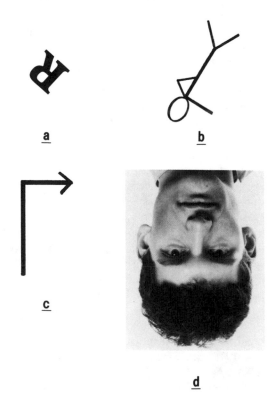

FIGURE 10.1. Examples of stimuli used in the experiments on disoriented patterns.

underlies performance in a given task. The operation of mental rotation is usually determined *a posteriori*, on the basis of the shape, and of the slope, of the function relating RTs to departure of the pattern from the upright. It is generally agreed that mental rotation implies a linear relation between RTs and departure from the upright, and an assumed rotation rate in the range of 200 to 800 deg/sec for two-dimensional patterns (Shepard & Cooper, 1982). However, as is illustrated later, qualitatively similar patterns of RTs may also be obtained in tasks involving the processing of disoriented visual objects even though mental rotation does not seem to be the operation underlying the correction of the disorientation (see Sergent & Corballis, in press).

Hemispheric Involvement in Mental Rotation

Although some reference to the capacity of brain-damaged patients to perform mental rotation was made in the 1930s, the first evidence of hemisphere asymmetry in mental rotation was presented by Levy-Agresti and Sperry (1968) who found that the right hemisphere of commissurotomized patients was the more adept at matching a solid object with an unfolded picture of this object. Additional evidence was reported by Ratcliff (1979) who observed that patients with posterior lesion of the right hemisphere were significantly worse than all other groups in judging whether inverted human figures were depicted with a disc on their left or their right hands. Because all the patients could perform the task normally when the figures were upright, Ratcliff inferred that the deficit was one of mental rotation.

Most investigations of hemispheric asymmetry in mental rotation in normal subjects have used the paradigm developed by Cooper and Shepard (1973) and involved the presentation of alphanumeric characters appearing in varying angular orientation and the measurement of the time it takes for subjects to decide whether a character is in its normal or mirror-reversed version. Studies that have used this task with lateral tachistoscopic presentations on normal subjects have not yielded clear-cut results. Thus, a predominant contribution of the right hemisphere has been found by Cohen (1975), whereas other experiments involving judgments about rotated patterns have failed to yield any significant differences between visual fields (Corballis, Macadie, & Beale, 1985; Corballis & McLaren, 1984; Jones & Anuza, 1982). On the other hand, Fischer and Pellegrino (1988) reported a right-field advantage when subjects had to match a lateralized disoriented character with a centrally located upright character.

This diversity of findings also characterizes results from studies in which physiological indexes of cerebral activation were measured in normal subjects. Ornstein, Johnstone, Herron, and Swencionis (1980), in an EEG study, reported greater activity over the left than over the right hemisphere when subjects engaged in a mental rotation task, whereas Stuss, Sarazin, Leech, and Picton (1983), in an event-related potential study, found a symmetrical involvement of the right and left parietal lobes in mental rotation. More recently, Deutsch, Bourbon, Papanicolaou, and Eisenberg (1988) measured cerebral blood flow in normal subjects performing a series of cognitive tasks, and found that, among a variety of visuospatial tasks, the most pronounced asymmetry favoring the right hemisphere occurred during performance of a mental-rotation task.

In a further attempt to examine this issue, we (Corballis & Sergent, in press-a) tested 133 college students on this mental-rotation task, and found a right visual-field superiority in overall performance, but similar rates of mental rotation in the two visual fields. The results are shown in Figure 10.2, and they illustrate the typical mental rotation functions resulting from an increase in reaction time with angular departure from the upright. However, we also found that 47 of the subjects (35%) displayed a left visual-field superiority. These findings are obviously inconclusive regarding the contribution of the cerebral hemispheres to mental rotation as such. While this lack of clear-cut findings with respect to cerebral asymmetry in mental rotation could be taken as suggesting an equal competence or involvement of the two hemispheres in performing this transformation (Cohen & Polich, 1989), such a conclusion does not necessarily follow from the results. In fact, it could as well reflect different hemisphere efficiency at performing the various operations that compose the mental-rotation task. In such a task, the subjects also have to encode the characters, to identify them in order to know where their normal upright orientation is, and to decide whether they are in their normal or backward version. An examination of the overall performance may thus not allow a specification of the respective efficiency of the hemispheres at carrying out each of these operations, and, consequently, hemisphere asymmetry in the mental-rotation task cannot be unequivocally attributed to the mental-rotation operation. It is noteworthy that, in some studies in which the subjects were tested with alphanumeric characters as well as with geometrical shapes, there was always a tendency toward a larger contribution of the right hemisphere with the latter than with the former, suggesting that factors other than mental rotation *per se* contribute to the overall pattern of visual-field asymmetry in the mental-rotation task. In addition, in all

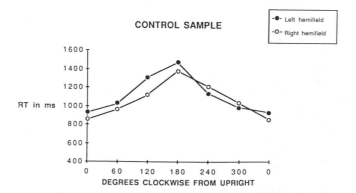

Figure 10.2. Mean RTs of 133 subjects as a function of visual field and orientation of letters.

the studies on normal subjects in which the mental-rotation function was derived, it was found that there was no hemisphere difference in the rate at which the patterns were mentally rotated, further suggesting that visual-field differences may reflect operations not directly related to mental rotation *per se*.

It is when faced with such a mixture of findings that the computational approach may become necessary in order to determine the lateralization of a given operation, as only through an examination of the respective competence of each hemisphere at carrying out each component operation is it possible to identify the stages at which the two hemispheres may be functionally unequal.

Mental Rotation in Commissurotomized Subject L.B. We have now examined this question in a commissurotomized patient known as L.B., and we have conducted a fairly long series of experiments in an attempt to isolate some the components of the task. Although commissurotomized subjects constitute a non-representative sample of the general population, the particular properties of their brain allow for the emergence of striking dissociations in hemisphere-processing competences if there are marked differences between the hemispheres in their ability to perform one or several components of a task. For instance, if the mental-rotation component is predominantly represented in one hemisphere, the absence of direct interhemispheric connections should give rise to a clear visual-field asymmetry because the less competent hemisphere would not benefit from the processing resources of the more competent hemisphere as it does in the intact brain.

Mirror-Image Discrimination of Disoriented Letters. In a first series of experiments on mental rotation (Corballis & Sergent, 1988), we carried out six sessions of 128 trials each, using as stimuli the letters *F*, *L*, *P*, and *R*, that appeared in eight different angular orientations, ranging from 0 to 315 deg clockwise from the normal upright in steps of 45 deg (see Figure 10.1a). Two letters were used within a session, and each letter could appeared in its normal or backward version in the left or the right visual field, and L.B. responded with two fingers of one hand, with the responding hand counterbalanced within a session.

The results of the six sessions are summarized in Table 10.1 (the "rates" refer to the speed-in degrees per second- at which a character is rotated, assuming that mental- rotation underlies performance). In all sessions, the right hemisphere performed in a manner essentially similar to that observed in normal subjects, and it proved much more adept than the left hemisphere at carrying out the mental rotation task. Accuracy was systematically higher after right- than left-hemisphere stimulations, and the mental-rotation rates for the right hemisphere were within the range typically obtained in such tasks with normal subjects. In contrast, in three of the first four sessions, the left hemisphere performed no better than chance, and the reaction times did not show the linear function typical of mental rotation. These functions are shown on the left side of Figure

Table 10.1
L.B.'s performance on 6 sessions of mental-rotation task

Session	Stimuli	L.V.F.				R.V.F.			
		% Correct	R.T	Rate	%Var.	% Correct	R.T.	Rate	%Var.
		deg/sec				deg/sec			
1	R,L	84.4	1042	800	0.23	57.8	1676	346	0.51
2	R,L	93.8	996	417	0.89	59.4	1623	-1179	0.02
3	R,L	96.9	1018	447	0.47	67.2	1928	-668	0.10
4	R,L	85.9	747	841	0.90	57.8	1011	18000	0.01
5	F,P	93.0	1137	285	0.63	78.1	1425	298	0.63
6	R,F	97.7	710	451	0.69	83.6	967	325	0.76

10.3 for the left and the right visual fields. While the function for the left visual field reflects the increasing RTs as the orientation of the character further departed from the upright, the right visual-field function does not provide a good approximation to an idealized mental-rotation. Even when L.B. performed significantly above chance in the right visual field, presumably as a result of learning through practice, his responses were still slower and less accurate than in the left visual field.

Although these findings suggest that L.B.'s right hemisphere has the ability to mentally rotate alphanumeric characters, they do not necessarily imply that his left hemisphere is deprived of such an ability. There are, in fact, at least two other operations, involved in the mental-rotation task, at which L.B.'s left hemisphere may have been defective. One such operation is concerned with the *identification* of disoriented letters, which is necessary in determining where the upright of the letter is and, therefore, in knowing the direction and the extent of the rotation to which the disoriented letter must be subjected. The other operation has to do with the *discrimination* between normal and backward versions of the letter, which presumably takes place after the letter has been rotated and constitutes the final decision of the mental-rotation task.

L.B. was therefore further tested on two control experiments, aimed at examining the capacity of the hemispheres at carrying out these two operations (Corballis & Sergent, in press-b). In one experiment, the task was almost identical to the mental-rotation task except that, instead of making a forward-backward discrimination, L.B. had to identify the letter (*F* or *R*). Evidence from

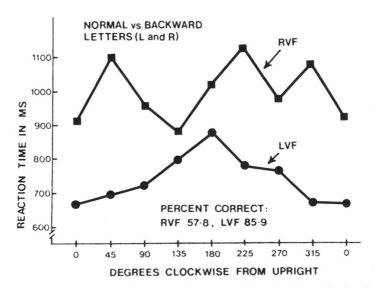

FIGURE 10.3 Mean RTs of L.B. for the mental-rotation task (session 4) in each orientation in each visual field.

normal subjects (e.g., Corballis, 1982) suggests that this task does not require mental rotation, and, therefore, that there is no linear relation between RTs and disorientation. The results of L.B. are depicted on the right side of Fig. 10.4, and they fail to show the typical increase in RTs as the orientation of the letter further departs from the upright, which would be expected if mental rotation underlay performance (as shown on the left side of Fig. 10.4). The results of this experiment therefore confirm that mental rotation is not required in the identification of disoriented characters. In addition, they indicate faster responses to right- than to left-hemifield presentations, suggesting that the left hemisphere could identify disoriented letters, in their normal or backward version, faster than could the right hemisphere. The superiority of the left hemisphere was also apparent in response accuracy, and it was significant for both dependent variables. In the other control experiment, L.B. had to decide whether an upright letter was in its normal or mirror-reversed version. The results showed that there was no visual-field difference in terms of response latency, but left-hemifield presentations produced more accurate responses than did right-field presentations, which nonetheless produced correct responses on 85% of the trials. In addition, there was an interaction between visual field and responding hand in this task. These results may then indicate that both hemispheres were capable of performing the discrimination between normal and mirror reversed letters, but it is possible that this component of the mental-rotation task also contributed to the overall superiority of the right hemisphere in addition to mental rotation itself.

The results of these two control experiments may thus provide indications that the main source of the superiority of L.B.'s right hemisphere in the mental-rotation task is the rotation component, as the identification of disoriented letters, as well as the discrimination between normal and backward versions, could be achieved without marked difficulties in the left hemisphere.

At this point, two main conclusions may be suggested. First, the mental-

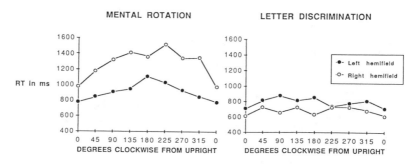

FIGURE 10.4 Mean RTs of L.B. for the mental-rotation task and the letter discrimination task, in each orientation in each visual field.

rotation task is composed of a series of operations that may not be performed equally efficiently by the two hemispheres. In the present case of L.B., when one of these component operations is poorly achieved in one hemisphere, the overall performance of this hemisphere is greatly affected because of the essentially isolated processes going on in each hemisphere of commissurotomized subjects. Although caution is required in generalizing from such subjects to the normal population, the pattern of dissociations observed in L.B. is nonetheless instructive and suggests a second point. The mixed results observed in the many studies of mental rotation in normal subjects do not necessarily bear on the mental-rotation component as such. Depending on the influence of experimental factors on the efficiency of the hemispheres at performing the other component operations, such as encoding of the letter, identification of the disoriented letter, normal-backward discrimination, the overall performance may reflect hemisphere asymmetry in these operations and may conceal genuine asymmetry in the mental-rotation operation. If no control tasks are carried out, it is impossible to determine whether or not the mental-rotation component is better performed by one hemisphere or the other. It may therefore be justified to suggest that the many studies on the laterality of the mental-rotation operation in normal subjects are inconclusive with respect to hemisphere specialization for this operation, whether or not significant visual-field, or hemispheric-activation, asymmetries were obtained.

As will be illustrated next, however, still other factors may contribute to the efficiency of the hemispheres at performing mental rotation.

Left-Right Discrimination. A subsequent series of RT experiments was carried out on L.B. in an attempt to examine mental rotation in tasks requiring left-right discrimination of disoriented patterns, using stimuli that did not require verbal identification of letters (Corballis & Sergent, in press-b). In one experiment, we used a stickfigure designed to represent a person holding out either the right or the left arm (see Fig. 10.1b). This figure could appear at varying angular departures from the upright as was done with the alphanumeric characters, and the task was to judge whether it was the right or the left arm of the figure which was raised. The results are depicted in Fig. 10. 5, and they again show a better performance of the right than of the left hemisphere. Although the reaction times for the left hemifield departed somewhat from an idealized mental rotation function, they nonetheless reasonably well fitted this function which accounted for more than 70% of the variance. By contrast, only 15% of the variance was accounted for by the mental rotation function in the right visual field, and the estimated rate of mental rotation was much too fast to suggest that mental rotation was involved in this task for the left hemisphere.

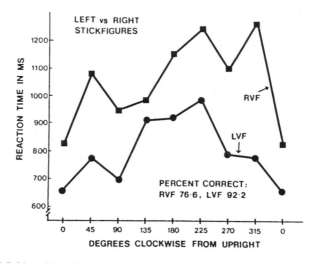

FIGURE 10.5 Mean RTs of L.B. for stickfigures in each orientation in each visual field.

In the next experiment, we tried to examine mental rotation in conditions where the subject would have to compare two stimuli presented at varying orientations ("double-stimulus task"). We first conducted a control task with only one stimulus that was made of a long and a short arm, with an arrow on the short arm pointing either to the right or to the left ("single-stimulus task"). The upright position was defined as the short arm at the top of the long arm in vertical orientation (see Fig. 10.1c). The stimuli were presented one at a time, in 6 different angular orientations varying in steps of 60 degrees, and each appeared either in the right or in the left visual field. The task was similar to that used with the stickfigure, and L.B. had to decide whether the short arm was pointing to the right or to the left after rotation of the figure to its upright.

The results are shown in Fig. 10. 6 and were totally unexpected. Accuracy was 99% in right visual field-left hemisphere presentations, but only 46% in left visual field - right hemisphere presentations. L.B. was operating completely at chance level when the stimuli were projected to his right hemisphere. This was rather surprising as this task did not appear very different from the stickfigure task. After two sessions, when it was obvious that L.B. was performing at chance in left-hemifield presentations, we inserted two new sessions of rotated stick-figures, to check that his right hemisphere was still able to perform mental rotation and, if so, hoping that it might prompt the right hemisphere to perform accurately. L.B. performed the stickfigure task as he had done earlier, with a right-hemisphere advantage in both speed and accuracy. We then ran two additional sessions with the initial stimuli, and left visual-field performance

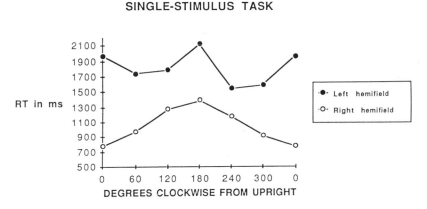

SINGLE-STIMULUS TASK

FIGURE 10.6 Mean RTs of L.B. for the "single-stimulus task" in each orientation in each visual field.

remained at chance level, with accuracy at 52%. Reaction times were also much faster in the right than in the left hemifield, and the mental rotation function accounted for only 5% of the variance in the left field, while it did for 96% in the right field.

This failure of the right hemisphere to carry out this task is rather puzzling. It cannot be attributed to a failure to tell left from right because this could be achieved accurately with the stickfigures. It cannot either be attributed to a failure of mental rotation as such, because L.B.'s right hemisphere had not experienced such difficulties in earlier tasks. It may be that L.B.'s right hemisphere failed to understand the instructions, but this seems rather unlikely. L.B. has shown the capacity to comprehend fairly complex instructions and to carry out demanding tasks in his right hemisphere, and it is not clear why this should be the case with this particular task. During the experimental sessions, we had suggested to L.B. that he might imagine the stimuli to be human figures, with the arrow representing the left or the right arm as with the stickfigures. Although he seemed to have tried, he replied he could not imagine the stimuli as human figures because there was no representation of the head. This should not be taken too seriously, however, because this comment must have emanated from his left hemisphere which had no difficulty with the task.

One possible explanation for L.B.'s right-hemisphere difficulty in performing this task may be related to the nature of the stimuli. By contrast with all the stimuli we had used so far, these simple stimuli had to be encoded and represented in terms of their categorical relations in order to determine the location of the short arm with respect to the long arm and thus to know where the upright stands, which was necessary to find out the direction of the arrow. While highly familiar stimuli, such as alphanumeric characters or the stickfigure, present little difficulty with respect to determining where their upright stands, the stimuli used in the present task had an arbitrary upright that was defined in terms of the relations between its two component arms. As a consequence, the determination of the upright may have required the capacity to encode these stimuli as a function of their categorical spatial relations. The failure of the right hemisphere to perform this task may then result from a deficiency of this hemisphere at encoding visual information as a function of the categorical relations of its component parts, which would be consistent with Kosslyn's (1987) suggestion of an asymmetry in the encoding capacities of the two hemispheres. Kosslyn has proposed that the right hemisphere preferentially encodes information along a coordinate system whereas the left hemisphere plays a critical role in encoding visual information on the basis of the categorical relations of its components. The absence of clear reference frame along which to describe the stimulus used in this task may have then made it difficult for the right hemisphere to achieve a reliable encoding of this stimulus that had to be subjected to additional transformations inherent in the operation of mental rotation. Although such an explanation is consistent with Kosslyn's (1987) theoretical developments, it is rather *ad hoc*, and further investigation would be required to determine the nature of L.B.'s right-hemisphere deficiency.

We also carried out a double-stimulus task in which the two stimuli were presented one above the other within the same visual field, and L.B. had to decide whether or not they were the same irrespective of angular orientation. In this task, in which the determination of the upright is not necessary because the two stimuli have only to be put in correspondence for matching, the left hemisphere again proved superior to the right hemisphere that, this time, performed significantly above chance. However, an examination of RTs (shown in Fig. 10.7) indicates that only the left hemisphere used mental rotation to perform this task. Performance by the right hemisphere yielded a negative estimate of mental rotation rate, and the shortest RT was obtained to stimuli separated by 180 deg, a condition that should have yielded the longest reaction time had L.B.'s right hemisphere used a mental mental-rotation strategy.

Irrespective of whether these results can be used to infer properties of functional lateralization in the general population, this series of experiments illustrate several points relevant for the study of hemispheric asymmetry. The merits of a computational approach seem to be fairly evident in that it allows a decomposition of a given function into its constituent operations and provides the opportunity to identify the respective competences of the hemispheres at carrying out each operation constitutive of a given task. Another point is that little can be taken for granted in the study of cerebral lateralization. The experiment involving the presentation of one stimulus composed of a long and a short arm was just designed as a control task for the double-stimulus task, and it was considered a simple formality. We had not thought for a moment that L.B.'s right hemisphere would be unable to carry out such a task that was conceived as a simplified version of the stickfigure task. Obviously, we were wrong and, this is a third

DOUBLE-STIMULUS TASK

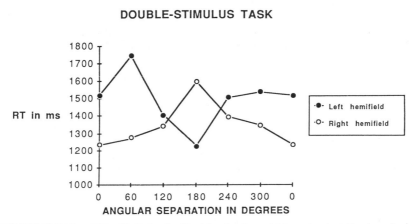

FIGURE 10.7 Mean RTs of L.B. for the "double-stimulus task" in each orientation in each visual field.

point, the study of a given function cannot be conducted irrespective of a consideration of the characteristics of the information to be processed. Even though the component operations of this task were exactly the same as those composing the stickfigure task, opposite patterns of hemisphere asymmetry were obtained in the two tasks. Thus, examination of component operations is not sufficient to understand the realization of a given function, and the structural properties of the stimuli also contribute to the respective processing efficiency of the cerebral hemispheres.

Processing of Disoriented Faces

Although the preceding series of experiments offer some insight into the distribution of processing competences between the two hemispheres, they are restricted to one commissurotomized subject and to one type of operation. In fact, two other commissurotomized patients (A.A. and N.G.) were tested on this task but they failed to perform the forward-backward and the left-right discrimination of rotated stimuli, even when the stimuli were presented for unlimited time. In addition, mental rotation is but one of the transformations to which visual objects can be subjected to correct for their disorientation, and, as noted earlier, the visual system may resort to different types of operations to achieve a correspondence between the retinal description of an object and the stored underlying invariants that characterize its uniqueness. To examine this issue further, a different approach was used that involved the processing of disoriented faces, which allowed the possibility to study the capacity of commissurotomized subjects to process disoriented stimuli without the requirement of telling left from right. In addition, to make the task not too difficult for these subjects, they were tested on their capacity to perform a male/female categorization of disoriented faces, as this categorization was thought to be less demanding than a face discrimination or recognition task. Before describing these experiments, some background information is required to outline the various factors inherent in this study along with the specific problems it addresses.

Upright and Inverted Faces

Faces are typically mono-oriented multidimensional stimuli hardly recognizable upside-down, and the spatial arrangement of the component features that uniquely defines the identity of each face may be too complex to be subjected to mental rotation without loss of relevant information. Rock (1973) suggested that faces overtax a system for rotating disoriented stimuli, and the difficulty in recognizing inverted faces may result from the impossibility to rotate each feature simultaneously. Thus, because the features of upside-down faces would have to be rotated one at a time, information about the spatial arrangement of the features (the configural information) cannot be recovered. There is a large body of findings showing that although the recognition of upright faces can be achieved with an efficiency superior to that involved in the recognition of other visual objects, inversion is more detrimental to the recognition of faces than to the recognition of other objects (see Sergent, in press-a, for further discussion).

Two issues are worth considering in the present context. One is concerned with the nature of the processes underlying the perception and recognition of inverted faces, and specifically whether inversion entails a qualitatively different process from the one underlying perception of upright faces. The second point bears on the respective capacity of the two hemispheres to process upright and inverted faces.

Processes Underlying Perception of Upright and Inverted Faces.
In addition to Rock's (1973) suggestion and demonstration that inversion of faces overtaxes a system for rotating disoriented stimuli, other evidence points to a qualitative difference in the processing of upright and inverted faces. Sergent (1984) examined the nature of the processes underlying the perception of faces at different orientations in same-different and dissimilarity-judgment tasks. Although the results showed that upright faces were compared on the basis of both component and configural information, there was no evidence that subjects made use of configural information in comparing inverted faces, suggesting that different informational contents of the faces were processed depending on the orientation of the stimuli. However, the artificial nature of both the task (same-different, and dissimilarity judgments) and the stimuli (Photofit faces) invites caution in drawing strong conclusions from these findings. They nonetheless indicate that the same faces are subjected to different processes depending on their orientation. Diamond and Carey (1986) have presented further evidence illustrating the difficulty in extracting the configurational

information from inverted faces. They argued that stimuli represented in terms of second-order relational information (i.e., distinctive relations among elements that define a common configuration of a class of objects) are highly vulnerable to disorientation in subjects who have learned to make use of this information. Presumably, all humans have learned to extract the configurational information from faces, and, although this learning makes them highly efficient at processing normally oriented faces, it also reduces their capacity to efficiently process inverted faces. Diamond and Carey tested recognition of upright and inverted dogs by dog experts and novices, and, in support of their suggestion, they found the same vulnerability to inversion for faces and dogs only in dog experts, while novice subjects showed the typical interaction of class of objects by orientation. These two sets of findings, along with Rock's (1973) suggestion, point to an inability of subjects to extract the configural information from inverted faces, and therefore suggest qualitative differences in the processing of normally oriented and upside-down faces.

However, Valentine and Bruce (1988) recently argued that upright and inverted faces are processed in a qualitatively similar manner. They based this suggestion on the finding of a linear RT increase as faces to be judged as familiar or unfamiliar further departed from the upright. Assuming that this increase reflected only the time involved in mentally rotating the disoriented face, they concluded that the process of recognition itself was constant across orientations and, therefore, that upright and inverted faces were subjected to the same type of recognition process. Although this may be the case, there is nonetheless reason to doubt that the linear RT increase reflected the operation of mental rotation. Valentine and Bruce (1988) did not calculate the assumed "mental-rotation" rate but, by extrapolating from the function depicted in their Figures, this rate can be estimated as being in the order of 1400 degrees per second. Such a rate is much faster than the fastest rate observed in typical mental-rotation tasks with stimuli much simpler than faces, and Shepard and Cooper (1982) never found rates superior to 800 degrees per second (see also Corballis, 1982). It is therefore unlikely that the linear relationship between RTs and departure from the upright reflects the operation of mental rotation, and it may instead indicate a qualitative change in processing upright and disoriented faces.

Hemispheric Competence at Processing Upright and Inverted Faces. The effect of inversion on the processing of faces in the two hemispheres has provided a clear example of a double dissociation in unilaterally brain-damaged patients. Yin (1970) reported that right-hemisphere patients were more impaired than left-hemisphere patients at recognizing upright faces, but were less deficient than left-hemisphere patients at recognizing inverted faces. Although Yin's study was not designed to infer the nature of the underlying processes, it nonetheless indicates a different contribution of the two hemispheres to the perception and recognition of upright and inverted faces. Leehey, Carey, Diamond, and Cahn (1978) have confirmed this finding in normal subjects, as they found that the usual right-hemisphere superiority in recognizing faces was eliminated when the

same faces were presented upside-down. Although this seems to be a robust
effect, there is no unequivocal account of this finding, because the manipulation
of face orientation also modifies the difficulty of the task, which, in turn, affects
the respective contribution of the two hemispheres (see Sergent, 1988, for further
discussion). Nonetheless, a critical issue in this respect concerns the effect of
inversion on the processing of faces, and, so far, this has been examined only in
face-recognition tasks. Whether this effect extends to other operations performed
on faces, and, if so, whether it is of the same nature across operations, will be
examined in the experiments reported below.

Gender Categorization of Disoriented Faces

A face conveys a large amount of information to an observer and, in addition
to the identity of the person, it also carries information about gender, race, age,
emotion of an individual that can be accessed independent of his/her identity (i.e.,
one does not need to know a person to infer the age, gender or emotion from that
person's face).

It was with the gender of the faces that the following study was concerned,
and specifically with the capacity of the subjects to categorize disoriented faces
into male or female. Such a categorization can be performed without accessing
individually stored representations, but it requires the extraction of specific facial
information that contains invariants characterizing its gender and that allows a
differentiation between the two categories. Evidence from multidimensional
scaling analysis of dissimilarity judgments between male and female faces
(Sergent, in preparation) indicates that the hair are the main feature on which
male/female categorization is based. However, two other dimensions are found to
significantly contribute to this categorization: One represents the configuration of
the internal features, and the other some form of interaction between the hair and
this configuration. These findings were confirmed in a RT study in which
subjects performed a male/female categorization on the basis of either the full
faces, of the hair of these faces, or of the internal features of these faces. The
results showed an increase in RT and error rates along these three conditions,
suggesting that efficient categorization is achieved by processing the whole face
and that, even if the hair is a sufficient clue in most circumstances, the
configuration of the internal features also conveys relevant information about the
gender of the individual and significantly contributes to this categorization. If the
inversion of faces is detrimental to the extraction of the configuration that
emerges from the relationships among internal features, as suggested by Diamond
and Carey (1984), Rock (1973), and Sergent (1984), but not by Valentine and
Bruce (1988), then a male/female categorization should be sensitive to the
disorientation of faces, and this should be reflected in the shape and the slope of
the function relating RTs to departure of the faces from the upright. It remains
true, however, that the hair constitute a highly distinctive feature of the face,
easily localizable, and, as such, may provide a reliable basis for categorization,
irrespective of orientation.

Evidence From Normal Subjects. Laterality studies on male/female categorization of upright faces have indicated that both hemispheres are competent at performing such a task and can do so equally efficiently depending on the conditions of stimulus presentation. For instance, Sergent (1982) observed a shift from left to right visual-field superiority as exposure duration was increased from 40 to 200 ms, but no field difference at 120 ms. In the present study, a relatively long exposure duration (180 ms) was used to minimize the number of errors and ensure a greater reliability of the RT data. Although such an exposure duration may inherently favor right-hemifield presentation of upright faces, the main concern of the study was with the effect of face disorientation. If the two hemispheres are differentially affected by this disorientation, one should expect an interaction of visual field by orientation.

The experiment consisted in the lateral presentation of one among 6 male faces and 6 female faces, each appearing in one of 6 different angular orientations, ranging from 0 to 300 degrees clockwise from the normal upright in steps of 60 degrees (see Figure 10. 1d). The subjects responded by manually pressing one of two telegraph keys. Figure 10. 8 presents the functions relating RTs to departure of the faces from the upright, for each visual field, along with the total number of errors. It shows an interaction between visual field and orientation, reflecting faster RTs to upright faces in the right than in the left hemifield while departure from the upright resulted in smaller increase of RTs for left than for right visual-field presentations. These results therefore suggest that the right hemisphere is better adept than the left at correcting for the effect of disorientation of faces, and that this effect is not due to an inherent advantage of this hemisphere at processing faces, since the left hemisphere was superior to the right hemisphere in categorizing upright faces.

However, even though disorientation of the faces significantly affected the speed at which the categorization was made in both visual fields, the cost of face disorientation was relatively small in this task compared to the identification of inverted faces (Rock, 1973), or the mirror-image discrimination of letters (see Figure 10.2). When the mental-rotation rate was estimated from the functions depicted in Figure 10.8, it was found to be 7500 and 2481 degrees per second for the left and the right visual field, respectively (as a comparison, the mental-rotation rates of letters estimated from the functions shown in Figure 10.2 were 320 and 345 degrees per second for the right and the left hemifield, respectively. These RT functions showed a linear increase with departure from the upright, and accounted for 89.3% and 93.5% of the variance in left and right visual fields, respectively. Despite this linear increase, the results are not consistent with the operation of mental rotation in this task, in neither hemisphere, because the rates have no common measure with those observed in typical mental-rotation task. Given that mental rotation, as currently conceived, is regarded as an analog simulation of corresponding real rotation (Bethell-Fox & Shepard, 1988), a 7500°-rate is incompatible with such a rotation (as a comparison, this rate would correspond to 21 revolutions of the handle of a clock in 1 second!).

It is nonetheless the case that disorientation significantly affected the speed of processing, and, if mental rotation cannot account for the increase in RTs, another explanation of the findings must be sought. In view of the evidence mentioned earlier that both the hair and the configuration of the internal features contribute to the gender categorization of faces, this RT increase may then reflect the increased difficulty in extracting the configural information from the face as it further departs from the upright. In this sense, the disorientation of the faces decreased the redundancy of the facial information normally used in male/female categorization, which, in turn reduced the speed at which the faces could be classified.

These results also provide information about the respective contribution of the cerebral hemispheres to the processing of disoriented stimuli. Upright faces were categorized faster by the left than by the right hemisphere, replicating earlier findings obtained under similar viewing conditions (e.g., Sergent, 1982). It must be noted that this finding is specific to the particular viewing conditions prevailing in this experiment and should not be regarded as an indication of more efficient left- than right-hemisphere face categorization. Nonetheless, the disorientation was better accommodated by the right than by the left hemisphere, and this was especially evident at orientations that most departed from the upright (120, 180, and 240 degrees, see Figure 10. 8). This finding suggests that the contribution of the right hemisphere may become more critical the further the presentation of objects deviates from their canonical perspective, which concurs with earlier findings by Warrington and James (1986). This right-hemisphere advantage does not seem to result from the operation of a mental-rotation component, however, and it may reflect a greater capacity of this hemisphere either to make appropriate decisions on the basis of restricted facial information or to extract the relevant information contained in disoriented stimuli. Either way, the findings may be consistent with the view that the right hemisphere is less affected than the left by a reduction in the normal redundancy of the incoming information (e.g., Sergent, 1984, in press-b).

It is noteworthy that the right-hemisphere superiority observed at orientations that departed most from the upright is opposite that found in the *recognition* of inverted faces (Leehey et al., 1978; Yin, 1970). It may thus not be the inversion *per se* that is the critical factor in the classical effect of face inversion on hemisphere processing, but the particular set of information that must be extracted from the inverted face depending on what characteristics about the individual have to be accessed. In addition, in so far as a male/female categorization and face recognition both require the processing of facial features, the hemispheric dissociation in processing upright and inverted faces cannot be due solely to the particular nature of faces as opposed to other visual objects. It may therefore be the difference in the operations that must be implemented depending on the information to be extracted that must account for the opposite hemisphere superiority in the recognition and categorization of inverted faces. One such difference concerns the informational demands inherent in the two

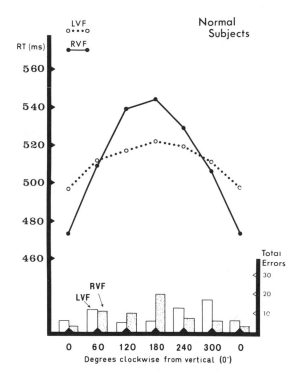

FIGURE 10.8 Mean RTs and error rates of normal subjects to categorize faces in each orientation in each visual field.

types of task. While male/female *categorization* may be adequately, though not optimally, achieved on the basis of a salient feature such as the hair, a distinctive feature may not be sufficient for face *recognition* which is typically based on the configuration that emerges from the interaction among the features (Sergent, 1984).

Evidence From Commissurotomized Subjects. The same study was undertaken on three commissurotomized subjects in an attempt to seek converging information about hemisphere competence at processing disoriented faces. In addition, the study of these subjects served the purpose of better specifying the source of visual-field asymmetry in categorizing disoriented faces observed in the normal subjects. If the left hemisphere is essentially unable to perform such processes and requires the resources of the right hemisphere, one would expect the disconnected left hemisphere to operate at chance in this task. By contrast, if the results of the normal subjects reflect unequal efficiency of the two hemispheres, then the patterns of results of the commissurotomized subjects should be qualitatively similar to that of the normal subjects.

The experiment was in all points similar to the preceding one, except that more trials were run in order to obtain sufficient data to carry out separate analyses of the RTs of each commissurotomized subject. The results are shown in Figure 10. 9 for each subject, in terms of RTs for each orientation and visual field, along with the percentage of errors for each condition.

All three subjects performed above chance in the two visual fields, suggesting that both hemispheres were capable of carrying out the categorization of the disoriented faces. In addition, the RT functions were essentially similar to that obtained with normal subjects, although their slopes were much steeper because of basic slowness in response time, and the results revealed an interaction of orientation by visual field. These interactions are clearly illustrated in Figure 10. 9 for each patient, and indicate that the difference in RTs between the two visual fields was smaller with upright faces (0°) than was the superiority of the left visual field with inverted faces (180°). In addition, the linear component of the functions relating RTs to orientation was significant in each visual field of the three subjects.

These findings provide converging evidence of a crucial role of the right hemisphere in correcting for disorientation of mono-oriented stimuli. The right hemisphere superiority was most pronounced the further the orientation of the face departed from its normal upright, suggesting that, as in normals subjects, this superiority cannot be attributed to inherently greater efficiency of the right hemisphere at processing faces. Nonetheless, the left hemisphere, although slower and less accurate than the right hemisphere, was capable of processing the disoriented faces at a level superior to chance, and this was achieved without the contribution of the right hemisphere. The superiority of the right hemisphere may thus be relative rather than absolute, and the left hemisphere is not totally bereft

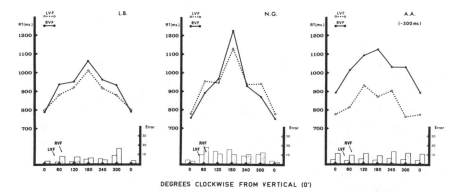

DEGREES CLOCKWISE FROM VERTICAL (0°)

FIGURE 10.9 Mean RTs and error rates of 3 commissurotomized subjects to categorize faces in each orientation in each visual field (300 ms have been subtracted from A.A.'s actual RTs).

of the capacity to perform at least some of the transformations required to access the relevant information from stimuli that depart from their canonical perspective. Considering that such a deviation from the upright reduces the possibility to extract the configural facial properties that are relevant for the differentiation of males from females, the smaller impairment resulting from disorientation in the right than in the left hemisphere may reflect a greater capacity of the former to accommodate itself of a loss of redundancy of the relevant information.

CONCLUSION

Advances in the understanding of the mapping of cognitive functions onto cerebral structures have relied on the development of new conceptual frameworks and experimental techniques, and, while much remains to be learned about functional cerebral lateralization, a computational approach may contribute to such an advance. This approach represents a significant progress over the more global evaluations of hemispheric functions, and it goes far beyond the characterization of hemisphere specialization along dichotomic dimensions. The identification of component operations underlying the realization of a given function is a necessary step in explaining the respective contribution of the hemispheres to cognition. It also imposes a rigorous experimental approach that takes nothing for granted in the study of hemisphere processing capacities. The merits of this approach were illustrated in the examination of the contribution of the cerebral hemispheres to the processing of disoriented stimuli. By focusing on specific operations inherent in the realization of a given task, it was possible to isolate, at least in the study of commissurotomized subject L.B., the actual source of a hemisphere superiority in a specific function. What was also illustrated by this approach was that many factors underlie the realization of a given operation, and the same operation was found to produce opposite patterns of hemisphere asymmetries a result of a simple change in the structural properties of the stimuli on which the operation had to be implemented. While this points to the necessity to consider conjointly the operations and the representations of the information being operated on (see Sergent, in press-c), it also suggests that advances in our understanding of cerebral lateralization of functions depend on a thorough, and rather tedious, examination of each single process and representation assumed to underlie the implementation of a function. A computational approach certainly provides a useful framework for carrying out such an examination.

However, while the decomposition of a function into its operational units allows a specification of the various stages through which information processing unfolds, this decomposition is posited a priori, irrespective of the properties of the organism that implements these operations. The brain certainly realizes the functions described at a computational level, but its way of implementing them may not correspond to the decomposition into processing modules postulated in computational models. Such models fall short of accounting for the parallel distributed nature of cerebral processing and the high redundancy of brain structures and processes, and they provide no clue as to how the two hemispheres are conjointly involved in the realization of any function (see Sergent, 1989). As an information processor, the brain possesses unique properties which impose specific constraints on the conditions under which computations are implemented, and factors such as state and process limitations, degradation, memory loads, task complexity, all modulate the respective efficiency of the cerebral hemispheres in non trivial manners. It may thus be through a conjoint examination of the actual operations underlying a given function and of the specific conditions under which those operations are carried out in the brain that significant advances in the understanding of cerebral lateralization will be made.

ACKNOWLEDGMENTS

The work reported in this chapter was supported by grants from the University of Auckland Research Committee, the Natural Sciences and Engineering Research Council of Canada, and the Medical Research Council of Canada.

REFERENCES

Allen, M. (1983). Models of hemispheric specialization. *Psychological Bulletin, 93*, 73-104.

Bethell-Fox, C. E., & Shepard, R. N. (1988). Mental rotation: Effects of stimulus complexity and familiarity. *Journal of Experimental Psychology: Human Perception and Performance, 14*, 12-23.

Cohen, G. (1975). Hemispheric differences in the utilization of advance information. In P. M. A. Rabbitt & S. Dornic (Eds.), *Attention and Performance V* (pp. 20-32). London: Academic Press.

Cohen, W., & Polich, J. (1989). No hemispheric differences for mental rotation of letters or polygons. *Bulletin of the Psychonomic Society, 27*, 25-28.

Cooper, L. A., & Shepard, R. N. (1973). Chronometric studies of the rotation of mental images. In W. G. Chase (Ed.), *Visual information processing* (pp. 75-176). New York: Academic Press.

Cooper, L. A., & Shepard, R. N. (1975). Mental transformation in the identification of left and right hands. *Journal of Experimental Psychology: Human Perception and Performance, 1*, 48-56.

Corballis, M. C. (1982). Mental rotation: Anatomy of a paradigm. In M. Potegal (Ed.), *Spatial abilities: Development and Physiological Foundations* (pp. 173-198). New York: Academic Press.

Corballis, M. C. (1988). Recognition of disoriented shapes. *Psychological Review, 95*, 115-123.

Corballis, M. C., & McLaren, R. (1984). Winding one's *ps* and *qs*: Mental rotation and mirror image discrimination. *Journal of Experimental Psychology: Human Perception and Performance, 10*, 318-327.

Corballis, M. C., Macadie, L., Beale, I. (1985). Mental rotation and visual laterality in normal and reading disabled children. *Cortex, 21*, 225-236.

Corballis, M. C., & Nagourney, B. A. (1978). Latency to categorize disoriented alphanumeric characters as letters or digits. *Canadian Journal of Psychology, 23,* 186-188.

Corballis, M. C., & Sergent, J. (1988). Imagery in a commissurotomized patient. *Neuropsychologia, 26,* 13-26.

Corballis, M. C., & Sergent, J. (in press-a). Hemispheric specialization for mental rotation. *Cortex,*

Corballis, M. C., & Sergent, J. (in press-b). Mental rotation in a commissurotomized subject. *Neuropsychologia,*

Deutsch, G., Bourbon, W. T., Papanicolaou, A. C., & Eisenberg, H. M. (1988). Visuospatial tasks compared via activation of regional cerebral blood flow. *Neuropsychologia, 26,* 445-452.

Diamond, R., & Carey, S. (1986). Why faces are and are not special: An effect of expertise. *Journal of Experimental Psychology: General, 115,* 107-117.

Eley, M. G. (1982). Identifying rotated letterlike symbols. *Memory & Cognition, 10,* 25-32.

Farah, M. J. (1984). The neurological basis of mental imagery: A componential analysis. *Cognition, 18,* 245-272.

Fischer, S. C., & Pellegrino, J. W. (1988). Hemispheric differences for components of mental rotation. *Brain and Cognition, 7,* 1-15.

Humphreys, G. W., & Riddoch, J. (1984). Routes to object constancy: Implications for neurological impairments in object constancy. *Quarterly Journal of Experimental Psychology, 36A,* 385-415.

Jolicoeur, P. (1988). Mental rotation and identification of disoriented objects. *Canadian Journal of Psychology, 42,* 461-478.

Jones, B., & Anuza, T. (1982). Effects of sex, handedness, stimulus, and visual field on "mental rotation". *Cortex, 18,* 501-514.

Kosslyn, S. M. (1987). Seeing and imagining in the cerebral hemispheres. A computational approach. *Psychological Review, 94,* 148-175.

Leehey, S., Carey, S., Diamond, R., & Cahn, A. (1978). Upright and inverted faces: The right hemisphere knows the difference. *Cortex, 14,* 411-419.

Levy-Agresti, J., & Sperry, R. W. (1968). Differential processing capacities in major and minor hemispheres. *Proceedings of the National Academy of Sciences (USA), 61,* 1151.

Ornstein, R., Johnstone, J., Herron, J., & Swencionis, C. (1980). Differential right-hemisphere engagement in visuo-spatial tasks. *Neuropsychologia, 18,* 49-64.

Ratcliff, G. (1979). Spatial thought, mental rotation, and the right cerebral hemisphere. Neuropsychologia, 17, 49-54.

Rock, I. (1973). *Orientation and form.* New York: Academic Press.

Sergent, J. (1982). Theoretical and methodological consequences of variations in exposure duration in visual laterality studies. *Perception & Psychophysics, 31,* 451-461.

Sergent, J. (1984). An investigation into component and configural processes underlying face perception. *British Journal of Psychology, 75,* 221-242.

Sergent, J. (1988). Some methodological and theoretical issues in neuropsychological research. In F. Boller & J. Grafman (Eds.), *Handbook of Neuropsychology, Vol. 1* (pp. 69-81). Amsterdam: Elsevier.

Sergent, J. (1989). Image generation and processing of generated images in the cerebral hemispheres. *Journal of Experimental Psychology: Human Perception and Performance, 15,* 170-178.

Sergent, J. (in press-a). Structural processing of faces. In A. W. Young & H. D. Ellis (Eds.), *Handbook of research on face perception.* Amsterdam: Elsevier.

Sergent, J. (in press-b). Ontogenesis and microgenesis of face perception. *European Bulletin of Cognitive Psychology, 9,*

Sergent, J. (in press-c). Image generation in the cerebral hemispheres: Facts and fancies. *Journal of Experimental Psychology: Human Perception and Performance, 15,*

Sergent, J., & Corballis, M. C. (in press). Categorization of disoriented faces in the cerebral hemispheres of normal and commissurotomized subjects. *Journal of Experimental Psychology: Human Perception and Performance, 15,*

Shepard, R. N., & Cooper, L. A. (1982). *Mental images and their transformations.* Cambridge, MA: MIT Press.

Stuss, D. T., Sarazin, F. F., Leech, E. E., & Picton, T. W. (1983). Event-related potentials during naming and mental rotation. *Electroencephalography and clinical Neurophysiology, 56,* 133-146.

Valentine, T., & Bruce, V. (1988). Mental rotation of faces. *Memory & Cognition, 16,* 556-566.

Warrington, E. K., & James, M. (1986). Visual object recognition in patients with right-hemisphere lesions: Axes or features? *Perception, 15,* 355-366.

Warrington, E. K., & Taylor, A. M. (1978). Two categorical stages of object recognition. *Perception, 7,* 695-709.

Yin, R. K. (1970). Face recognition by brain-injured patients: A dissociable ability? *Neuropsychologia, 8,* 395-402.

11 Symmetries and Asymmetries in the Processing of Sinusoidal Gratings

Frederick L. Kitterle
Stephen Christman
University of Toledo

Research with normal subjects using lateral tachistoscopic techniques has shown that some visual tasks may be performed better if the stimuli are presented in the visual field to the left of fixation (LVF) whereas other tasks are performed better if stimuli are presented in the visual field to the right of fixation (RVF). Because the visual pathways arising from the temporal hemiretinas in humans pass directly to the ipsilateral cerebral hemisphere and the pathways arising from the nasal hemiretinas project to the contralateral cerebral hemisphere (Davison, 1972), visual stimuli that are presented in the LVF, are, initially, represented in the right hemisphere (RH) of the brain. Stimuli presented in the RVF, on the other hand, are represented in the left cerebral hemisphere (LH). Thus, the dependence of performance on visual-field presentation has been assumed to reflect information-processing asymmetries between the two cerebral hemispheres. The precise way in which to characterize hemispheric differences in processing, has led to a proliferation of models that attempt to categorize asymmetries in terms of a high-level task dichotomy (e.g., analytic/holistic or verbal/visuospatial) (Bradshaw & Nettleton, 1981; and reviews in Beaton, 1985; Cohen, 1982; Hardyck, 1986; Sergent, 1983).

Attempts to account for functional differences between the two hemispheres solely in terms of high-level dichotomies are insufficient (see Sergent, 1982). Recent studies indicate that the magnitude and direction of visual information-processing asymmetries not only depend on the nature of the task, but also on the interaction of task variables with characteristics of the visual stimulus and the mode of presentation. For example, for a variety of tasks variations such as the size, contrast, retinal eccentricity, luminance, energy, and exposure duration of the stimulus can reverse or reduce the relative processing efficiency of one hemisphere over the other (see Sergent, 1983 for a review). Sergent (1983, 1987) has made the point that in the study of cerebral laterality effects, methodological and procedural questions such as how large to make the stimuli, how long to make the exposure duration, and how far from fixation to present the target, rather than being incidental in nature, are of central theoretical importance. These manipulations influence the nature of the visual input, and thus, the conditions under which the brain has to operate. Further, it is of theoretical importance to consider how visual information is represented because a particular representation will determine the type of operations that can be carried out. Specifying the nature of the visual input is crucial for understanding how the brain processes visual input. This is particularly the case in studies using lateral tachistoscopic techniques where the brain is presented with inputs unlike those found in normal situations.

Sergent and others (e.g., Christman, 1987; Jonsson & Hellige, 1986; Sergent, 1982a, 1982b, 1983, 1986, 1987; Sergent & Hellige, 1986) have suggested that the aforementioned effects of input characteristics on hemispheric asymmetries may be attributed to the differential hemispheric processing of spatial frequency components of the input. Specifically, it has been proposed that there is a right-hemisphere advantage in the processing of low spatial frequencies and a left-hemisphere advantage in the processing of high spatial frequencies.

The basis for describing a visual stimulus in terms of its spatial frequency components derives from Fourier Theory, which states that the image of any object can be mathematically analyzed as a set of spatial frequencies at various orientations, amplitudes, and phases (see Weisstein, 1986, for a review).

Psychophysical studies have determined the sensitivity of the human visual system to sinewave gratings by measuring the contrast threshold to detect gratings at a number of different spatial frequencies. The resulting curve describes a contrast sensitivity function where contrast sensitivity (the inverse of contrast threshold) is plotted as a function of spatial frequency. Several studies have shown that this curve reflects the activity of a number of multiple mechanisms, each selectively sensitive to a narrow range of spatial frequencies. These and other data support the view that the human visual system contains filters that are selectively sensitive to the spatial frequency content in the visual input (Campbell & Robson, 1966; see Harris, 1986, for a collection of papers on this topic as well as Thomas, 1987). Because the processing of higher versus lower frequencies is segregated in the visual system, it is reasonable to hypothesize hemispheric differences in the processing of different ranges of spatial frequency.

Kitterle (1986) has provided a review of the literature that indicates how the shape of the contrast sensitivity function is influenced by exposure duration, retinal locus, mean luminance, and grating size. For example, at brief exposure durations the visual system is more sensitive to low spatial frequencies, whereas, the reverse is true for high spatial frequency (Arend & Lange, 1979). Lowering mean luminance decreases contrast sensitivity to the high spatial frequencies, which carry the information about edges, and peak contrast sensitivity shifts to the lower spatial frequencies. With increases in retinal eccentricity, contrast sensitivity shifts to the lower spatial frequencies. Thus, all of these manipulations may be expected to produce greater impairment of LH relative to RH performance.

Several studies testing the hypothesis that the cerebral hemispheres are differentially effective in processing spatial frequency information have attempted to directly manipulate the spatial frequency content in the visual stimulus through spatial filtering by blurring the image. This manipulation on the input reduces the high spatial frequency content in the visual stimulus. For example, Jonsson and Hellige (1986) had subjects indicate whether two letters presented in either the right or the left visual field were physically identical. They found that blurring letters was more detrimental to LVF-RH than to RVF-LH performance. However, defocusing a stimulus may not only reduce the contribution of the high spatial frequencies but also diminish the contribution of the low spatial frequencies as well as making the stimulus less perceptible. Thus, Jonsson and Hellige (1986) have proposed an alternative explanation, namely, the "perceptibility hypothesis." They argued that because blurring reduces the perceptibility of the stimulus it may be the case that the right hemisphere is more sensitive to stimuli that are defocused or less perceptible rather than to low spatial frequencies per se. Research attempting to dissociate between the perceptibility versus spatial frequency hypotheses has yielded ambivalent support for both hypotheses (Michimata & Hellige, 1987; Taylor & Hellige, 1987). Perhaps the perceptibility hypothesis pertains to task, not input, characteristics.

The spatial frequency hypothesis receives additional support from research on patients with unilateral cerebral vascular accidents (CVA) that explores letter-matching performance with blurred and degraded stimuli presented foveally. Wolcott, Saul, Hellige, and Kumar (in press) found that letter-matching with blurred or masked stimuli results in poorer performance for patients with CVAs in the RH in comparison to controls or patients with left CVAs. Thus, when the LH is intact, but not the RH, and the stimulus contains only low spatial frequency information, performance is impaired.

Christman (submitted) examined the effects of dioptic blur in a temporal integration task in which recognition was dependent on the summation of information contained in two successively presented stimuli. With dioptic blurring attenuation is greater at the high spatial frequencies and can be quantitatively specified. Two conditions of blur (1 diopter and 2 diopters) were used. The former attenuated spatial frequencies above 9 c/deg and the latter above 3.5 c/deg. Christman showed that attenuation of the high spatial frequencies above 9 c/deg resulted in selective impairment of LH performance only. These results are quite consistent with the spatial frequency hypothesis.

Stimuli have also been digitally filtered as a way of selectively altering the spatial frequency content of the visual input. Sergent (1985) found that a left-hemisphere superiority in the identification of faces that contained a broad range of spatial frequencies was reversed to a right-hemisphere advantage when the faces were low-pass filtered. Sergent (1987) also found an interaction between visual field and spatial frequency in a same/different judgment task on broad-pass and low-pass filtered faces.

The shift in hemispheric dominance on a given task as a result of blurring can also be accomplished by varying the exposure duration of the stimulus (e.g.,

Sergent, 1982). Based on the temporal properties of the low and high spatial frequency channels it appears that the extraction of spatial frequency information from a visual stimulus takes place at different rates (Breitmeyer & Ganz, 1977). At brief exposure durations the visual system is more sensitive to low spatial frequencies, whereas the reverse is true for high spatial frequency (Arend and Lange, 1979). In addition, psychophysical studies have shown that temporal integration is faster for low than for high spatial frequency and this holds at both threshold (Breitmeyer & Ganz, 1973) and suprathreshold levels (Kitterle & Corwin, 1979). Hood (1973) compared the effects of exposure duration on visual sensitivity for detecting a sharply focused and blurred bar and found that increases in exposure duration had a greater effect on sensitivity for detecting the sharply focused bar. At brief durations there was little difference in sensitivity between the two stimuli due to the fact that detection of targets was primarily mediated by the shorter latency, more sensitive low spatial frequency channels that responded to the low spatial frequencies in the targets. At longer durations, the longer latency, high spatial frequency channels could be activated and mediate detection resulting in further increases in sensitivity. However, with the blurred bar the high spatial frequencies were not present and consequently, increases in exposure duration did not benefit the detection of this stimulus.

The implication of the aforementioned is that in a cerebral laterality experiment, if a task can be performed with either high or low spatial frequencies, variations in exposure duration should alter hemispheric dominance. For example, if the exposure duration is brief and a task can be performed with low spatial frequency information, there should be a RH advantage. On the other hand, increases in exposure duration should result in enhanced performance for RVF-LH presentations. These findings have been confirmed in a number of studies (e.g., Hellige & Sergent, 1986; Sergent, 1983; Sergent & Hellige, 1986; however see Christman, in press; Diehl & McKeever, 1987; Sergent, 1987). Curiously, Sergent (1987) found, with low-pass filtered faces, that increases in exposure duration benefited RVF/LH presentations more than LVF/RH presentations. One might argue that the LH can also process low spatial frequencies but the temporal properties of these channels differ from that of the RH and/or processing times for cognitive operations based on this information differ for the two hemispheres. Longer exposure durations may define optimal processing conditions and consequently both hemispheres can perform the task even when there are no high spatial frequencies in the stimulus, although the LH may require longer exposure durations for optimal processing of lower frequencies.

Sergent (1987) has pointed out a number of methodological reasons why other studies with filtered images have not confirmed the spatial frequency hypothesis. In part, studies may have failed to adequately control for the spatial frequency content of the stimulus. For example, Boles and Morelli (1987) used squarewave gratings to test this hypothesis. This stimulus is a complex waveform whose composition can be mathematically described as the sum of a series of sinusoidal components including the fundamental as well as higher frequency odd harmonics.   Because squarewave gratings contain a broad range of spatial frequencies that are available for both hemispheres to process, Hemisphere by Spatial Frequency effects would not be easily interpretable.

Moscovitch and Radzins (1987) attempted to vary the strength of the spatial frequency content of their targets by masking.   The mask, however, was composed of dots spatially distributed to determine a specific spatial frequency. Dots themselves are represented by a wide range of spatial frequencies and, thus, are ineffective as a filter for a narrow band of spatial frequencies.   In addition, there were uncontrolled changes in mean luminance in this study and others (e.g., Boles & Morelli, 1987; Szelag, Budhoska, & Koltuska, 1987) that may have counteracted any spatial frequency effects.

Changes in mean luminance can differentially mask high and low spatial frequencies.   As a result the evaluation of hemispheric differences in spatial frequency may not be straight forward.   That is, hemispheric processing of spatial frequency may be confounded by potential differences in hemispheric susceptibility to masking (Badcock & Sevdalis, 1987; Green, 1981; Kitterle, Beasley, & Berta, 1984; Kitterle, Corwin, & Berta, 1979).

Finally, Glass, Bradshaw, Day, and Umilta (1985) used digitized faces and assumed that they were sampling the low spatial frequency range.   Based upon the size of the elements comprising the stimulus, it is not clear that high spatial frequency information was effectively removed.   In fact, spurious high spatial frequencies may have been introduced into the stimulus display.   However, in Experiments 2 and 3 they used blurring as an alternative means of filtering the high spatial frequencies and, in this case, found a greater RVF/LH impairment. This finding supports the spatial frequency hypothesis.

In summary, evidence from blurring experiments is generally consistent with the spatial frequency hypothesis by showing that a reduction in the contribution of the high spatial frequency channels significantly reduces RVF performance.   On the other hand, research has not shown that there are shifts to RVF superiority when there is a reduction in the contribution of low spatial frequency channels (see Hardyck, this volume).   This raises the possibility that the right hemisphere may more sensitive to degraded images than the left rather than differentially sensitive to spatial frequency *per se* (Jonsson & Hellige, 1986). The spatial frequency hypothesis, however, has the advantage that the frequency content of input can be quantitatively specified, whereas the perceptibility of input cannot.

As we have noted earlier, studies using filtered images have manipulated the spatial frequency composition of the stimulus and, thus, provide an answer to this criticism.   Generally, these studies support the spatial frequency hypothesis. There are, nevertheless, several difficulties when testing the spatial frequency hypothesis with filtered images.   As Sergent (1987) has pointed out

> it is not presently possible to specify apriori the respective values of relevant procedural variables that would systematically result in a given visual field superiority.   This is not simply due to the interaction among procedural variables in determining the resolution level of the input, but also to our

ignorance about which spatial frequencies convey the relevant information for optimal performance in a particular task. (p. 424).

Thus, the approach taken by our laboratory has been to study differences in performance between the hemispheres for psychophysical tasks which are clearly defined and in which the task-relevant spatial frequency information is clearly specified (i.e., when the stimulus consists of a single spatial frequency component, that frequency, by definition, is the only frequency that can be available in the input as well as required for processing by task demands). Our experiments required subjects to either detect or identify sinusoidal gratings presented in either the LVF or RVF. We varied spatial frequency, exposure duration, and contrast.

EXPERIMENTS WITH GRATINGS

Methological and Procedural Considerations

In our experiments we used a Picasso image generator under computer control to produce the sinusoidal gratings on the face of two Tektronix 608 monitors (P-31 phosphor). A black matte screen was placed in front of the two spatially adjacent monitors and the screens of both monitors were visible through the circular openings in the surround. A fixation point was placed midway between the circular apertures. With the exception of the mean luminance of the monitors the room was dark. In all experiments subjects received a warning tone and the stimuli followed at some variable foreperiod. Throughout the experiment, daily photometric readings were taken to assure that both monitors were matched in mean luminance and contrast. A viewing hood limited the subject's field of view and with a chin rest helped to stabilize the head. In all of our experiments we carefully stressed the importance of maintaining fixation and the importance of responding both quickly and accurately. Prior to all experiments subjects were given a handedness inventory. Only right-handed males with no history of sinistrality and with normal or corrected to normal vision participated in the experiments.

In all of our experiments there were no changes in the mean luminance of the stimulus display when the gratings were presented; level of adaptation was held constant. Studies have shown that changes in mean luminance can have very dramatic and differential effects on the processing of spatial frequency information (Green, 1981; Kitterle, Beasley, & Berta, 1984; Kitterle & Corwin, 1979). It should be noted that some studies using gratings that did not support the spatial frequency hypothesis failed to control for mean luminance (Boles & Morelli, 1988; Szelag, Budhoska, & Koltuska, 1987).

DetectionTasks

Our initial work was designed to test whether the cerebral hemispheres differ in sensitivity to detect the presence of sinewave gratings (Kitterle & Kaye, 1985). The gratings were flashed for 100 msec and there was a 900 msec intertrial interval between presentation. In this procedure we determined the high spatial frequency cutoff (i.e., the highest spatial frequency that can be resolved at a given contrast level). We did not find any hemispheric differences in contrast sensitivity.

Although some studies have shown that there may be hemispheric differences in contrast sensitivity (Beaton & Blakemore, 1981; Rao, Rourke, & Whitman, 1981, Rovamo & Virsu, 1979), they have not been replicated (Blake & Mills, 1979; Kitterle & Kaye, 1985; Peterzell, Harvey, & Hardyck, 1989; Rijsdijk, Kroon, & van der Wildt, 1980; Rose, 1983). It is quite possible that these earlier findings may be the result of individual differences in nasal and temporal sensitivity because only monocular viewing was used.

It is quite possible, however, that the failure to find laterality differences in the aforementioned studies may result because of the following reasons. First, hemispheric differences may only arise when there is a limited capacity for handling information or allocating attention and this was not the case in detection tasks just discussed. Second, differences in hemispheres may be revealed in processing time rather than in contrast sensitivity and all of the above studies only measured contrast thresholds. Third, laterality effects may occur only at suprathreshold levels, consequently, they would not be found at threshold levels. Fourth, the detection of gratings occurs at an early stage in the processing of information and laterality effects may only occur at a later (cognitive) stage. The next experiment considers the first two possibilities. A later section of this chapter addresses the latter two possibilities.

Detection Under Uncertainty. As we noted earlier, it might be argued that the detection of a grating is a relatively simple task for the visual system and hemispheric asymmetries arise only when there is a limited capacity for handling information or for allocating attention (Rose, 1983). In detection experiments, it is typically the case that a grating is randomly selected and then that grating is presented in the same visual field on a number of trials until contrast threshold is determined. This process is repeated for several spatial frequencies. Thus, there is a fair degree of certainty on each trial as to the nature of the visual stimulus and visual field of presentation. If, on the other hand, the spatial frequency and visual field of presentation were to vary randomly over trials, then there would be maximal uncertainty in both the nature of the stimulus and in spatial position. This should limit the capacity for allocating attention and for handling information. It is interesting that this sort of uncertainty about stimulus identity and hemifield location is typical of visual laterality experiments using more complex stimuli.

Davis (Davis & Graham, 1981; Davis, Kramer, & Graham, 1983) has shown that when subjects are uncertain about which spatial frequency will be presented on a given trial and/or spatial position in which it will be presented, contrast thresholds rise. Davis has argued that the uncertainty effect occurs because more visual channels must be monitored under uncertainty conditions and these channels are noisy, resulting in an increase in false alarms. Consequently, performance deteriorates relative to conditions when an observer can devote all resources to the monitoring of a single channel.

With these things in mind, we (Kitterle, Christman, & Hellige, in preparation) determined contrast thresholds for sinusoidal gratings whose contrast and spatial frequency varied randomly over trials and that were randomly presented in either the left or the right visual fields. On a given trial, following a warning tone, a grating or blank field was presented and subjects depressed one key if they thought a grating was presented and another key if they thought a blank field was presented. We also determined RTs for detection. Ten right-handed males were paid to serve as observers in this experiment.

The results of this study are summarized in Fig. 11.1 where contrast sensitivity is plotted as a function of spatial frequency for a detection criterion of 75%. Filled circles present the data for the LVF/RH and the open circles the RVF/LH results. It is readily apparent that there is no difference in contrast sensitivity between the two visual fields. A similar conclusion applies to the RT data. As can be seen in Fig. 11.2, there is no interaction between visual field and spatial frequency. The apparent trend toward an overall RVF/LH advantage was not significant. Thus, despite increases in uncertainty, hemispheric differences in contrast sensitivity and RT were not found.

Despite the procedural changes that we incorporated in our experiment, we were unable to find hemispheric differences in contrast sensitivity. These results, taken together with studies mentioned earlier, strongly suggest hemispheric symmetry obtains in contrast detection. These findings have been interpreted to indicate that detection may be mediated at an earlier (sensory) stage of information processing and that hemispheric asymmetries arise at a later (cognitive) stage (e.g., Moscovitch & Radzins, 1987; Sergent, 1983).

Suprathreshold Detection (Simple Reaction Time). The failure to find hemispheric differences in threshold detection experiments may be due to the fact that typical laterality experiments employ suprathreshold stimuli while the aforementioned detection experiments are at threshold levels of stimulation. In order to provide some insight into this question, we examined suprathreshold detection by determining simple RTs to gratings presented at suprathreshold levels. For this task, sinusoidal gratings of either 1 or 9 c/deg were randomly presented in either the RVF or LVF after a random foreperiod and subjects were required to depress a key as soon as the stimulus was perceived. The gratings were exposed for either 50 or 200 msec. and were presented at one of three contrast levels (.05, .2 and .5). The results of that experiment are shown in Fig. 11.3. Open circles plot the results for RVF/LH and the open circles plot the results for LVF/RH presentations. As can be readily seen, there is no evidence for hemispheric asymmetries in simple reaction time. Rather, there are spatial frequency effects with faster RT to low than to high spatial frequency gratings and small increases in RT with increases in contrast for the high spatial frequency gratings. We did not find any main effects of exposure duration, nor did exposure duration interact with visual field or with visual field and contrast. The results of the experiments at threshold and suprathreshold levels provide further supporting evidence that the LH and RH are equally efficient at tasks requiring the simple detection of spatial frequency.

Identification Tasks

There are suggestions that differences in hemispheric processing may occur in psychophysical tasks that require relatively extensive computation by the visual system (Christman, 1988; Greenwood, Rotkin, Wilson & Gazzaniga, 1980; Rose, 1983). Thus, it is quite possible that hemispheric asymmetries may arise in psychophysical tasks such as discrimination and identification that require the activity in two or more channels to be monitored and compared (Cohen, 1976; Kitterle, 1986; Rose, 1983).

Identification 1. In order to test this possibility, we measured RT to identify the spatial frequency of briefly flashed suprathreshold sinusoidal

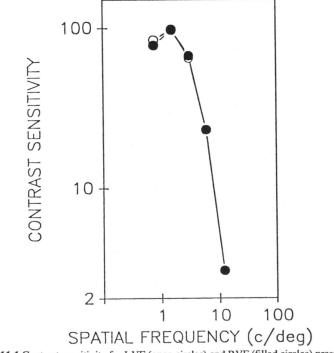

FIGURE 11.1 Contrast sensitivity for LVF (open circles) and RVF (filled circles) presentations.

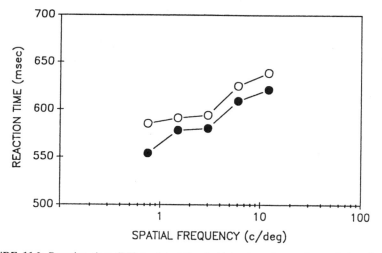

FIGURE 11.2. Reaction time (RT) to detect threshold level gratings. Open circles plot LVF presentations and filled circles plot the data for RVF presentations.

gratings. On any trial either a 1 or 9 c/deg vertically oriented grating was presented in either the LVF or RVF and subjects were required to press one key if it was the 1 c/deg target and another key if it was the 9 c/deg target. The gratings were exposed for either 50 or 200 msec and were presented at a variable foreperiod after a brief warning tone. The contrast and the exposure duration of the targets were randomly varied. For this experiment six right-handed males with normal vision who were naive about the purpose of this study served as subjects.

The major question of our experiment was whether visual field of presentation interacted significantly with spatial frequency. If there are differential processing efficiencies between the two cerebral hemispheres, then the identification of the low spatial frequency grating should be faster when presented in the LVF/RH, whereas time to identify the 9 c/deg target should be faster if it is presented in the RVF because the LH is hypothesized to process high spatial frequencies more efficiently.

Because the effect of duration and the interaction of duration with any of the other variables was not significant, we have averaged over duration and plotted RT as a function of contrast for the 1 c/deg grating in Figure 11.4 and for the 9 c/deg grating in Fig. 11.4. The filled circles plot the results for the RVF/LH and the open circles show the results for the LVF/RH. There is a significant second order interaction between spatial frequency, visual field, and contrast. For the 1 c/deg grating, RTs are faster when the grating is presented in the LVF than in the RVF and these differences are greater at a contrast of 10%. With increases in contrast to 20% there is a corresponding decrease in RT for LVF and RVF presentations. However, increase in contrast from 20% to 40% had no effect further on RT and the visual field differences remained relatively constant over this range.

The pattern of results with the 9 c/deg grating is quite different. With this target RT is faster for RVF than for LVF presentations.   In addition, reaction times become faster with increases in contrast and there is no evidence of asymptotic performance.

The results of this study provide clear evidence that the left and the right hemispheres are differently sensitive to spatial frequency information. A low spatial frequency grating was identified more rapidly when presented in the LVF, whereas more rapid identification was found for RVF presentations of a high spatial frequency grating.   Moreover, as we mentioned earlier, there is no ambiguity about the relevant information needed for the task. The identification paradigm that we used was relatively simple and the visual targets contained only one spatial frequency at a specific orientation.

Very few experiments have explored the effects of contrast in laterality studies (Christman, in press; Davidoff, 1977; Rose, 1983; Sergent, 1984). Most have explored the effects of changes in mean luminance while holding contrast constant (see Christman, submitted; Hellige and Sergent, 1986; Sergent, 1983; Sergent and Hellige, 1986). With grating patterns we are able to independently vary both contrast and luminance. It might be useful in future work with gratings to study the effects of manipulations of contrast and mean luminance on the magnitude and direction of hemispheric asymmetries.

In summary, we have demonstrated a spatial frequency by visual field by contrast interaction that supports the hypothesis that the processing efficiency of the cerebral hemispheres depends upon the spatial frequency and contrast of the stimulus.   There were no interactions of any of these variables with exposure duration.

Identification 2. It might be argued that the durations that we used did not sample the range of exposures over which differential hemispheric effects are found. That is, the shortest exposure duration was, in fact, too long. As noted in other work, temporal summation at suprathreshold levels occurs over a shorter range of durations (see Kitterle & Corwin, 1979) than found at threshold (e.g., Legge, 1978). Consequently, we repeated the identification experiment holding contrast at 10% and used exposure durations of 20, 40, and 160 msec. Ten right-handed male subjects participated in this experiment. They were required to depress one key of the wide bars were presented and another key if the narrow bars were presented.

The results of this experiment are presented in Fig. 11.5a and 11.5b where RT is plotted as a function of exposure duration for the 1 c/deg grating (Fig 11.5a) and the 9 c/deg grating (Fig 11.5b).   Filled circles plot the data for RVF/LH presentations and open circles for LVF/RH presentations.

Statistical analysis of these data indicate that there is a significant interaction between spatial frequency and visual field. Reaction times were faster to the 1 c/deg grating when it was presented in the LVF, whereas faster RTs were obtained to the 9 c/deg target when it was presented in the RVF.   There was no

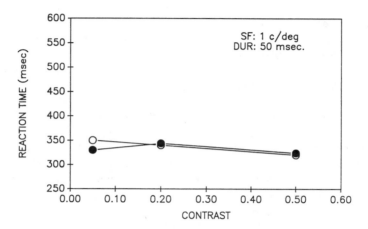

FIGURE 11.3A. Reaction time measures to detect a 1 c/deg suprathreshold grating as a function of contrast presented for 50 msec. Filled circles plot the results for RVF/LH and the open circles plot the results for LVF/RH presentations.

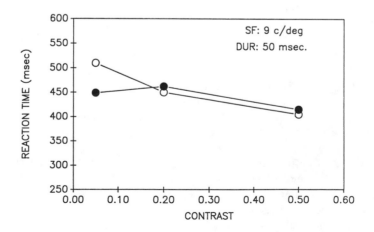

FIGURE 11.3B. Same as 3A for a 9 c/deg grating presented for 50 msec.

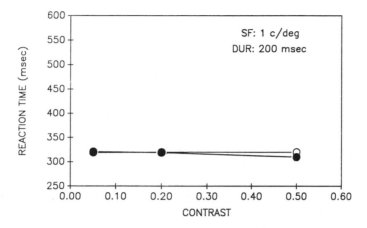

FIGURE 11.3C. Same as 3A for a 1 c/deg grating presented for 200 msec.

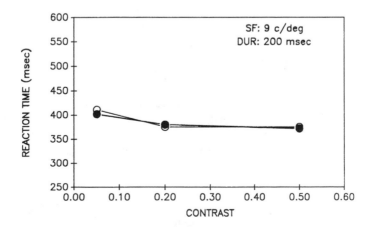

FIGURE 11.3D. Same as 3A for a 9 c/deg grating presented for 200 msec.

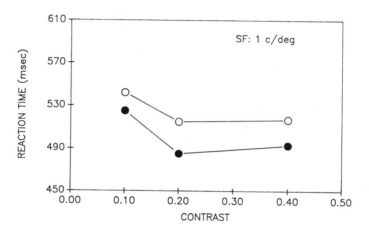

FIGURE 11.4A. Reaction time to identify a 1 c/deg grating as a function of contrast level for LVF (filled circles) and RVF (open circles) presentations.

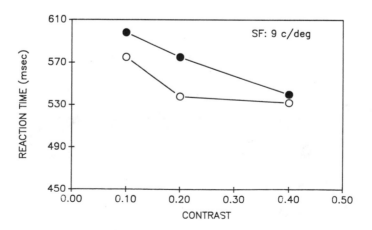

FIGURE 11.4B. Same as 4A for a 9 c/deg grating.

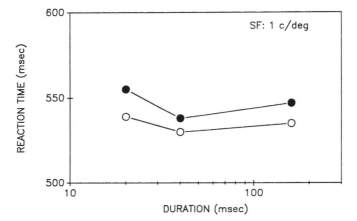

FIGURE 11.5A. Reaction time to identify a 1 c/deg grating at 10% contrast as a function of exposure duration for LVF (open circles) and RVF (filled circles).

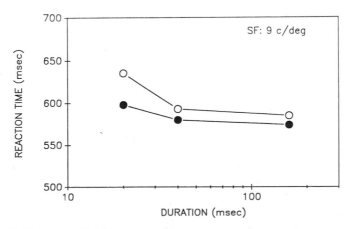

FIGURE 11.5B. Same as 5A for a 9 c/deg grating.

significant second-order interaction between duration, spatial frequency, and visual field. However, duration and spatial frequency did interact significantly and there was a main effect of duration. Consistent with studies indicating that the temporal summation varies with spatial frequency, we have shown that reaction times decrease with increases in exposure duration; the rate of decrease being more gradual with the 9 c/deg grating than with the 1 c/deg sinusoidal grating.

The failure to find an interaction between visual field and exposure duration contrasts with other studies that have shown differential effects of duration. Generally, increasing the exposure duration of a complex stimulus such as a face or a letter benefits the LH more than the RH (Christman, in press; Sergent, 1983; Sergent & Hellige, 1986; but see Diehl & McKeever, 1987; Sergent, 1987). In such situations, increases in exposure duration benefit the integration of high relative to low frequencies. Unlike the previous studies, however, we used simple sinusoidal gratings and consequently one may not expect to find differential effects of exposure duration on hemispheric processing of spatial frequency.

Identification of Sinewave Gratings at Threshold. The previous experiment has shown that laterality effects can arise in sinewave grating identification experiments at suprathreshold levels. This finding is consistent with the conclusions of several researchers that laterality effects arise under conditions which involve extensive computations (e.g., Christman, 1988; Kitterle, 1986; Kitterle & Kaye, 1985; Rose, 1983). If this is the case then cerebral asymmetries may also exist at threshold levels for grating identification because the nature of the computation required for identification is the same regardless of contrast level. On the other hand, it may be the case that hemispheric asymmetries will arise only when extensive computation needs to be performed on suprathreshold input. To date, all studies examining hemispheric processing of threshold stimuli have failed to find asymmetries (Blake & Mills, 1979; Fiorentini & Berardi, 1984; Kitterle & Kaye, 1985; Peterzell, Harvey, & Hardyck, in press, Rao, Rourke, & Whitman, 1981). All of these studies, however, employed detection tasks, which may not have had sufficient computational complexity to allow the emergence of hemispheric asymmetries. Therefore, we (Kitterle, Christman, & Hellige, in preparation) examined the ability of the RH versus LH to identify high and low spatial frequencies at threshold.

Eight right-handed males participated in this experiment. Each subject participated in two conditions. In the low frequency condition, subjects identified which of two possible low frequency stimuli (0.75 or 1.5 c/deg) occurred; similarly, in the high frequency condition, they identified which of two high frequency gratings (6.0 or 12.0 c/deg) occurred. Each grating was paired with five contrast levels spanning a range from subthreshold to slightly suprathreshold. Although the particular physical contrast levels varied for each spatial frequency, they were equated in terms of effective contrast (i.e., the physical contrast at each contrast level were chosen so as to provide equivalent detectability for all four frequencies).

The percent-correct identification performance for the low and high spatial frequency conditions are plotted in Figs. 11.6a and 11.6b respectively. The corresponding RT data is graphed in Figs. 11.7a and 11.7b.

Inspection of Figs. 11.6a and 11.7b shows that there were no marked differences in the abilities of the LH and RH to identify low frequency gratings at threshold. There is a hint in the accuracy data, however, toward an emerging RH advantage at the highest contrast levels. Figs. 11.6b and 11.7b, on the other hand, demonstrate a robust LH advantage in terms of accuracy and RT for the identification of high spatial frequency gratings at and near threshold. A significant hemisphere X spatial frequency interaction for the identification of spatial frequencies was thus obtained, in accord with predictions of the spatial frequency hypothesis. The absence of a double dissociation (i.e., RH advantage for low spatial frequencies and LH advantage for high frequencies) stands in contrast to the results of the suprathreshold identification experiment discussed previously. However, the two experiments differed in a number of methodological factors that limit direct comparisons. Nonetheless, we can conclude that hemispheric asymmetry in the identification of low versus high spatial frequencies exists at both suprathreshold and threshold levels.

CONCLUSIONS

The present experiments were designed to test the hypothesis that the cerebral hemispheres are differentially sensitive to the outputs of spatial frequency channels. We have explored this problem by investigating detection and identification performance using sinusoidal gratings that were presented in the right or left visual fields. Using this technique we were able to avoid some of the problems of earlier research. With letters or faces it has proven difficult to specify, a priori, the relevant values of the procedural variables in determining the resolution level of the input and also the spatial frequency frequencies that convey the information relevant for optimal task performance in a given task. In our studies we were able to clearly define the spatial frequencies relevant for effective task performance and avoid these ambiguities.

Several studies have shown that the hemispheres do not differ in their sensitivity to spatial frequency in detection tasks. We cannot account for the failure to find hemispheric differences in earlier studies as simply due to the fact that the task was relatively easy. Our results indicate that hemispheric symmetry still obtains when the detection task is made more difficult by introducing both stimulus and position uncertainty. Nor can we argue that the hemispheric differences only arise at suprathreshold levels because we found evidence for hemispheric asymmetries in the identification of gratings at threshold and suprathreshold levels.

Sergent (1983, 1987) has suggested that hemispheric differences emerge when processing takes place beyond the sensory level, at later cognitive stages.

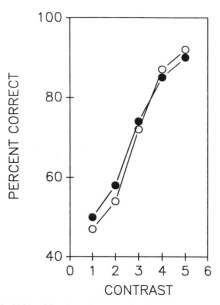

FIGURE 11.6A. Threshold identification of low spatial frequency gratings (.75 and 1.5 c/deg) as a function of contrast (arbitrary units) for LVF/RH (open circles) and RVF/LH (filled circles) presentations.

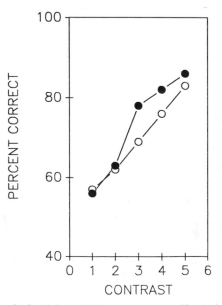

FIGURE 11.6B. Same as 6A for high spatial frequency gratings (6 and 12 c/deg).

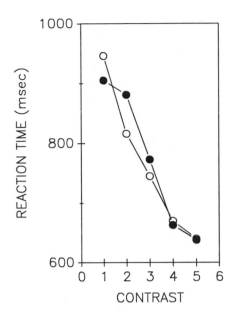

FIGURE 11.7A. Reaction times to identify low spatial frequency gratings (.75 and 1.5 c/deg) as a function of contrast (arbitrary units) for LVF/RH (open circles) and RVF/LH (filled circles) presentations.

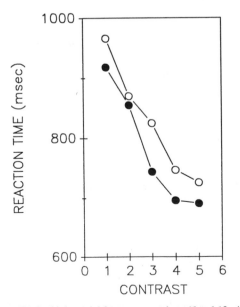

FIGURE 11.7B. Same as 7A for high spatial frequency gratings (6 and 12 c/deg).

identification reflects activity at a higher (cognitive) level of information processing (Christman, 1988; Kitterle & Kaye, 1979; Sergent, 1983).

One way to conceptualize the notion of processing beyond the sensory level is in terms of the nature of the decision process rather than differences in level of processing. In other words, these differences are not in terms of the information available to the RH and LH; rather, hemispheric differences arise as a function of the type of processes applied to that information (see Peterzell et al., in press). This conclusion derives from recent models of identification and detection of sinusoidal gratings that argue that detection and identification processes operate on the same level of sensory information (Thomas, 1985, 1987; Thomas, Gille, and Barker, 1982). It is also consistent with recent unpublished work in our laboratory that has found a spatial frequency by hemisphere interaction in the time to discriminate differences in spatial frequency.

In general, formal models of detection and identification assume that there are two stages: an encoding stage followed by a decision stage. The encoding stage describes how the physical stimulus activates spatial frequency tuned pathways and how the stimulus is represented within the visual system by the set of pathway responses. The decision stage describes how these responses are combined and tested against a decision rule in order to select a judgment to be made. For example, a true detection occurs if at least one pathway is activated (see Thomas, 1978). This model suggests that the detection process involves very little computation.

However, when the task is identification, the judgment may be based upon more extensive computation requiring a quantitative comparison among the magnitudes of the responses in each pathway. For example, a probabilistic approach to identification regards the response of each pathway in terms of likelihood functions that relate activity in a pathway to each of the possible stimuli to be identified. This information is used to estimate, for each possible stimulus, the likelihood that the stimulus produced the observed set of pathway responses. The stimulus identified is the one that is the most likely source of the response set. Although these models have not been developed to account for RT data or laterality effects, the additional computation involved in identification is consistent with the longer RTs for identification than for detection that we found in the current experiments. To account for hemispheric asymmetries, perhaps the RH and LH differ in the values signalled by the active pathways as a function of spatial frequency or they may differ in the likelihood functions that relate activity in low versus high spatial frequency pathways to each of the possible stimuli to be identified.

In summary, our results suggest that hemispheric asymmetry in the processing of spatial frequency arises as a function of the computational demands of the task, with the additional complexity of the decision stages involved in identification and discrimination tasks compared to detection tasks leading to the emergence of hemispheric asymmetries in the former conditions only. Thus, the hemispheres do not appear to differ in terms of the nature of their sensory input; rather, asymmetries arise in terms of the efficiency with which the LH versus RH perform perceptual and cognitive operations on input of varying spatial frequency. This finding not only has implications for models of cerebral laterality, but can also help address basic questions regarding the unfolding of processes operating upon the initial representations of visual information. Mathematical models of visual detection, discrimination, and identification (see Thomas, 1987; Wilson & Gelb, 1984) have been developed, and an approach based on determining the parameters on which the hemispheres do or do not differ will help constrain and refine such models.

ACKNOWLEDGMENTS

This research was partially supported by an Academic Challenge Grant to the Experimental Psychology Program to enhance research in Cognitive Psychology and provided funds to support a postdoctoral fellowship for Dr. Christman.

REFERENCES

Arend, L.E. Jr., & Lange, R.V. (1979). Influence of exposure duration on the tuning of spatial channels. *Vision Research, 18*, 195-200.

Badcock, D. R., & Sevdalis, E. (1987). Masking by uniform field flicker: some practical considerations. *Perception, 15*, 641-647.

Beaton, A. (1985). *Left side, Right side: A review of laterality research.* Yale University Press: New Haven.

Beaton, A., & Blakemore C. (1981). Orientation selectivity of the human visual system as a function of retinal eccentricity and visual hemifield. *Perception, 10*, 273-283.

Blake, R., & Mills, J. (1979). Pattern and flicker detection examined in terms of nasotemporal division of the retina. *Perception, 8*, 549-555.

Boles, D., & Morelli, M. (1988). Hemispheric sensitivity to spatial frequencies. *Bulletin of the Psychonomic Society, 26*, 552-555.

Bradshaw, J., & Nettleton, N. (1981). The nature of hemispheric specialization in man. *Behavioral and Brain Sciences, 4*, 51-91.

Breitmeyer, B., & Ganz, L. (1977). Temporal studies with flashed gratings: Inferences about human transient and sustained channels. *Vision Research, 16*, 861-865.

Campbell, F.W., & Robson, J. (1968). Application of Fourier analysis to the visibility of gratings. *Journal of Physiology, 197*, 551-566.

Christman, S. (1987). Effects of perceptual quality on hemispheric asymmetries in visible persistence. *Perception and Psychophysics, 41*, 367-374.

Christman, S. (1988). Task factors and hemispheric asymmetries in visible persistence. Presented at the 16th Annual Meeting of the International Neuropsychological Society, New Orleans, 1988.

Christman, S. (in press). Perceptual characteristics in visual laterality research. *Brain and Cognition.*

Christman, S. (submitted). Effects of luminance and blur on hemispheric asymmetries in temporal integration.

Cohen, G. (1982). Theoretical interpretations of lateral asymmetries. In Beaumont, J., (Ed.) *Divided visual field studies of cerebral organisation.* Academic Press: London, 87-111.

Davidoff, J. (1977). Hemispheric differences in dot detection. *Cortex, 13,* 434-444.

Davis, E., & Graham, N. (1981). Spatial frequency uncertainty effects in the detection of sinusoidal gratings. *Vision Research, 21,* 705-712.

Davis, E., Kramer, P., & Graham, N. (1983). Uncertainty about spatial frequency, spatial position, or contrast of visual patterns. *Perception and Psychophysics, 33,* 20-28.

Davson, H. (1972). *The Physiology of the Eye,* Academic Press: New York.

DiLollo, V., & Woods, E. (1981). Duration of visible persistence in relation to range of spatial frequencies. *J. Experimental Psychology: Human Perception and Performance, 7,* 754-769.

Diehl, J., & McKeever, W. (1987). Absence of exposure time influence on lateralized face recognition and object naming latency tasks. *Brain and Cognition, 6,* 347-359.

Fiorentini, A., & Berardi, N. (1984). Right-hemisphere superiority in the discrimination of spatial phase. *Perception, 13,* 695-708.

Glass, C., Bradshaw, J., Day, R., & Umilta, C. (1985). Familiarity, spatial frequency and task determinants in processing laterally presented representations of faces. *Cortex, 21,* 513-531.

Graham, N. (1980). Spatial frequency channels in human vision: detecting edges without edge detectors in Harris, C. S. (ed) *Visual Coding and Adaptability,* Lawrence Erlbaum Associates: New Jersey.

Green, M.A. (1981). Spatial frequency effects in masking by light. *Vision Research, 21,* 861-866.

Greenwood, P. M., Rotkin, L. G., Wilson, D. H., & Gazzaniga, M. S. (1980) Psychophysics with the split-brain subject: On hemispheric differences and numerical mediation in perceptual matching tasks. *Neuropsychologia, 18,* 419-434.

Hardyck, C. (1986). Cerebral asymmetries and experimental parameters: Real differences and imaginary variations? *Brain and Cognition, 5,* 223-239.

Harris, C. S. (Ed.) (1980). *Visual Coding and Adaptability,* Lawrence Erlbaum Associates: New Jersey.

Hood, D. (1973). The effects of edge sharpness and exposure duration on detection threshold. *Vision Research, 13,* 759-766.

Jonsson, J., & Hellige, J. (1986). Lateralized effects of blurring: A test of the visual spatial frequency model of cerebral hemisphere asymmetry. *Neuropsychologia, 24,* 351-362.

Kitterle, F. (1986). Psychophysics of lateral tachistoscopic presentation. *Brain & Cognition, 5,* 131-162.

Kitterle, F., Christman, S., & Hellige, J. (in preparation). Identification and detection of spatial frequency in the left and right cerebral hemispheres.

Kitterle, F. L., & Corwin, T. (1979). Enhancement of apparent contrast in flashed sinusoidal gratings. *Vision Research, 19*, 33-39.

Kitterle, F., Corwin, T. R., & Berta, J. (1979). Masking of sinusoidal targets by uniform fields of unequal duration. *Journal of the Optical Society of America, 69*, 1445.

Kitterle, F. L., Beasley, E.M., & Berta, J. (1984). The effect of luminance decrements upon the detection of sinusoidal gratings. *Perception and Psychophysics, 35*, 221-228.

Kitterle, F. L., & Kaye, R. (1985). Hemispheric symmetry in contrast and orientation sensitivity. *Perception & Psychophysics, 37*, 391-396.

Legge, G. (1978). Sustained and transient mechanisms in human vision: Temporal and spatial properties. *Vision Research, 18*, 69-81.

Michimata, C., & Hellige, J. (1987). Effects of blurring and stimulus size on the lateralized processing of nonverbal stimuli. *Neuropsychologia, 25*, 397-407.

Moscovitch, M. (1986). Afferent models of visual perceptual asymmetry. *Neuropsychologia, 24*, 91-114.

Moscovitch, M., & Radzins, M. (1987). Backward masking of lateralized faces by noise, pattern, and spatial frequency. *Brain and Cognition, 6*, 72-90.

Peterzell, D., Harvey, Jr., L., & Hardyck, C. (in press). Spatial frequencies and the hemispheres: Contrast sensitivity, visible persistence and letter classification. *Perception and Psychophysics*.

Rao, S., Rourke, D., & Whitman, R. (1981). Spatio-temporal discrimination of frequency in the right and left visual fields: A preliminary report. *Perceptual and Motor Skills, 53*, 311-316.

Rijsdik, J., Kroon, J., & van der Wildt, G. (1980). Contrast sensitivity as a function of position on the retina. *Vision Research, 20*, 235-242.

Rose, D. (1983). An investigation into hemisphere differences in adaptation to contrast. *Perception and Psychophysics, 34*, 89-95.

Rovamo, J., & Virsu, V. (1979). An estimation and application of the human cortical magnification factor. *Experimental Brain Research, 37*, 495-510.

Sergent, J. (1982a). The cerebral balance of power: Confrontation or cooperation? *Journal of Experimental Psychology: Human Perception and Performance, 8*, 253-272.

Sergent, J. (1982b). Influence of luminance on hemispheric processing. *Bulletin of the Psychonomic Society, 20*, 221-223.

Sergent, J. (1982c). Theoretical and methodological consequences of variations in exposure duration in visual laterality studies, *Perception and Psychophysics, 31*, 451-461.

Sergent, J. (1983). Role of input in visual hemispheric asymmetries. *Psychological Bulletin, 93*, 481-512.

Sergent, J. (1984). Role of contrast, lettercase, and viewing conditions in a lateralized word-naming task. *Perception and Psychophysics, 35*, 489-498.

Sergent, J. (1985). Influence of task and input factors on hemispheric involvement in face processing. *Journal of Experimental Psychology: Human*

Perception and Performance, 11, 846-861.

Sergent, J. (1987). Failures to confirm the spatial-frequency hypothesis: Fatal blow or healthy complication? *Canadian Journal of Psychology, 41*, 412-428.

Sergent, J., & Hellige, J. (1986). Role of input factors in visual-field asymmetries. *Brain and Cognition, 5*, 174-199.

Szelag, E., Budhoska, W., & Koltuska, B. (1987). Hemispheric differences in the perception of gratings. *Bulletin of the Psychonomic Society, 25*, 95-98.

Taylor, A., & Hellige, J. (1987). Effects of retinal size on visual laterality. *Bulletin of the Psychonomic Society, 25*, 444-446.

Thomas, J.P. (1985). Detection and identification: How are they related? *Journal of the Optical Society of America A, 62*, 1457-1467.

Thomas, J. P. (1986). Seeing spatial patterns. In Boff, K.R., Kaufman, L. and Thomas, J.P. (Eds.), *Handbook of Perception and Human Performance*, (Vol 1), John Wiley and Sons: New York.

Thomas, J.P., Gille, J., & Barker, R. (1982). Simultaneous visual detection and identification: Theory and data. *Journal of the Optical Society of America, 72*, 1642-1651.

Wolcott, C. L., Saul, R. E., Hellige, J. B., & Kumar, S. (in press). Effects of stimulus degradation on letter-matching performance of left and right hemisphere stroke patients. *Journal of Experimental and Clinical Neuropsychology*.

Wilson, H. G., & Gelb, D. J. (1984). Modified line element theory for spatial frequency & width discrimination. *Journal of the Optical Society of America, 1*, 124-131.

Weisstein, N. (1980). The joy of Fourier Analysis. In Harris, C. S. (Ed.), *Visual Coding and Adaptability*, Lawrence Erlbaum Associates: New Jersey.

Author Index

Subject Index